MACROPOLITICS

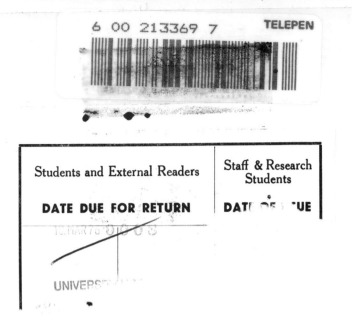

MORTON A. KAPLAN

University of Chicago

MACROPOLITICS

Selected Essays on the Philosophy
and Science of Politics

ALDINE PUBLISHING COMPANY

CHICAGO

First published 1969 by Aldine Publishing Company, 529 South Wabash, Chicago, Illinois 60606

Library of Congress Catalog Card Number 68-8153

Designed by Chestnut House

PRINTED IN THE UNITED STATES OF AMERICA

ACKNOWLEDGMENTS

The author wishes to thank Alan Gewirth, Duncan MacRae, Jr., Nathan Leites, Donald Reinken, and Charles Wegener for helpful comments on an earlier draft of the philosophical essay presented in this volume.

I am grateful to those below for permission to republish the following items:

to *World Politics* for "Traditionalism versus Science in International Relations", October 1966 (Copyright © 1966 by Princeton University Press), and "The International Arena as a Source of Dysfunctional Tension", July 1954 (Copyright 1954 by Princeton University Press).

to James C. Charlesworth for "Systems Theory" from *Contemporary Political Analysis* (Copyright © 1967 by the Free Press).

to *Social Research* (Spring 1968) for "Systems Theory and Political Science" (Copyright © 1968 by The New School for Social Research).

to *Ethics Journal*, Vol. 70, pp. 228–32 (Copyright 1960 by the University of Chicago Press) for "Some Problems of the Extreme Utilitarian Position"; and Vol. 71, pp. 301–02 (Copyright 1961 by the University of Chicago Press) for "Restricted Utilitarianism".

to John Wiley for the two appendices and the chapter on the national interest from *System and Process in International Politics* (Copyright © 1957 by John Wiley and Sons, Inc.).

to the Hudson Institute for "A Nightmare" from Herman Kahn and Anthony J. Wiener, *The Year 2000* (Copyright © 1967 by the Hudson Institute, Inc.).

to the Center of International Studies, for *The Communist Coup in Czechoslovakia*, Research Monograph Number 5, January 1960 (Copyright 1960 by the Center for International Studies, Princeton University).

to St. Martin's Press for "The Systems Approach to International Politics" from Kaplan, *The New Approaches to International Relations* (Copyright © 1968 St. Martin's Press, Inc.).

to Doubleday for "Some Problems of International Systems Research" from *International Political Communities* (Copyright © 1966 by Doubleday & Company, Inc.).

To Azie
with love

PREFACE

When the idea of publishing a group of my essays in book form first arose, it had only a limited interest for me. As I thought about the project, the idea of composing an introductory essay in which I sketched some philosophical ideas underlying my thought arose and enthusiasm began to develop. I have believed for a long time that social scientists take too narrow a view of scientific method, that the implications of a scientific philosophy for value theory are ordinarily misconceived, and that these misconceptions are relevant both to political science and political philosophy.

Although I am neither a professional philosopher nor an expert on the philosophy of science, the essay that follows has obvious relevance and great importance for some issues of political science.

We cannot ignore the philosophical foundations of many issues in political science, hoping that the issues will go away or that others will solve them for us. If the essay is something less than the full-length and detailed treatment that might be desired, it nonetheless I hope raises the right issues and adumbrates some of the answers.

The philosophical essay that opens this book combines two strands of thought: a philosophical pragmaticism related to positions developed by Charles Sanders Peirce, and the type of systems theory that evolved from the neurological work of W. Ross Ashby and W. Grey Walter. The approach that I take to value theory, and that is presented in *System and Process*, represents a break with the earlier position I took in "An Introduction to the Strategy of Statecraft" and was produced by the integration of systems theory into my philosophical pragmaticism. The Freudian influence on my philosophy of values will become obvious.

For those who see a scientifically oriented philosophy as inaugurating a break with past philosophical traditions, it is important to point out that Peirce was strongly influenced both by Kant and by Hegel. Morris R. Cohen, on whom I wrote my doctoral dissertation, has called his own pragmaticist philosophy neo-Aristotelian. The elements that relate my philosophic position to some of the important chains of influence from Aristotle through Hegel to Peirce and Cohen are evident in the essay itself. The classic philosophic tradition is the beginning of a great chain of thought that extends to the present, and to forget this would make modern political science shallow. To recognize the greatness of the classic writers, however, does not require making a fetish of the specific positions they took. It does them little credit to suggest that nothing that has occurred since their deaths, if known to them, possibly could have influenced their world view. The world views of many of the great philosophers were affected by discoveries in science both before and during their lifetimes. Although Hegel is reputed to have thought that the owl of Minerva took wing with the completion of his *Encyclopedia*, time chips away at even the greatest achievements.

My essay begins with some obvious and well-known remarks, expressed elsewhere with greater precision than I have reproduced here. The development of the essay brings the reader along a path that leads to conclusions that run against the current grain. The perspective will appear wrong, or unfamiliar, and some of the examples may seem shocking. I am aware of a lack of prudence in this respect, but I could not make the points I wish to make without running this risk. The tough-minded will follow me, and they will use from this work what suits them and can be integrated into their own thought. Some of the more tentatively held positions and some of the more "daring" speculations are deliberately included in fragmentary form.

I did not intend in this essay to begin a dialogue with my colleagues in Eastern Europe; however, now that the essay is completed perhaps the debt to Hegel and to Marx that we share may help to facilitate such a dialogue. Although the dogmatic elements in the Hegelian tradition have long been understood and rejected in the West, we may too easily have dismissed those elements of that tradition that can be vital in our own thinking. Perhaps Eastern European thinkers will find in the Peircean development of Hegelian philosophy empirically meaningful viewpoints better suited than they think to the newer perspectives in Eastern Europe. In addition, although this also was not my intention in writing the essay, it may help to dispel the false dichotomy between status quo and revolutionary philosophies. The present always needs to be overcome in order to sustain and to develop justice. The present, however, also has its claims; and a future that is reached unwisely, whether by revolutionary or by incremental steps, could become a nightmare.

As my work on the philosophic sketch evolved, I decided to restrict the number of essays in this volume and even occasionally to break them up and reorganize some sections to bring them into closer relationship with chosen themes. As a consequence, I have included none of my writings on specifically strategic topics, on foreign policy, or on the interpretation of classic political thinkers. Moreover, it became important to include a few selections from *System and Process*. Thus the volume serves less to display the range or scope of my writings than to expand or illustrate a number of the points raised in this opening essay. They represent a position that may be called, for want of a better term, systemic pragmaticism.[1]

[1]Peirce coined the term "pragmaticism" after William James misused "pragmatism".

CONTENTS

PART I

On Philosophy

I

GLIMPSES INTO A

PHILOSOPHY OF POLITICS

Much of philosophy is concerned with the warrant whereby mind asserts knowledge; much of the turmoil in modern philosophy is related to Hume's attack on causality. Hume's attack was not as self-evident as often believed, for he started with an unstated hypothesis as to how the mind acquired knowledge and how it developed notions of causality. He assumed sequences of events as factual givens and neglected to notice that the elements of the sequence were not directly observed. Kant accepted many of Hume's assumptions but mandated causality as a necessary principle of mind that applied to representations rather than to things-in-themselves. Despite the grandeur of Kant's edifice, the notion of things-in-themselves was soon recognized as untenable within the framework of his own philosophy. Hegel sought, among other things, to restore the basis for empirical knowledge. Things revealed themselves to others through their manifestations under changing conditions. Final truth existed only in the Absolute. Relative and partial truths—and only such—became manifest in history, where both necessity and accident played their parts.

The influence of Hegelian philosophy, even after its breakdown, upon historicism and existentialism need not be told here, where, in any event, we are both simplifying and adumbrating only those elements essential to our own account. It was, however, the Hegelian notion of knowledge acquired through use and action from which derived Marx's notion of *praxis*, F. H. Bradley's idealistic philosophy, and Peirce's concept of pragmaticist meaning. In Peirce's view, humans acquired and refined knowledge by acting upon the world. Objects, events, and relations were real and had their own modes of existence. Need and knowledge influenced behavior and values. Man learned about himself and about society and developed values through participation in society—a Hegelian viewpoint shared with Marxism. We will attempt to show how the fusion of this framework with concepts from systems theory can be used, with the addition of certain informational concepts, to make value choices empirically meaningful in a sense that even Peirce did not anticipate. Although the framework within which the world is known is the central concern of what follows, we begin with a few remarks on science in order to reach that goal.

PROCEDURES OF SCIENCE

There is a common understanding that there is a method of science, that those who follow this method operate scientifically, and that those who do not do so operate unscientifically. In a general sense this is perhaps true; but in more specific senses it can be misleading. Lord Kelvin, for instance, has said that science is measurement and that the better the measurement the better the science. His was a parochial induction from the world of physics and has proved misleading in the world of politics.

Even in physical science, some acute observers of the scientific scene argue that scientific method is discovered by observing what scientists do. Obviously, this can be equally misleading. We do have standards for scientific research. We reject fake cancer cures or the formulations of witch doctors because there is something about the methodology of these self-designated "scientists" that is not accepted as proper according to the criteria of science. They do not seek empirical confirmation according to accepted standards.

Science at the propositional level entails what might be called a set of road maps. An assertion that by following a particular route from a particular place one will reach some other particular place or that by eating a certain food one will be nourished entails a set of directions and a predicted result. Neither the language nor the directions are esoteric; anyone capable of following directions and with appropriate training is capable of duplicating the result. The mode of operation therefore is a public one entailing a faith in a minimum level of order in the universe and in the ability of human beings to communicate with each other by means of symbolization.

To this extent, the method of science is the method of common sense. The failure of a set of directions to hold would then constitute either a disproof of the relationship asserted or an event requiring some sort of explanation. The tools used in conducting these common sense experiments would themselves follow equally public rules; for instance, the syntax of language or the rules of mathematics or of logic. In this usage, the ancient Egyptian metalsmiths, for instance, could be called practical scientists, for they understood the combinations of various metals that made better or worse alloys, even if they did not understand why these results were produced from the more theoretical standpoint available to scientists today. Even contemporary metallurgy has some of the same quality of pragmatic experiment that characterized the ancient Egyptian craft, for it is only when the theory of molecular structure is much farther advanced that metallurgists will be able to produce metals to order. Even so, modern science, as distinguished from ancient science, is characterized by the theoretical.

The theoretical was a category familiar to the ancients, although their meaning of the term differed from ours. For Aristotle the theoretical was that which could be derived from premises known by the mind to be true. The truth of the conclusions was guaranteed syllogistically by the truth of the premises. Thus the proof of theory would not be determined by experiment or by experience.

Aristotle distinguished the various sciences according to how theoretical they were. Thus mathematics and physics ranked as the most theoretical; biology, for instance, was much less so; and politics was an entirely practical discipline. This meant that knowledge of truth in politics rested upon experience and depended upon circumstances. Despite his supposed modernity, Hobbes accepted Aristotle's definition of the theoretical but differed with him primarily in claiming that politics was a theoretical subject.

The break with the classical notion of the theoretical involves a number of changes in perspective and method. Galileo accepted the classical, and perhaps even the Platonic, notion of the theoretical, but in his search for order in the universe chose a simple problem, such as the motion of a body, rather than the problem that preoccupied the Greeks: the mathematics of perfect motions. He thus moved from a complexity that he was not capable of solving to a simple problem that the mathematics of his age could solve. With the discovery of non-Euclidean geometry in the nineteenth century, the notion that the mind was capable of distinguishing true premises from other premises with certainty was challenged so strongly that few would assert it today.[1] From this point forward, an empirical theory would be judged "true" only if it were confirmed—or not falsified—by empirical evidence. Theory remains a deductive schema—a system of mutual implications concerning a set of variables and their relations—but the schema is now tentative only. It is accepted as true only if the predictions to which it gives rise are not falsified. Empirical evidence is the warrant for belief.

Further shocks were in store for moderns with Heisenberg's uncertainty principle, Godel's proof that mathematical systems of sufficient complexity are necessarily incomplete, and Born's proof that if there are measurement errors, then after some period of time predictions are no longer possible, even in the absence of the uncertainty principle.

[1]Not all accepted it even earlier. Cf. Georg W. F. Hegel, *Encyclopädie der Philosophischen Wissenschaften, Die Wissenschaft der Logic* (Leipzig 1920, Verlag Felix Meiner #71), "There is nothing shorter and more convenient than making the bare assertion that I find a content in my own mind along with the knowledge of its truth. . . ." Of course, we now reject the dialectic as a mode of confirming knowledge. To the extent that Hegel used the dialectic as a metaphor, as some believe, in the effort to show that nature "overflows" our formal categories, it is a useful heuristic device, although perhaps more harmless intellectually when translated into Morris Cohen's term, "polarities". The principle of polarity, according to Cohen, asserts that in all determinate events or things there are opposing elements or categories, such as unity and plurality, identity and difference, and so on. These are conceptual derivatives necessary to meaning, not "panlogistic" propositions. Nature includes indetermination as well as determination. There is nothing in either logic or nature that issues a fiat against the existence of entities in which contrary tendencies are conjoined. The law of contradiction requires only that a distinction of the aspects in which the contraries hold be clearly made.

The combination of these factors disrupted the naive seventeenth-century view of science in which God as the master mathematician would be able to predict any event in the world.

Ours is not an age of grand designs or highly general theories. The order that relativity physics has introduced into macrophysics is less than complete. Some aspects of macrophysics seem special and cannot be encompassed within the framework of grand design. Many engineering applications of physics involve trial and error or experimentation; building bridges or airplane design are cases in point. If the sciences still exhibit the descending order that Aristotle established, they do so less neatly than in the Aristotelian case. And even in the queen of the empirical sciences, macrophysics, some of our knowledge is either non-theoretical, incompletely theoretical, or theoretical but restricted to a narrow subject matter. Many of these qualifications are even more true in microphysics.

The greater the simplicity the theorist can achieve, the more theoretical he can make his subject matter. The present complexity of microphysics results from the fact that no simplifying theoretical scheme has yet worked. Despite the seeming multitude of particles at the micro level, the prospect of a simplifying breakthrough cannot entirely be discounted, nor can the prospect of a theory unifying the micro and macro levels.

Even in relatively simple areas of macrophysics, however, an increase in the number of variables creates difficult problems. Two-body problems can be solved by means of general formulas. Three-body problems require considerable paperwork. Interaction problems among large numbers of bodies require the most modern computers for solution. And the solutions turn out to be for the particular case rather than general solutions for multi-body problems. As the number of variables is increased, the generality of solutions diminishes.

The case of the social sciences is even more obdurate. In the first place, physical theory asserts a number of rules of mechanical equilibrium that are meaningful because the variables in the equalities asserted are independently measurable. The concept of mechanical equilibrium is therefore most useful for predictive purposes, although it is propositional rather than theoretical. The assertion that a system is in homeostatic equilibrium—and social and political equilibria are only of this type—is at best a device for categorizing systems rather than for explaining their behavior. There are no independent measures for homeostatic equilibria; thus attempts to use the concept for explanatory purposes in the social sciences are tautological in the worst sense. In addition, efforts to use simple equalities to explain general social or political behavior, when they are not merely meaninglessly tautological, are truistic. A proposition such as "demands and supports within a system must be in balance" is at best a truism, for no conceivable observation can ever falsify it. Maintenance of the system is *ipso facto* proof of balance and *vice versa*. We can have a theory for social or political systems only when the propositional structure is sufficiently rich and related to distinguish different characteristic modes of behavior for systems in which the other variables take different values.

In the second place, the relationship between the micro and macro elements is different in the political and social sciences from what it is in the physical sciences. Although macro behavior is undoubtedly dependent in some ways upon the nature of the micro elements in physics, the laws of macro physics are apparently independent of new discoveries at the micro level. Although there are large-scale political and social events in which variations at the micro level can be assumed to cancel out, such as the rate of suicide in particular societies, for many important macro systems in the political or social sciences the number of actors is small enough so that variations in the characteristics of the actors or environmental accidents affect the behavior of the macro system. Thus, for instance, in oligopolistic situations in economics or in subsystem dominant systems in international politics, theoretical assertions concerning the quality of the equilibrium or the prognosis for stability depend upon specification of actor characteristics that are known to differ among actual systems as well as upon environmental constraints or accidents.

Third, all political and social theories require, for that degree of simplicity compatible with theoretical depth, analytical distinctions between physically inseparable components of behavior. Economic theory, for instance, has its greatest power when certain parameters— such as psychological motivation, cultural values, political constraints —are held constant at particularly chosen values. Psychology, for another instance, abstracts from the variations of economic, social, and political settings, as well as from the accidental factors that characterize individual events.

Apart from the fact that there is no general theory for any of the social sciences, it is also true that each theoretical system is applied to a particular subject from its own perspective, so that, as among the physical sciences, there is no way of unifying the points of view in order to create a single theoretical perspective from which any particular event may be viewed. Although it is true that a physical event such as starting an automobile on a cold day is, in terms of predictive statements, dependent upon a number of particular constraints and is not merely derivable from a simple theory of physics or mechanics, the situation with respect to social or political events, although superficially similar, is radically different because the parameters cannot be filled in numerically to derive the result.

Although social science theory can be engineered to account for the effects of at least some extra-systemic factors, the derivations are only plausible rather than necessary. Thus it can be shown that changes in French public opinion after the cession of Alsace-Lorraine are consistent with the changes in alignment patterning and war objectives that followed.[2] However, other factors reinforced this tendency and still other factors operated against it. Such engineering of theory in the social sciences usually is a matter of judgment that is not fully demonstrable, although in the Alsace-Lorraine case the subsequent pattern of events is partly explainable by the theory and the observed parameter change. In still other cases, no theoretical schema is central and we "fit" propositions together into a pattern to explain the particular case plausibly. At other times, when we attempt to account for specific micro events rather than macro systemic factors, international relations theory may not be central to the explanation. Although the Cuban missile crisis is an event in international politics, the personalities, perceptions, and military strengths at the disposal of the key leaders may dominate the decision process. Because of little information and diverse perspectives, the element of intuitive judgment may play a much larger role in both decision and interpretation of the event than could warrantably be encapsulated within a scientific perspective.

Furthermore, in some kinds of bargaining situations it is not clear that we know what we mean by a "rational solution". If this is so—and I would argue that it is so—the elements of actuality must rest upon

[2]See the section on the engineering of theory in the selection "The Systems Approach to International Politics".

items that are surds from the standpoint of any interpretative schema
and that are thus to a significant extent unknown and unknowable.
These would be accidents not merely by falling outside the particular
interpretative framework, but accidents in the much more radical sense
of falling outside of any interpretative framework.[3]

Until the development of modern game theory, applying statistics to
gambling in the individual case involved several deep philosophical
problems. Charles Sanders Peirce, for instance, argued that applying
the appropriate odds for the class of events to the single-shot case
involved a faith in the entire community of gamblers. It is the virtue
of modern game theory that it provides solutions for single-shot cases
rather than statistical rules designed to optimize some average expectation. Even so, some caution must be applied to this assertion. The
numbers in the payoff boxes are utiles rather than physical outcomes.
The utilities for the outcomes may themselves represent expectations
based upon statistical inferences. In games where the minimum of the
maxima and the maximum of the minima do not coincide for the pure
strategies, the expected outcome of the game in terms of utiles is
determined on the basis of the odds, and in fact will not coincide with
the utility of any of the possible payoffs.

[3]From the standpoint of a man walking along Broadway in New York on a
winter's morning whose head happens to come into contact with a falling milk
bottle, the event is an accident in that it was not predictable within the framework
of any statement applying to individuals, rather than to classes, walking along
Broadway on a winter's morning. On the other hand, from the standpoint of one
who sees a cat knock the bottle over, it is predictable that it will fall upon the head
of anyone who is standing on a certain spot at a certain number of seconds after the
bottle leaves the windowsill. In the same sense, a bad harvest that leads to the failure
of a military campaign that leads to an instability in the international system is an
accident from the standpoint of international politics. It is not, however, an accident
if one takes into account the conditions of weather and harvest. It is an accident
merely from the standpoint of a theory of international politics. It is somewhat in
this sense that Hegel refers to history as the realm of accident. We are, however,
asserting that the social and political world includes accidents in an even more
fundamental sense, namely, in the sense that the specific events are not predictable
from the standpoint of any theory or rational reconstruction. Thus, for instance,
when two people fail to reach agreement in bargaining games for which there are
strict solutions, we can say that the failure results from stubbornness, from lack of
understanding of the game theoretical elements, or from some other assignable
cause. When, however, two men fail to agree in an asymmetric Nash bargaining
game, then, since there is no uniquely determined rational or even "fair" bargain
we can explain the event only in the negative sense of pointing to the absence of a
solution. Moreover, we cannot predict that they will not reach an agreement.

It is not clear that the class frequency concept of probability is appropriate for understanding or explaining many important events at the micro level in international politics or in politics generally. Nor is it clear that the concept of probability apart from class theories of probability, for example, subjective probabilities, has a clearly imputable meaning for many such events. Although selected aspects of such events may be treated according to class probability theories—as, for instance, the probability that the president of the United States will respond to particular kinds of domestic pressures, the probability that so many missiles will misfire in a volley, or the probability that a concession will be met by a counter concession—the relationship of the class to the specific case is even more tenuous than in the case of Peirce's gambler; the absence of any framework within which to unify the various probabilities may render meaningless the concept of prediction and perhaps even of explanation for at least some of these specific micro events. That is, to the extent that the specific case is distinguished from the class of cases by particular parameters that do not cancel themselves out, the validity of the class assertion for the particular case either in terms of a probability distribution or in terms of subjective probabilities may be misleading.

Since in subsystem dominant systems, such as international systems, it is possible, even if not necessarily likely, for individual decisions to transform radically the matrix of future decision-making (consider an erratic decision to launch a full-scale nuclear war), subsequent events cannot be said to be fully explainable by prior events. We are not arguing that there is some method of understanding superior to scientific method for understanding such events, but rather that such events are unexplainable. We do not mean that they are "uncaused", but only that we do not know whether the sequence of events is in any sense representative, that we do not know what the sequence depended upon well enough either to assert that our speculative explanation is better than many others or to assess its probability in class terms.

THE STATUS OF SCIENTIFIC STATEMENTS

The status of simple propositions is not seriously open to question. A set of directions for getting from New York to Chicago is in some understandable sense a direct statement about the external world. Theories are not merely directions in this sense, however, although at one time the Vienna School of logical positivism had hoped that scientific theories could be built cumulatively from sets of observation, or protocol, statements. Although it was well known that scientists did not construct theories as the logical positivists would have advised, Hempel has shown that the very effort is logically contradictory and that scientific theories must include some elements which are not themselves capable of empirical verification. Any social science theory using dispositional statements would be of this type, but there is a danger that social scientists would use this truism to camouflage meaningless concepts.

Questions have therefore arisen about the nature of the relationship between a theory and the world which the theory is designed to explain. Is a theory merely a set of conventions that organizes existing knowledge, or does it somehow penetrate to the truth of external reality?

Although one can point out that scientific experiments can validate a particular proposition only within the framework of a philosophy that accepts the method of validation,[4] human beings who have seen trains run over individuals will not be misled by such philosophical verities into doubting the empirical truth value of common sense propositions. The status of scientific theories is apparently different. The view of theory as a conventional systematization of existing knowledge is not unthinkable according to common sense standards.

Nonetheless, even though this is not a philosophically conclusive argument, it is fair to point out that our expectation of the deflection of light in a strong gravitational field or of the decay rate of the meson, as predicted by relativity theory, can be explained only because scientists expect that relativity theory, in addition to making coherent the existing body of knowledge, has predictive value for natural events other

[4]Cf. F. H. Bradley, *Appearance and Reality* (London: Swan Sonnenschein, 1899), p. 128, to the effect that thought requires an assumption about reality; C. S. Peirce, *Chance, Love, and Logic* (Harcourt, Brace), 1923, p. 124, to the effect that without a tendency toward comprehending reality, the mind could never develop; Stephen C. Pepper, *World Hypotheses* (University of California Press, 1942), pp. 67-69, for the specific argument that the canons of science can never verify the methods of science, for the verification of hypotheses is dependent upon the prior assumption that using evidence in this fashion is legitimate. Thus the cumulative development of scientific proofs adds nothing to the truth of the method, although it does add to the truth of the body of knowledge if the validity of the method is assumed.

than those considered or known when the theory was formulated. The failure to unify the corpuscular and the wave theory of light, for instance, seems to justify the view that theories consist only of conventional summations of human knowledge or of alternative perspectives for examining the same phenomena. Yet the many occasions on which theories have in fact led to correct predictions of previously unknown facts seems to support the view that theories do have truth value, that is, they are analogues or models that do capture some of the "stuff" or structure of reality. Such verifications suggest that examples dependent on seemingly inconsistent explanatory theories await some further form of reasonable reconciliation. In any event, although I am not competent to pass judgment on the matter, possibly some of the difficulty in attempting to reconcile such diverse views as the wave and particle theories of light stems from the attempt to translate scientific theories at the micro level into an imagery that has meaning only representationally or anthropomorphically, and/or from a failure to articulate adequately the context of the experiments.

Still other attacks have been made upon the truth value of theoretical science. According to the paradigm theory, science depends upon a set of agreed maxims and canons of interpretation; science is therefore an intersubjective rather than an objectively communicable process; and a paradigm is retained until replaced by some other paradigm. Unless this position is a restatement of the truism that all empirical knowledge is probable only, it seems grossly misleading in its implications. It is true that scientists will often not "see" events that conflict with preconceived theories, and that many such "events" even if "seen" will be held invalid because they conflict with the accepted scientific paradigms. Where, however, this is not merely a case of the ability of humans to misperceive or to misreason, it seems rather to indicate a reasonable conservative rule that holds that the entire body of science is more probable than a seemingly inconsistent observation.

This rule requires a significant body of evidence, collected according to still more general canons of science, to call into question the accepted framework of scientific thought. Were this not so, scientists would spend most of their time tracking down half-baked notions. A rule of thumb that conserves time incurs the risk that important new information will be disregarded, at least until the accumulation of evidence forces reconsideration. Any reasonable scientific system would be programmed to operate in this fashion, although one might want to vary the weight of the evidence required to force reconsideration of existing "paradigms".

Thus science is genuinely an objective publicly communicable process, for it is in the long, or even the intermediate, run self-corrective. Moreover, it is unlikely that existing paradigms will be found wrong in that they must entirely be discarded. Newtonian physics was not entirely invalidated by relativity theory. It is now seen as locally true but as interpretable within a different framework that gives rise to some different conclusions. New frameworks may be radically different and yet many of our "homespun truths" will remain true in that they provide a glimpse, even if a partly mistaken one, of the character of the external world.

Occam's razor is generally viewed as a convention whereby the most economical hypothesis is regarded as the preferable explanation for a set of observations. We will argue that its status is somewhat better than this and that it is a necessary corollary, if not a derivative theorem, of the basic rule of scientific confirmation. Consider a student's thesis that his low grade in school is a product of the teacher's dislike of him rather than of his poor work. Generally the former would be regarded by an independent observer as the more complicated of the two hypotheses. If, however, one reads the tests and the answers appear correct, if the teacher were overheard to make prejudicial remarks about him, and so forth, the pupil's hypothesis would be the simpler for accounting for the set of observations. If, however, evidence appears that the pupil had substituted this set of answers for the test actually turned in, if it turns out that the teacher's remarks were a consequence of the pupil's having engaged in a similar dishonesty in the past, the original hypothesis would be simpler for the new, and more complete, set of facts. This process, however, would not likely go on forever; at some point, accumulations of evidence would begin to fit into one hypothesis simply while attempts to retain the other hypothesis would require increasingly complicated explanations, each element of which is selected on a purely *ad hoc* basis, regardless of ordinary plausibility, in order to sustain the hypothesis. At this point acceptance of the more complicated hypothesis would involve a determination to ignore or to "explain away" disconfirming evidence. The truth of the premise would be assumed and the evidence juggled to fit it. Although it is possible that

discovery of new evidence would make the seemingly more complicated hypothesis simpler, there would be no warrant for regarding it
as plausible at this point unless one rejects the modern conception that
evidence is used to test hypotheses rather than the other way around.
The simpler hypothesis makes our experience more coherent, and this
is what we mean when we ascribe empirical truth to it. Occasionally
it is difficult to decide what we mean by the simpler hypothesis.

The truth value of theories, as explained above, has a similar basis.
It is possible that different theories may make the existing body of
observations equally coherent, or may even stimulate similar or different
observations that would not have been predicted in their absence, or
a wider range of phenomena may later be comprehended more simply
by a different theory. Nevertheless, our ascription of empirical truth
value to a theory is an assertion of its usefulness to interpret a given
body of observations and to operate in the empirical world, even with
respect to previously unobserved events. To deny that this is what is
meant by a warrant of empirical truth is to assert that some other
warrant can be issued. Yet there is no other warrant consistent with
basic scientific methodology.

DISCOVERY VERSUS PROOF

We ought to distinguish between the processes of discovery and of
proof. The process of discovery, or intuition, generally occurs at the
preconscious level. How it works is at present unknown; but we can
indulge in some speculations. There is probably a preconscious facility
in the mind capable of scanning for "fits" between previously observed
data and newly observed data, such that a person is "recognized" as
"so-and-so" or a situation as similar to some other situation. Or alternatively the components of a set of propositions are recognized to
"fit" together, that is, to be coherent, and to have consequences that
are also coherent with observations. This is a more complicated form
of patterning. We do not know what kind of "language" the preconscious mind uses, whether it employs a deductive or inferential
logic, or whether the mind uses a kind of kaleidoscopic process that
keeps moving parts of the jigsaw around. The latter process would use
preconscious criteria for closeness of "fit". When the elements of the

pattern are coherently close enough to what is desired, then perhaps a signal is transmitted that permits the inflow of the information to the conscious level.

The process of proof, unlike the process of discovery, is publicly communicable and conscious. It involves first the analysis of the elements of the patterning into component parts to establish consistency and rigor. It then involves the establishment of criteria with respect to the kinds of observations that will be accepted in confirmation of propositions or theories and the search either for such evidence or for disconfirming evidence.

Deductive elegance, of the type obtained in physical theory, is rarely if ever attained in the social sciences. Quite often, however, fully general theory is not attained in the physical sciences either. Kepler's laws for planetary motions, for instance, apply only to our solar system.

No theory, no matter how elegant, can assure us that we know all the conditions accounting for the regularities expressed within it. In the social sciences, however, we quite often find situations where we cannot even express our propositions within a completely clarified deductive framework. In these situations, we may employ deductive methods for some parts of the problem. For instance, the economist can show the relation between marginal cost and marginal income for purposes of profit-making. He does this at the price, however, of completeness. His variables may be related to variables not treated within his system and from which they are not separable, for instance, political or cultural variables. His discussion does not deal with political interference, consumer boycotts, or cultural factors inconsistent with the operation of the system in the form described by him.

Sometimes, as in many political hypotheses, the propositional structure is so complicated that we have not found ways, and perhaps cannot, to simplify them so as to permit complete deduction. In these cases, the social scientist looks for evidence that seems to support a given point of view or at least is consistent with it. Many cases of historical explanation are of this character. The assigned cause of a given event is that which seems most consistent with the available evidence; the event in most cases, however, could not properly be deduced from what is assumed to be the cause, for there is not sufficient closure to the argumentation.

Sometimes the methods are purely paradigmatic. For instance, Apter presents a paradigm distinguishing value types into instrumental and consummatory, and authority types into hierarchical, pyramidal, and segmental, thereby producing a set of six combinations related to success in modernizing and developing new nations.[5] But we are less than secure with this type of paradigmatic information until we can assimilate to it certain other hypotheses as to why these particular factors interact with development and modernization. In the process, we get a set of relationships in which at least partial deductions are possible.

We are all aware of the poverty of statements about the world attempting to derive particulars from a single deductive scheme. Thus theories of "economic man" or of "power-oriented man" are usually recognized as caricatures, although in some particular cases they seem to account for much of man's behavior. More often, we find it necessary to fit together evidence from many perspectives but are not always aware that the criteria for this "fitting" are less than transparent, that we are unable to articulate fully or precisely the relationships among the inferential or deductive structures. The sketchier and the more complex this process becomes, the correspondingly less we are able to communicate our reasons to others or to articulate them for ourselves. Yet, in some cases, this may reflect the obdurateness of nature rather than defects on the part of our inquiry.

The Humeian argument that cause is merely a disposition of the mind to act upon accumulated examples of association, itself assumes a causative model of the mind's operations. If things are observed as concomitant and if they are then asserted to be causally related, we are left with the inference that the brain produces the impression of relationship. It could not do this, however, unless there were something about the mind, that is, about the operations of the brain system, that produces this effect. (The decomposition of events into elements of sequences is itself a hypothesis.) The fact that the human mind is capable of showing that some associations it makes are incorrect also tells us something about the nature of the mind. Using such examples to show that association is distinctive from cause also assumes causality.

[5]David E. Apter, *The Politics of Modernization* (University of Chicago Press, 1965), pp. 81 ff.

Thus, although this illustration does not prove the existence of causality, it shows at least that the Humeian attempt to disprove it rests upon the assumption of some form of causality. Hume's thesis thus contradicts itself, although cause cannot be proved for any single observed event.

This is related to the so-called induction problem posed by Hume: the induction of a universal from a particular. It is true that no summations of inductions can prove the existence of a universal. It may even be true—Peirce pointed to its possibility—that the laws of nature may be slowly changing. Yet we would seek to assimilate these changes to a new form of "lawful" behavior. The oscillatory cosmological hypothesis would appear to represent one such attempt. Yet the concept of law in the scientific sense of mutual implication is necessarily that of an invariant. We cannot "know" such invariants, but we do postulate them. Our postulations are often wrong or incomplete. Yet the evidence that confirms hypotheses according to the basic rule of science confirms the universal, although only in the sense of probable rather than of absolute knowledge. This is what we mean by knowledge of the universal; it is putative rather than apodictic. The assertion about the individual case is deductive, not inductive.

MEANING AND ITS CIRCULARITY

Peirce has stated that the meaning of something is revealed by the infinity of experiments that can be performed upon it. This statement should be interpreted to refer to the object language, and not to statements about the object language, i.e., statements in metalanguage, except insofar as these in turn are discussed as objects of still a higher metalanguage. The philosophy of science, therefore, can be viewed as a form of metaphysics, for it talks about the methodology of science rather than about scientific statements. According to Russell's theory of types, statements in the metalanguage do not apply to themselves. Carnap's assertion that a complete definition would be infinitely long should be interpreted in the same light.

The distinction just made implies that philosophy and science are separate endeavors, and that philosophy deals with metastatements. Thus philosophy would include metaphysics, metapsychology, metapolitics, metaethics, and metalanguage, among others. If this statement is correct, it would be a mistake to attempt to reduce philosophy to linguistic analysis.

Attempts to explain the meaning of meaning rather than to explain meaning lead in turn to a meaning of meaning of meaning. In Russell's sense, however, this is a nonvicious regressus of implications rather than a vicious regressus of meanings. In a less sophisticated analysis, this process would be viewed as circular, for there is an appeal from one form of statement to another. Circularity is particularly the case when we wish to exhaust meaning by an analysis involving episte-mology. Observations always involve relations among the observer, that which is observed, and the context of observation. Attempts to exhaust these always force the observer to consider the matter from some other standpoint, which in turn is not observed.

The scientist must observe the instruments that measure experi-mental results; sometimes we must explain that he has misobserved them. These explanations concerning his faulty observations may be psychological, perceptual, physinlogical, or even physical. Yet to do so requires still other observations using still other instruments made by still other people whose own observations and perceptions must be accounted for. Thus we come full circle; each observation and each explanation depends upon others. Our common sense ignores this process and we shift our system of explanation as we move from one aspect of the problem to another. We use our human senses to observe instruments that are then used to assess the human physiology, etc. The eye and the hand construct the ruler, which then is used for measurement, and the measurements are then observed by humans.

Time, length, color, and so on, are characteristics not of objects alone but of objects, context, and measuring instruments. The complete system can never be defined within the same framework. The entire system is dependent upon a form of knowledge that precedes the experiment. This is the basic but misleading truth that underlies the Platonic observation that nothing can be learned and that we merely remember what we had forgotten.

It is thus clear that a pragmaticist theory of meaning controverts the Lockean distinction between primary and secondary qualities, for al-though the primary qualities are in some sense more universal than the so-called secondary qualities, they also depend upon the characteristics of the object about which the statement is made, the context in which it is made, and the qualities of the measuring instrumentation. To view color as somehow less real than distance because blue may be seen as green through a yellow filter or because a colorblind man may not discriminate different colors is to fail to understand that ascriptions of qualities necessarily include the relational element. When we say that something is really blue even though seen as green, what we are really stating is that in what we regard as a normal environment normal observers would see it as blue.[6]

To argue that the color "yellow" is subjective but that light waves or frequencies of light are objective is to miss the point that light waves are themselves inferences. To argue that we have only sensory inputs and that what we perceive consists of subjective representations created by the mind overlooks that these so-called sensory inputs are themselves inferences from representational observations. Each assertion, whether of a representation or of a "sensation", is an assertion concerning some aspect of "something" "out there" as observed by an instrument or a series of instruments in a particular context. Each assertion is testable as to its veridicality, and for such testing requires the assumption that other observations are veridical.

The self and its physical constitution are known through observations and through inferences from these observations. The self stands on exactly the same basis as all other empirical objects. Indeed, the arguments on solipsism are at base faulty for they can arise only after a distinction between self and environment on the basis of observations. Just as it was early pointed out by Trendelenburg that Kant's *ding an sich* could be dispensed with, for representations of others would themselves generate observations by the representational self, so the solipsistic self can be dispensed with, for it is superfluous. The observations that present others also present the self and are judged by the

_____

[6]Even many of our most common observations are dependent upon this context, instrument, object relationship, although we tend to ignore this, as a consequence of our reifying what we regard as the normal environment. We regard man as self-reproducing; but man would not reproduce himself in an environment that lacked food or oxygen. We would not regard a wrench as self-reproducing. But if there were an automated wrench factory set into motion by a wrench operated by a man, the wrench would be self-reproducing. The example seems ludicrous to us only because we do not regard a man so motivated and the factory as part of the "normal" environment of a wrench.

same sorts of tests. The existence of the self is a hypothesis to be judged by the same criteria as the existence of others.

Obviously such observations can never exhaust the meaning of objects (as contrasted with the meaning of sentences), for there can always be other observations, other interpretative frameworks, and other observers alien to our understanding. But insofar as "objective", "empirical truth", and other such terms have meaning to us, they mean that objects external to us (or the predictions of theories) are capable of arousing representations in us of the stated kinds under the stated conditions.

By subjective as distinguished from objective, we mean not that which is unrelated to observer and context but that which cannot be confirmed by tests as external to the observer. Subjective experiences may be produced by defects in the functioning of the observational system, as in hallucinations, by an abnormality in the context, as in a mirage, or by private notions. The existence of an hallucination can be confirmed by independent observations of behavior and produced under controlled conditions. They are objective, but the putative external objects cannot be confirmed by other tests and the assertion or belief that they are "out there" is merely subjective. Mirages are objective in the same sense as hallucinations, though caused in part by light rays external to the person, but the beliefs to which they give rise are merely subjective. The private notion of many individuals, for instance, that they were adopted is, when independent evidence will not sustain it, a merely subjective notion, although the assertion that people hold such notions is objective. A merely subjective notion of values would be one which could not become manifest under the specified conditions or which, if made manifest, would have bad consequences.

It is a proposition of communication theory that structure is merely more slowly changing process. Josiah Royce pointed out that we see the planets as moving and the stars as fixed but that a creature with a span of perception of a millennium would see the planets as an ellipse of light and the stars as moving. Is either or both set of experiences subjective? Both are objective, for no test will controvert them under the specified conditions of tolerance. That is, the planets do constitute an ellipse for a time period of millennial length. An object placed in their path and held there for that length of time would undergo collision. The planets are also moving; objects moving at ordinary velocities will bypass them unless intercept occurs during the specific relevant segment of their travel. The human organism is a constant with respect to some observational tests and a changing organism with respect to others. Whether a system is in stable equilibrium depends upon the duration of time, degree of perturbation, variable to be investigated, and so forth, that are relevant to the particular investigation or purpose. Thus a system may be both stable and unstable with respect to the same dimension, or, for instance, an object may be all green or all yellow at the same time. These seeming inconsistencies result from the fact that the context of the statement is ellipticized. They are relative but not merely subjective, for each of the seemingly inconsistent statements can be confirmed and publicly communicated and will become appropriately meaningful if the context and relationship is specified.

When we assert that "x is a chair", we are asserting that x is used as a chair by a class of beings and that it meets certain standards that so permit it to be used. If x is used as a chair by a particular person and not by others, the statement "x is a chair" is an elliptical expression for "x is not ordinarily used as a chair by others but I so use it because of personality differences or physical differences". In this form, the statement is an assertion of an objective implication and is capable of being independently confirmed. If one says, "This *is* a chair", it is an elliptical expression for, "This is my idea of what a chair really ought to be." In this case, the idea might be held only by a single individual. It is objective, however, in the sense that we can find out whether he really holds the opinion, e.g., by a lie detector test, for instance, and by testing to see if the chair meets the specifications for "real chairness" that he articulates.

It is important to distinguish the cases of color and chairness. When we say that "x" is yellow, we state that no equivalent research design will reveal it as anything else, even though a different design or a different receptor may lead to its designation as blue. The choice of research design is related to human purpose, but each research design reveals something "true" about the object independent of our purpose. Even a creature with a different set of receptors would conclude that "x" has the stated color when seen by humans under the specified experimental conditions. When we state that "x" is a chair, however, that statement has no meaning apart from usage. The meaning is dependent upon use rather than merely revealed by it. It was William James' confusion of the concept of use in pragmatist philosophy that led Peirce to coin the term pragmaticist.

Nonetheless, in each of the examples cited there is at least some element that is objectively verifiable. We would argue that this statement must be true for all publicly communicable statements in language rather than in metalanguage. Even though scientific theories must contain elements that are not confirmable in this sense, the theory must produce statements that are. Moreover, by raising the level of language —a regressus of implications rather than of meanings—we can apply similar tests to assertions that this is a true statement about theories. Observational "circularity" is of a similar order. There is always some observer or observation outside the system of statements, but this observer or observation can be brought within it by extension to another observer or another observation.

In the *Thesos on Feuerbach*, the Marxist position is that contemplating the world should be forsaken for changing it. The pragmaticist systemic position can be stated as asserting that observations involve an interaction with the world, that the interactor must observe and study the world, and then he must change the world and himself in accordance with his needs, his capabilities, and his understanding. This is multistable regulation.

MEANING AND ITS SOURCE

The pragmaticist theory of meaning is dependent upon pre-experimental knowledge as well as on contextual and relational operations. The Lockean notion of the mind as a *tabula rasa* is inconsistent with how we acquire knowledge. Just as every logical, mathematical, or theoretical system begins with definitions and axioms, so every observation begins with an observing system and a set of accepted concepts in which the inflow of information is interpreted.

Despite the circular nature of the process and thus of our knowledge concerning it, gaining knowledge is neither opaque nor mysterious. The computer that operates on the simplest discrimination between "zero" and "one" or "no" and "yes" shares an equivalent "mystery" with man. If the computer is built so that it cannot discriminate between the inputs "zero" and "one", its operations are meaningless, unrelated to the external world and the problems fed to it. Animals unable to receive information appropriately from the environment lose out in the evolutionary struggle.

Man has been programmed by successful evolution to discriminate data from the external world in a reasonably veridical fashion. More than this, man has been endowed with the capacity to carry out experiments such that he can recognize and correct his own mistakes. He is built with multiple negative feedback loops.

The Platonic metaphor is misleading. Man begins with knowledge of the external world, a knowledge both of objects and of relations that is programmed into him. The capacity of man to use negative feedback, to question the input of data, and to reprogram (multistability) himself as a consequence of negative feedback operations enables man to move from the known through the unknown to the newly known.

Thus man starts with an inbuilt body of notions, probably both of form (as in Plato) and of content (e.g., Whitehead's eternal objects). A theoretical epistemology would no doubt desire to explore this problem further; the sketch is sufficient for our purposes here. The crescive nature of knowledge explains the extrapolative curve of invention. As the mind has more to operate upon, the number of permutations increases geometrically, thus permitting not only quantitative progressions but qualitative reformulations and breakthroughs.

MEANING AND DISPOSITION

A pragmaticist test for meaning may be related to what Carnap called a disposition-type statement. It may be said, for instance, that liquids have a disposition to behave one way under normal conditions of temperature and pressure and still another way under extreme conditions of temperature or pressure—the phenomenon known as superconductivity. Thus it may be said that vegetables have a tendency to grow and to multiply under some conditions and to putrefy under others. It may be said that men have a disposition to behave nobly under some circumstances and corruptly under others; and also that the dispositions of individual men under the same circumstances differ. Some men either have a higher threshold, that is, a lesser disposition, to engage in certain kinds of activities than do other men; or a disposition to do so under different sets of circumstances. Such statements also imply a relationship between the object, the context in which it is placed, and the instrumentation through which it is perceived.

So far, words such as "putrefaction", "health", "nobility", "corruption", merely signify that the observations satisfy the criteria for the definitions of the terms. The evaluative elements, however, also involve a relationship among the object, the context, and the observing instrument, in this case man. We will argue later that propositions of this kind have been misunderstood in the literature and that they are also objective. That is, just as colors imply an observing system capable of perceiving that aspect of the object in the context, so evaluative statements also imply a relationship among the observing instrument, the object, and the context.

Although Carnap certainly and probably also Peirce never intended this conclusion or used the concept of either pragmaticist meaning or disposition sentence in the way we use them here, we will argue that the present usage provides useful understanding of the character of the kinds of statements we actually make and of their relationship to the external world and to us.

SYSTEMS CONCEPTS

There are a few basic concepts of systems theory that have special relevance for our analysis. Since these concepts are defined and used by the author elsewhere,[7] only a few statements will be made here. An ultrastable system is a system that can employ negative feedback both to reduce disturbances in the environment and to reorganize itself in a way that maintains some system variable within defined limits. A multistable system is a system that has one or more part systems that are themselves ultrastable. The term actor is always employed to refer to a system that participates in a larger system. Thus a man may be an actor within a group, a group an actor within a nation, and a nation an

[7]See the selections on systems theory.

actor within an international system. The most inclusive framework of analysis is not referred to as an actor because all action, by definition, occurs within it by actors participating in it.

A system consists of a set of variables related by one or more functions. Although the world is open, the systems model is always closed. Otherwise we could not know, to use Morris Cohen's phrase, how its variables are mutually implicated. The parameters of the system are held constant. We can vary the parameters selectively, however, to assess how the system will behave under different conditions. This is preferable to including the parameters in the system as variables, for we would then have a system so complicated that we could not explicate its behavior—that is, we could not specify the rules for the relations of the variables and work out their implications. Similar reasons preclude our building much, if any, feedback into our explanatory systems models. Systems models, when suitably interpreted, are tools for explaining empirical events.

Purpose, thought, and consciousness may not be as closely related as is sometimes thought. Grey Walter's little machine that plugs itself into a wall socket to charge its batteries or that fills its tank from a pump in order to acquire energy to run its engine may be said to have purpose, at least as we usually use that term. The machine will go around obstacles placed in its way—it uses feedback—to reach particular end or resting states. Yet apparently it cannot think and lacks consciousness.

Ordinarily we think of purpose as something reported to us by other people or as something we introspect from our own behavior. Nonetheless, in this post-Freudian era, we know that there are such things as nonconscious and preconscious purposes, and we infer these from other people's behavior, aspects of which they themselves may be unaware, or retrospectively from analyses of our own behavior.

Grey Walter's little machine is an extremely simple system and we are thereby able to infer its resting states from its behavior without knowledge of its manufacture. It does employ feedback—a seemingly essential element of what we mean by purpose—but is not even ultrastable. Ultrastability gives purpose much of its poignancy, as we shall see when we turn to the consideration of values, but does not seem essential to the concept.

It is illogical to argue, as some would wish to, that Grey Walter's little machine has only the purposes that men have built into it. If a similar machine fell together accidentally—very unlikely no doubt but not impossible—would we be willing to say that this machine has purpose but that Grey Walter's does not? Suppose we could synthesize sperm and ovum and grow a human being: would we say it has no purposes of its own but only those the maker placed in it? If so, we would justify the creation of a class of slaves indistinguishable from human beings in every way except by origin.

Thought is a process of reasoning that makes use of class statements and inferences. Some computers can be said to think in this sense, although they obviously think in a decidedly primitive fashion and only upon external signals; many human thought processes occur at a preconscious level. Thus thought cannot be said to require consciousness.

Consciousness is a reflex awareness of self and apparently arises mysteriously in the cortical processes. It is analytically distinct from both purpose and thought. Consciousness is not merely response but awareness of awareness. The self is perceived as an object within consciousness.[8] Thought is required, however, either to communicate the existence of consciousness or to infer it from the behavior of others. The "I" with which human beings identify themselves is apparently dependent both upon consciousness and upon its singleness.

The concept of self is so closely bound to this singleness of consciousness and the collection of memories connected to it that one wonders whether a person should be referred to as the same person if his memory structure is erased and replaced by another set of memories, attitudes, and dispositions, or whether he should be referred to as a single person if a duality of consciousness occurs within the biological system. For instance, are multiple personalities part of the same person? What of the case where the brain hemispheres are severed? We know that one hemisphere can acquire information that the other hemisphere cannot communicate directly because there are leakages of information. Suppose no leakages occurred?

The questions are not trivial. We wish to make the point that consciousness is not an attribute of the entire biological system and that the relationship between the conscious subsystem and the rest of the

[8]This may make sense of what Fichte meant when he said the self acquires consciousness by striking a barrier and rebounding against itself.

system may be complex. Suppose that the hemispheres of the brain could be severed, and that the bundles of attitudes and dispositions that help constitute personality differed between the hemispheres. The two hemispheres might then have to communicate and bargain with each other in order to produce a pattern of behavior permitting survival for the physical organism and thus for the independently regulative, but physically dependent, hemispheres. We might then perhaps wish to consider the biological system a single system with two subsystem dominant actors within it.[9]

The example may seem frivolous, for many may doubt either the possibility or the importance of the depicted situation. Yet apart from the fact that the example may merely complicate the way in which consciously or unconsciously we weigh competing motivations within the individual, it may have a distinctive heuristic value for contemplating the status of social and political systems.

THE STATUS OF ORGANIZATIONS

Social and political systems do differ from biologically bounded systems in important ways. The multistable components of political and social systems are capable not merely of being detached and transplanted, as in the case of eye corneas, but of regulating their own transfer from one social system to another.[10]

[9]All objects receive information. A coin has information impressed upon it. It may be that there are merely gradations of "awareness" from physical impressment through neurological inputs to cortical reflexive awareness, and that what we call consciousness consists of the information processing of the reflexively aware ultrastable subsystem dominant cortical centers of the physiologcal system. If this is correct, then there would be different levels of information processing in the human system. In this case, there might be other levels of "aware" but nonreflexive neurological processing. This would make some sense of Spinoza's conatus, except that it would be difficult to understand how the concept could be applied to any objects that are not at least ultrastable.

[10]If we wish an extreme example, and in pursuing principles there is no objection to an extreme example, we could in fact deny the distinction we have just made. If we were to visualize an era in which brain transplants could be made, and if these transplants could be made by largely robotic devices, then it would be possible for one brain to order its body to seize an alien, but superior, body and to initiate the process of its own transplantation. We would thus be forced to an alternative, and perhaps more valid, distinction between biological and social and political systems.

We shall now argue that organizations are real and that they can legitimately be referred to as actors. Organizations are not merely reifications or circumlocutions. The fact that people exist and that organizations cannot exist apart from the existence of people is hardly an argument against the reality of organizations. Flesh and blood, hands and feet, hearts and livers and stomachs, skeletal and musculature systems exist, and people cannot exist apart from these. Yet we do not regard the statement that "x" is a person as a circumlocution for "x" consists of the several components previously mentioned. Nor would we attempt to reduce the statement that "x" picked up a phone to a statement that an arm attached to "x's" body reached toward an instrument called a telephone and lifted the receiver. It is also true that organizations cannot exist except for human perceptions. If this necessary, but not sufficient, condition is meant to imply, however, that individual human beings can decide not to perceive an organization and that henceforth the organization will not persist, it is at best a serious overstatement of the case against the reality of organizations. Indeed the argument against the reality of organization would not be pursued anywhere other than in the social sciences. An astrophysicist would throw up his hands at the suggestion that the solar system does not exist but only the sun, the planets, and the other satellites. Only if the units can be described satisfactorily without mention of their relationships could the system be argued not to exist.

The cultural system, for instance, may be said to exist. The fact that children born and raised in the United States become Americans and that children born and raised in India become Indians is a fact of utmost consequence, for these statements imply much more than mere nationality. If the actions of the United States, for instance, are in some sense a product of the motivations of individual Americans within the context of the American environment, the kinds of motivations Americans have and the elements that satisfy these motivations depend upon how Americans have been socialized within the context of the American cultural system.

Socialization is not uniform throughout the United States, of course; not all biological systems are equally disposed to the socialization

---

Political and social systems have within them not merely one or two but an extremely large number of ultrastable, purposive, and conscious subsystems. This would surely make for important differences.

pattern. There are various thresholds. That two Kwakiutls engage in a potlatch can be explained by their aggressiveness in a particular context, but their aggressiveness in the particular context cannot be explained except insofar as Kwakiutl culture rewards that type of aggressiveness. The Hopi would not behave in the same way.

Explanations at the macro and at the micro level are complementary. We can dispense with neither if we want a complete explanation. That John Jones married Mary Smith can be explained on the basis of their individual motivations within their particular context, but the fact that John Jones and Mary Smith enter into a monogamous relationship based upon the concept of romantic love cannot be explained on this basis. It would happen differently in other systems. The fact that a petrochemical plant in the Soviet Union refines petroleum, then combines the components into its cruder forms, again to refine it, can be explained on the basis of a shortage of storage facilities and a quota based upon the amount of crude petroleum that is refined. The fact that plant managers can be so motivated, however, can be explained only within the context of a Communist economic system.

The micro and the macro systems, of course, do interact. The traditional Japanese cultural system is breaking down as industrialization leads to a vast increase in apartment dwelling in sprawling urban complexes. Traditional Japanese dress and customs are forced to change under this impact. The macrosystem is not a huge brooding omnipresence unrelated to what occurs at the micro level. We are not arguing that the macro level has independent reality but only that it has interdependent reality. And the explanations of behavior at the two levels are necessarily different.

A bank president may endorse the bank's lending money because he likes the borrower or because earning more money for the bank will satisfy his ambitions. The bank, however, lends money to earn income. This is not a functionalist fallacy, as some believe, for the operation of the bank within the economic system constrains the officers of the bank to satisfy their individual motivations. whether pecuniary or non-pecuniary, in ways consistent with the bank's equilibrium role in the economic system—or this bank will fail and be replaced by some other bank that will properly fulfil the role, except, again, in a situation of transition to some other kind of economic system. Although an individual loan may be best understood—

understood in the fullest sense—by looking at the motivations of the lending officers, the lending policy of the bank can best be understood by an analysis of the bank's situation within the economic system.

There is a relationship between the levels of activity that cannot be understood apart from an analysis that includes both levels. Even at the micro level, the micro activity cannot be understood without using collective words such as bank. To state that John Jones made the loan is not to convey information unless others understand that John Jones is an official of the bank. Although John Jones, officer of the bank, may make a loan to a friend and lose money for the bank, it will be precisely this dereliction of his duty as an officer of the bank that requires explanation at the micro level, so that even in this case the normalized role expectations are an essential part of the explanation at the micro level. Lending to a friend, even if it is not profitable, does not require explanation at the micro level if it is a purely personal transaction.

The behavior of the group, moreover, is not necessarily similar to the behavior of the individuals who compose it. An analogy may help to make this thought somewhat more explicit. Paperclips are individually relatively rigid. If, however, they are linked together in a band, the band is flexible.

The more subsystem dominant a system is, the greater the extent to which explanations of system behavior must incorporate items of information relevant to the subsystems. A theory of international politics in most cases will therefore likely say less of importance to the statesman concerning the decisions he must make than will a theory of economics, particularly with respect to those aspects of economics coming close to perfect market formulations. To this extent, therefore, politics will be less theoretical than economics, its theories will be more limited in scope, and they will have lesser depth and power. Aristotle's insight that politics is a practical science rather than a theoretical science, and that it must proceed on the basis of experience, does incorporate at least some elements of truth.

We have called organizations real. Are they conscious? The question is the wrong question. Is man conscious? The common sense response that man is a conscious creature should perhaps be reformulated. Man can "think" when not conscious, and in any event his whole body is not conscious. The intimate tie that exists between the center of consciousness and the physical organization of human kind, together with the fact that personality almost invariably has singleness of organization, has tended to identify two elements that are analytically distinguishable.

The science fiction writers have been well ahead of the philosophers in this respect. Their stories of brains encased in mechanical environments or transplanted into other bodies or linked into a colony of pure intelligence, although containing many elements of pure fantasy, also make some required distinctions. The body contains a conscious subsystem; "it" is not conscious. And society contains consciousness, although there are multiple centers of it. The president may not be conscious of himself as the United States; but he is conscious of himself as president of the United States. Information pours into him from many sources in the system, even if it becomes distorted in the process, as the information that comes to individuals is distorted during the process of perception. The linkages between the president, other officers of the government, and the sources of information is neither as direct physically, nor as close to the original source in mode of entry, nor organized along as constant a set of linkages as is true in the case of individuals; but then the system is different.

Does the organization have purpose? For reasons already discussed, it does have purposes that can be understood only as organizational purposes. If a state goes to war and acquires territory, usually the territory satisfies given needs of the state. Of course, the state will not pursue this territory unless this objective also satisfies certain needs, whether similar or of an entirely different type, of the actors within the state. If the discrepancy is too great, the state will fail to survive or will be reorganized on a different basis. But what this tells us is not that the purposes of the state are the purposes of individuals but rather that the state is a subsystem dominant type of organization in which a multitude of constraints at system, subsystem, and individual levels must be satisfied if the system is to persist.

We are confronted by a simple failure of logic by the effort to show that there is no such thing as a public interest but only group interests. On the same basis one could argue that there are no group interests but only individual interests within groups. And one might finally argue that there are no such things as individual interests but only conflicting motivations within individuals. Many, if not all, public decisions in the United States, or in any other country, must satisfy some organizational needs as well as sub-organizational or individual needs.

That these needs will not be perceived if some individual does not perceive them and is not motivated to pursue them is a truism. The motivation occurs because the group exists; and where the motivation is not induced, the organization will decline and die.

None of this implies that the organization is superior to the individual or that the individual should sacrifice himself to the organization. There are different levels of organization and the individual is multistable. He can under many circumstances detach himself from one organization and move to another. But surprising numbers of individuals do sacrifice themselves for the organization, even during periods when the organization is not at war as a consequence of the socialization process. It has been asserted that society is a pyramid with a mass of people at the base and a few at the top and that those at the top receive a disproportionate share of the values of the system. One could argue, however, that just as soldiers are socialized to sacrifice themselves in war, as a consequence of individual dispositional factors that make them more vulnerable than other individuals to the appeals of the nation, leading statesmen, for instance, are inveigled, not by medals but by other honors, to engage themselves in a demanding activity that leaves no time for personal life by certain dispositions within their own personality systems. Other leading positions probably carry comparable burdens.

Another important distinction that Aristotle makes incorrectly can be related to the concept of system. The classic writers distinguish between what they call the natural and the artificial. The artificial is that which man makes by convention according to classic writers. According to this distinction, if modern biology were to synthesize a sperm and an ovum, to fertilize the ovum with the sperm, and to grow the fetus in a human-constructed womb, the resulting product would be artificial despite our inability to distinguish it from a living human being other than by knowing its origin.

This conclusion is, of course, outrageous both morally and theoretically; moreover, the usage distinguishes between artifice and nature on the wrong basis. Man and society are multistable and this fact governs their interaction with each other and with their environments in important ways. Man and society can change the environment to reduce disturbances, and they can also change themselves to keep other essential values of the system constant. Society can be changed and man's personality pattern and cultural values can be modified. Conceivably we can build machines capable of the same kind of interaction patterns; but we are not trying to make the distinction between convention and nature that the classic writers made. Instead, we distinguish between ultra or multistable interactions with the environment and merely stable interactions.

WHENCE VALUES?

The position developed in this essay has distinct implications for a philosophy of values. The position generally accepted by those who take a scientific viewpoint is that values exist in a normative realm that is not subject to scientific methods of proof. Although many writers will concede that values are not preferences in the meager sense of a decision whether to buy a chocolate ice cream cone, the general supposition is that alternative values are not challengeable in the way scientific premises are challengeable.

Some writers do attempt to develop what they regard as a philosophy of values for common discourse, namely those values which must be accepted if people are to discuss values among themselves. Such writers often argue that such statements must be generalizable or universalizable. Thus if there are admission standards to a university, these should be applied to all individuals regardless of such extraneous differences as race, color, or religion.

The further argument might be made that it could be shown that none of these differences is relevant to performance in the type of society we live in. Thus the restriction of Negro rights bears no reasonable relationship to Negro citizenship performance capacities.

Such reasoning should not be entirely dismissed, for it does put some kind of closure on the argument. Moreover, arguments of this kind can sometimes demonstrate to people that what they thought was a disagreement over values really consists of a disagreement over factual premises, and that the disagreement is now resolved by further evidence.

The practical virtue of such agreements is not to be denied. Nonetheless it should be recognized that such standards could be rejected in ascriptive and particularistic societies. Although factual arguments were sometimes used to buttress the myth of Aryan supremacy, the basic argument was rather an ascriptive argument that Aryans were superior because they were Aryans. Moreover, although Americans do not share the particularistic values characteristic of southern Italians, even in the United States it is recognized that members of families have greater obligations toward each other than toward their fellow men at large. These obligations may be attenuated in a largely universalistic, achievement-oriented society; but they will continue to exist even there.

Moreover, the nation itself has an ascriptive base. We do not believe that we should open the doors of the United States to unlimited immigration in order to permit equalization of the world's wealth nor are we willing to distribute our assets in such fashion. The reasons against this, moreover, go beyond the fact that such large distributions in short time would disrupt the economy and social system, thereby undermining the objective to be served. Even if this were not so, very few Americans would agree to such ends, and indeed very few writers on ethical theory would agree.

It might be argued that the historical trend is toward societies that are universalistic and achievement-oriented, so that universalizing arguments will have greater and greater force over time. This may indeed be true; but the argument has no ethical force unless we can argue that such societies are better societies. The fact that as societies are transformed in this direction more people find this argument congenial is hardly an argument of philosophical merit unless placed within a framework other than that employed by the advocates of this position.

Utilitarian arguments also suffer from a serious deficiency. An ethics of consequences seems fairly reasonable to this writer. But consequences always have to be judged. Utilitarian arguments always raise the question: utilitarian for what end? The appointment of Hitler was utilitarian for bringing about a Nazi state. Flagellation is utilitarian for those who have masochistic needs.

Although utilitarians generally advocate altruism or the good of society, there is no reason to act for the good of society except on the basis of some ethical principle that is not demonstrable within the framework of utilitarianism. Moreover, even if one agrees that he should not act in a way that harms society, there are many important circumstances in which one can better his personal lot or produce good for some other person without injuring society in any measurable way; yet if all act in this way society will be injured. Thus, for circumstances of this kind, even those act utilitarians who accept the good of society as a criterion would require at least one moral rule to achieve that good: namely, that all act as they would wish others to act in like circumstances.[11]

Although the acceptance of a moral rule of the kind described would be reasonable for a race of gods, most of the rest of us are subject to the distortions that Hobbes talked about. Give us a standard so broad and we will begin to perceive all our private vices as public virtues. Although any set of specific descriptive moral standards will soon include at least some that are dysfunctional, it can perhaps be argued that society is generally better off with such standards—although wise administrators seem to know that rules are made to be broken in exceptional circumstances. Articulation of this truism would likely be dysfunctional.

A SYSTEMS APPROACH TO VALUES

In any event, none of the previous positions takes us any appreciable distance toward a philosophical understanding of the problem of values. We have left the instrument, the system of perception, out of account. We have failed to understand that value-laden activity involves a relationship among a perceiving instrument, an experiment, and a setting. The judgments by the perceiver of values are much more complicated and subtle than judgments of color. Some of the early Renaissance writers, who took a natural-law view of values, were wrong when they regarded right and wrong as simple matters that could be as easily perceived as black and white. Values are much more

[11]See the selection "Some Problems of Restricted Utilitarianism".

complicated and involve multistable relationships among the perceiving instrument, the experiment, and the environment.

The human system is unlike Grey Walter's little machine in several respects. It is complicated and its resting states are difficult to distinguish in a complex and changing environment. It is also ultrastable; it can produce changes in both itself and its environment. Moreover, it is not programmed to maximize a single variable. These last two characteristics imply that it has choice with respect to values and, insofar as these problems are dealt with consciously according to the processes of thought, moral choices. Moreover, the instrument operates on the basis of imperfect information. Thus its judgments are subject to considerable distortion and misinterpretation.

Essentially what is being proposed here is a standard relative to conditions but not merely a matter of preferences. We argue that the observing instrument, in this case a human being, is a valuational instrument whose needs in any given set of circumstances are better satisfied by some possible changes than by others.

There would be an element of historicity in the processing of values. Placing certain individuals in favorable positions within the social or political system creates in them expectations deeply imbedded in their personality structure and their relationship to their immediate environment. Any rearrangement of the social structure that would threaten these expectations, though promising that they would be better off or at least not worse off, would not likely prove acceptable to them even were they to agree in some abstract sense that the resulting social or political system would be better in general.

The fact that men value, and that their valuations have some objective relationship to their systemic characteristics, does not in and of itself imply altruism. On the other hand, if one assumes that the dominant subsystem of man (the subsystem that acts as the ultrastable regulator for the entire system) lies in the cortical layer of the brain and that this layer has an inherent tendency toward generalizing at an abstract level, then there would be a tendency toward ratiocinations destructive of any particular historicity. This tendency need not be paramount; it need only function as a minor modifier at each particular time to have a great long-term effect, everything else being equal. It would then be reinforced by cooperative needs, socializational tendencies, and linguistic propensities to generalize or to universalize. If so, these tendencies would result in the modification of the external environment in ways permitting larger proportions of the population to function autonomously as metastable systems without threat to the functioning of those in the more central political, social, and moral roles. The thought expressed here is in some ways similar to Hegel's, when he viewed history as the march of freedom in the world, or Marx's, when he spoke of the transition from the realm of necessity to the kingdom of freedom.

Apart from the problematic character of the central assumption, an optimistic view of history is much easier to accept if one can assume either a *weltgeist* to overcome the accidents of history, or a dialectical tendency in which institutional processes will negate human irrationalities. The view presented in this essay is not completely consistent with such optimism. In order to satisfy human needs in a world of conflict, social, political, and moral institutions must be capable of surviving conflict in that world. It is not self-evident that those institutions best adapted to this type of survival are also best adapted to other human needs.

In short, the world is complex, with much and complicated feedback, and the concomitants of success in one area of activity may possibly be unfavorable in other areas.

Because the processes which socialize and integrate individuals into the roles of the system also influence moral perceptions, putative defects might be viewed by them as advantages. In order to survive in his crippled condition the paraplegic requires some form of neurotic structure. The neurotic structure of a paraplegic serves to rationalize his condition. But at least the paraplegic is confronted with the world of "normal" people. He cannot easily argue that the condition of being a paraplegic is "normal" or superior. Yet it is exactly that condition, that is, of being able to argue that the inferior is "superior", that characterizes the group or social condition. The ultrastable regulator within individuals, rather than acting to regulate the environment, may change itself to bring it into closer concordance with external requirements. It is difficult enough to control social processes seen directly as evil, such as the ways modern society pollutes its airs and its waters; it is immensely more difficult to control group processes, because of the ways in which individual decision-making is related to group behavior, where the evil is not manifestly apparent.

Many changes are incremental in small steps. In at least some cases, each transition from a "better" to a "worse" state may on balance be desirable, although, were one able to visualize the end of the process, it might be rejected with horror. Unfortunately the perceiving instrument changes as it changes the external environment; it is socialized to the changes it produces, it channels information in different ways, and it censors inconsistent types of information.

Let us attempt to recapitulate the position. Values are real. They are not relative in the sense of mere preferences, however, but are related to the characteristics of man, his relationship to his environment, and his environment. Values do not exist independently of the interaction between man and his environment any more than space or time have physical meaning apart from certain physical operations and the instruments used to carry out the operations on the experimental objects. The *weltgeist* and the historical dialectic introduce standards that cannot be brought into relationship to the real historical process.

JUSTICE

Justice is the extension of a system of values from the individual to the group, or from the group to a more inclusive grouping. It extends the concept of the good to a formal framework within which an external observer can decide whether an action accords with standards that are independent of person. The Nazi system, for instance, may have been believed to be good by Nazis, but it was destructive of a community of justice between Nazis and other people. If utilities are interdependent, justice is a genuine natural need. Justice, however, is not something that can exist independently of man's activities. In a world where information is imperfect and resources scarce, justice is something that can only slowly be created.

Although the concepts of justice and of injustice are, of course, definitionally inseparable, the empirical assertion that something is not just does not imply that there is a just alternative. The Arabs who have been displaced by the creation of the state of Israel have a claim that their losses are unjust. Their relationship to the soil of their ancestors is deep and their need for a cultural community under their control on that land is real. The needs of the Jews of Europe were no less real, however, and inconsistent with the Arab needs. Displacing the Jews from Israel or driving them into the sea would not bring about a state of justice. In situations of this kind one may prefer one injustice to another on the basis of reasoned arguments about which injustice is the least bad precedent for the future, and so forth.

If we do not argue that justice is always possible under existential conditions, we also do not argue that any single standard has univocal merit, even assuming objective standards. Thus we might agree that people should be rewarded according to merit, or, alternatively, according to production. Yet there may be different notions of both and conflicts between the concepts. We can recognize that any real social system will produce some injustices and that some choices between values and between systems will be marginal or doubtful. If the concept of justice is to be meaningful, however, it is essential that at least some values and some social systems be clearly worse than others.

It is also necessary to recognize that all systems and all values may do irreparable harm to at least some people. Soldiers are killed in war, one group deprived in favor of another, the present deprived in favor of the future, or the future deprived in favor of the present. And all cry justice.

If the environment is favorable enough, then perhaps we can agree upon a minimal standard for all as a prerequisite for justice, and also upon minimal deprivations of existing expectations for those who are to be taxed or penalized. If we are lucky and the environment favorable, it may even be that lesser present deprivations of those favorably situated will be consistent with greater future productivity, so that all are served best by such lesser deprivations.

The future is problematical. The killings, the tortures, the imprisonments, the deprivations of living individuals by totalitarian regimes are very difficult to justify on the dubious expectation that a better world will be created. Social science is not that powerful and the intuitions of the self-appointed leaders of the historical process not that convincing. Although any real social system must do some harm, one may indeed question where any men acquire the rights to deprive the present generation in major and radical ways. At a more modest level of inquiry, one may adopt some of the devices of modern bargaining theory in order to create minimum conditions of fairness for social outcomes. But in the end some injustices will result. The ineradicability of injustice, however, does not deprive the concept of justice of meaning.

SUGGESTED TEST FOR VALUATIONS

Those values would be best that brought man closest to his resting states. Presumably there would be certain tests for this in which the indicators would consist not merely of the actual responses to the environment but also of the functioning of the instrument, including the processing of information, the physiological responses, and the psychological state of health of the system.[12]

If this hypothesis is correct, then under conditions of perfect information man will designate those things as "good" that are consistent with his eufunctional behavior according to the suggested test. If interdependence of utility is a correct hypothesis, then under conditions of perfect information and of benign material environment, the preferences of most men for political and social institutions will agree, largely irrespective of social role. The content of the good would depend upon circumstances, although differences in preferences would be possible for nearly equivalent systems in which marginal trade-offs between roles are for the most part equivalent but different in sign. This last conclusion indicates that some preferences would remain related to role functions in even the best of worlds, although these likely would not be of major importance.

Since in any particular material environment that is less than benign, alternative social, political, or moral arrangements would satisfy some men better than others and *vice versa*—genuine conflicts of interests would arise concerning not merely the organization of the social, political, and moral world but of the principles that should govern its organization. If material circumstances are less than benign, some men may have genuine vested interests in social or political solutions that are bad for most other men. Presumably, however, their feelings for their fellow man under conditions of perfect information would create costs for them that would be detectable.

[12]This point is developed at greater length in the selection "The Realm of Values".

If the material environment is sufficiently harsh, a man may then be in the position of the paraplegic; he may be forced to shut out the information for his own mental health; and he may be forced to behave in ways that severely deprive others. But then we could presumably demonstrate the operation of pathological mechanisms and thereby have a standard for judgment that refers to him as "crippled" and to life circumstances or forms of social organization as the "crippling" agents. Presumably, if he decides against himself, he is equally "crippled". He is a victim.

Perfect information concerning the material environment and alternative choices is not available. There are ways it can be approached, however, at least in thought. Consider a situation in which a man would be able to relive his past in thought. He could be confronted with each of the branching points of his major life decisions and allowed subjectively to live the alternative lives. If individual choices could be tested in this fashion, social and political and moral choices could be tested in analogous fashion by confrontations with different patterns of social, political, and moral organization under similar and under different environmental constraints.

Presumably this would confront men with choices that are meaningful. Thus, where the material environments of the social and political systems are presented as "givens", the individual would observe the consequences of different positionings and different circumstances within the systems. He could observe which roles he would prefer if he could choose his roles and how much he would like or dislike the system if roles were chosen for him. Within his own life patterning, he could compare choices over those things where he in fact had the freedom to choose differently. Within these constraints, his conceptions of the good depend upon the limitations of institutional life and environment. In the second form of testing, he could vary institutional life and material environment, again in two ways. He could compare systems as to which he would prefer if he could choose his role and which he would prefer if his role were assigned to him. On the basis of a more limited freedom, he could compare differences in the existing institutional structures with respect to his past decision points, where he had had some freedom to effect changes in them.

After experiencing these alternatives, the individual would return to his actual situation. He would then have to choose in the present on the basis of the limited alternatives available to him. He now has a standard against which to judge his practicable choices; if he has interdependent utilities, it will be too uncomfortable for him not to make some effort to move the system closer to alternatives that are practicable, not too deprivational for him, and better for others as well. Presumably he will not confuse himself about the harm he does to others because of his needs under existing constraints.

If we are dissatisfied with the concept of a standard for values that is asserted to be meaningful but perhaps not empirically testable, we might propose the following kinds of quasi-tests. Children could be raised under controlled conditions and then compared in aspects of their functioning. Alternatively, if the future provides methods whereby memories may either be erased or impressed upon the mind, it would be possible to run experiments in which separate memory tracks could be impressed simultaneously and compared on an A, B basis. Since the order might not be entirely transitive, discarded sequences might be recompared with seemingly dominant patterns.

If these suggestions seem too fantastic, we could consider the more limited kinds of comparisons that we in fact make when we talk about propositions of this kind. These do not have the fullness of comparison suggested above and they suffer from the defect that we are constrained by our own local conditions in making comparisons. Nonetheless we can and do make at least limited comparisons and occasionally we even decide against our own social system on this basis, as many Germans did during the time of Nazi Germany. The degree of confidence to be placed in such localized comparisons must be quite low, for we do not fully know what conditions the system consequences are dependent upon. However, our ability to relate positions to life and social experiences is itself a solvent and does produce a broader set of comparisons. In any event, our concept of the nature of man as a valuating system is meaningful, the conception of limits to plasticity and costs for wrong choices is meaningful, and therefore at a minimum the concept of local comparisons is meaningful.

If the good is that which is appropriate to achieve man's resting states, if the resting state is multistable self-regulation, and if interdependence of utility is an aspect of man's nature, then, under conditions of perfect information and benign material environment, man will regard as categorical imperatives those things necessary for just social and political systems in which all men can regulate themselves in a multistable fashion. If the environment is less than benign and if information is perfect, individual men will recognize that what is good for them will to some extent be inconsistent with justice; however, they will also recognize a moral imperative to improve the material environment and social institutions so that the conflict between the good and justice will be reduced or will become at least less extreme than it would otherwise become. If information is less than perfect, then assertions of moral imperatives as well as of the good will differ from those that would have been asserted under conditions of perfect information. These can be called incorrect by the ordinary canons of science, to the extent that we are able to make such discriminations. What is good for individual men will depend upon their characteristics and circumstances; just social and political systems, however, will increase the probability that individual men will be able to achieve what is good for them.

Particularistic groupings would achieve goods for the members of the group. There would be costs in breaking up existing groups or in forming new groups. But groups would be of instrumental value only. Membership in a group would be accidental (parentage or location) and not related to the characteristics of the members in a human sense. Thus generalized arguments pointing out disparities of circumstance or treatment would have moral effectiveness. Reducing these disparities would become a moral imperative. There will almost always be some disparity between the good and the just, if the just be regarded as that which can be generalized regardless of individual human or particular group circumstances. There will almost always be a tension between man's need to do what is good for himself, as it is weighed independently of its effects upon others, and of his need to help sustain others. In addition, apart from the intrinsic worth of other people, there will be an essential instrumental need to secure the cooperation of at least some other people and to employ justifications that are generalizable as well as materially sound. Therefore there will be a tension that helps to produce the just as well as the good. Moral "oughts" represent these tendencies in man's nature as they emerge in speech. They are future-oriented and usually generalized. In benign material environments and under conditions of perfect information, if our hypotheses are correct, there should be considerable agreement among men on both the formal and material (or content) characteristics of moral statements. The categorical character of moral statements from this point of view represents their human necessity, that is, their grounding in human nature. Those who are morally crippled have had their human nature irreversibly changed. But, again, if our hypotheses are correct, they would not have chosen that state if confronted with full alternatives under conditions of perfect information. Thus, although the existential moral bond between them and other people has been attenuated, the independent observer can call their state of being "inferior" or "crippled".

AN ASIDE ON EXISTENTIALISM

Raising the question in this way forces us to the question of what we are. Hillel, the ancient Jewish sage, once asserted, if I may paraphrase him, "If I am not for myself, who will be? If I am not for others, what am I?" That is, after all, the ultimate question. Life is a process during which we both discover and make ourselves. Unlike an existentialism, however, that retreats from classical philosophy down the slopes of historicism, and in the absence of any real philosophical or scientific standard submits to the sentimentalism of so-called deprived classes or races, systemic pragmaticism sees within the absurdity and despair of existence a ground for rational discourse. We may be wrong to believe that interdependence of utility is part of the nature of human being, or to believe that the generalizing capacity of the ultrastable regulator is subversive of particularistic distinctions; we may mistake our own misconceptions for the true nature of man. But we do not make the jejune mistake of believing in our absolute freedom to make of ourselves whatever we will without costs. The sentimental despair of existentialism is not new. In a somewhat different form, it represents the quest of the French revolutionaries for absolute freedom, to which Hegel in his *Phenomenology* gave the cutting philosophic response that absolute freedom is meaningless, as meaningless as absolute death, as meaningless as quaffing a glass of water or cleaving a head of cabbage. Man is bound by his own necessity. He can remake himself, but only at a cost.

The sentimental despair of existentialism serves to justify the most arduous tyrannies in the name of an ideal divorced from an immanent standard related to the nature of man. The criteria for morality become external to man and related to fictional classifications such as class or race that lack organizational reality. Genuine organizations have instrumental value for men. If men have interdependent utilities, then they do have moral obligations to sustain organizations that protect worthy values, even if these organizations fail to match some standard of moral perfection. The notion produced by existential despair, however, that men should lose themselves in service to a class or to a race, which is barbaric except insofar as ideas connected with these classifications have worthy organizational and human consequences, is used to justify the most brutal repressions and perversions of morality in such pseudo-philosophies as that of Jean-Paul Sartre. Promethean notions that men are gods who must entirely create themselves from nothing, although they bear a superficial resemblance to the Hegelian notion of the development of morality over time, foster nonsensical limitless notions of freedom and produce genuine slavery.

Man cannot escape his moral responsibility in choosing because he is a moral creature. He is not free to make himself what he wills. Some choices, however, involve situations in which uncertainty and surprise can play major roles. Here man can be guided only by good motives and prudence. The results can be judged, and if possible efforts can be made to change them should they be judged bad. Much of tragedy involves situations where, regardless of what one does, injustice must be done, or situations where man must hew a road into an uncharted wilderness. Still he has at least a retrospective standard, to the best extent to which he can reason about it, to judge what he has done and to attempt to mitigate his mistakes.

Man has the power to pervert his nature, to change himself in such irreversible ways that he would be as morally crippled as the paraplegic is physically crippled. Any particular assertion that he has done so may be wrong, for such judgments are to a considerable extent acts of faith; but they are meaningful. And thus man's acts of faith, no matter how wrongly conceived, are grounded in a rational faith.

There is an important difference between being unable to demonstrate the content of a standard and being unable to argue that there is a standard. The latter is a counsel for genuine despair. The systemic pragmaticist point of view provides at least an opening for assertions concerning the content of a standard, even if not with high confidence.

We can then begin to judge individual acts, criteria for these acts in a particular context, and social, political, and moral systems, as to whether they bring us closer to or farther away from circumstances that do more to actualize the potentiality inherent in the kinds of human systems we are talking about.

In Marx's language, we would claim that existentialism, the philosophy of despair, is a false consciousness of the human condition. The world is a surd in the sense that its existence is a brute fact and that no reason can be given for its existence. The character of social organization produces results that are irrational from the standpoint of individual human motivation. Individual human motivation is often quite irrational from the standpoint of desirable social orders. We intend to deny none of these surdities. We claim only the existence of a human potentiality for reducing injustice, for reducing irrationality, for bringing order out of disorder.

The good, in the abstract, is the creation of a social, political, and moral environment in which individual human beings are provided with the facilities to regulate and to reduce the disorder in their own area autonomously, that is, with ultrastable self-direction. That they will do so is not a law of the universe; in this respect modern philosophy must differ from classic philosophy. That men have the potentiality to do so if they are capable of recognizing their own necessity—that is, if they can find their freedom in their own necessity—is an assertion that modern philosophy can hold in common with the classic stream of philosophy from the early Greeks through Hegel and Marx. We would agree with Aristotle's thesis that man's end is not life but the good life.

FRAGMENT OF A THESIS

If all organic material were multistable, or at least ultrastable, then all organic material would have regulatory components. If this were so, it would be possible for the systems to regulate not only to maintain the value of some essential variable but also to increase some aspect of it. This selectivity need not be intelligent. Structural changes might, in the earlier forms of organic life, occur as a consequence of random mutation. There might, however, be selectivity based not merely on efficiency with respect to environmental adaptation but also with respect to the satisfaction of the programmed regulatory goals of the system. If this were the case, then there might even be a hierarchical order in the universe, not as a matter of necessity or of law, but in that there would be certain tendencies toward this ordering. This would make sense of Spinoza's conatus or of Hegel's process of historic transformation. However, there would be no cunning of history to necessitate such developments. And since regulation is dependent upon information, there would be no guarantee that even seemingly intelligent choices would over the long run move toward better or "higher" rather than worse or "lower" forms. There is no evidence I know of that supports a hypothesis of telic adaptivity, but it is neither meaningless nor inconsistent with scientific procedure. If such a hypothesis were correct, then even if wrong choices were made there would be some tendency toward retrospective corrections of incorrectly chosen paths, not merely for man but for organic nature as well. Such a hypothesis would give content to Aristotle's concept of final cause. This striving "upward" would be the search for God, not in a pantheistic sense, but in the sense of immanent becoming.

PART II

On Systems

This section includes a part of an article on science and traditionalism in the October 1966 issue of *World Politics*, my chapter on systems theory from Charlesworth, *Comparative Political Analysis*, and short excerpts from my article on systems theory for the Spring 1968 issue of *Social Research*. The excerpts from the last of these emphasizes that systems theory is not a theory but rather a set of concepts useful for building empirical theory, that where systems concepts are used to treat events as if they were systems they are misleading, and that simple models are often both more useful for exploring reality than simulation models and closer to the "stuff" of reality. This article also takes over the definition of task and metatask function that was developed in *System and Process*.

The concept of crisis as a focus for research is very popular nowadays. The definitions of task and metatask functions permit a precise definition of a crisis. A crisis consists of the overloading of a system's capacity either by environmental disturbances or by the expectation of such disturbances. Capacity is then drained from metatask to task functions, thereby undermining the ultrastable regulator of the system and producing instabilities (see *System and Process*, Chapter 4). Crisis always involves the relationship of a system to its environment or context. The meaning of a crisis is therefore also so related.

2

TRADITIONALISM vs. SCIENCE

IN INTERNATIONAL

RELATIONS

Over the past decade traditionalists have launched a series of attacks on scientific approaches to international politics. Most of the arguments employed against the scientific approach stem from those used earlier by E. H. Carr in *The Twenty Years' Crisis*.[1] The general arguments that have been employed include these among others: that politics involves purpose in a way that physical science does not; that scientific knowledge is applicable to facts, but understanding, wisdom, or intuition are required for areas where human purpose is involved; that those pursuing scientific models tend to mistake their models for reality; that scientific method requires high precision and measurement and therefore is incapable of coping with the most important elements of international politics; and that the practitioners of scientific method can never be sure that they have not left something out of their model.

[1] 2nd ed. (Macmillan, 1956).

I

According to Carr, "The laboratory worker engaged in investigating the causes of cancer may have been originally inspired by the purpose of eradicating the disease. But this purpose is, in the strictest sense, irrelevant to the investigation and separable from it. His conclusion can be nothing more than a true report on fact. It cannot help to make the facts other than they are; for the facts exist independently of what anyone thinks about them. In the political sciences, which are concerned with human behavior, there are no such facts. The investigator is inspired by the desire to cure some ill of the body politic. Among the causes of the trouble, he diagnoses the fact that human beings normally react to certain conditions in a certain way. But this is not a fact comparable with the fact that human bodies react in a certain way to certain drugs. It is a fact which may be changed by the desire to change it; and this desire, already present in the mind of the investigator, may be extended, as the result of his investigation, to a sufficient number of other human beings to make it effective".[2]

The two cases cited by Carr are different, but Carr has mistaken the nature of the difference. Carr's inapt distinction results from a prior failure to distinguish between the facts he initially holds constant (system) and the facts he allows to change (parameters). It is a fact that rattlesnake venom injected into the blood system will normally kill a person. It is also a fact that the proper antidote administered in time will negate the destructive action of the venom. The cancer worker also desires to change some facts, namely, those relating to the development of cancer. He does this by changing, perhaps by drugs or perhaps by irradiation, the system in which the cancerous cells are embedded. The politician who desires to change the world must also change the state of a system—in this case, the political system. He may do this by the use of force, by the allocation of resources, or by means of verbal persuasion. The system may undergo radical change. Its characteristic operation may be different from what it was before the new inputs, including information, were embedded in the system. But then a similar kind of change in characteristic behavior occurs when, for instance, opium is injected into the human physiological system or flowers are hybridized (step functions).[3]

[2]*Ibid.*, 3-4.   [3]W. Ross Ashby, *Design for a Brain* (Wiley, 1952), 80 ff.

II

If the traditionalist has confused the distinction between the facts of physical science and the purposes of politics, then it is clear that he must also have confused the relationship between intuition and scientific knowledge.

There is a large literature on the subject of intuition in physical science and mathematics. Great discoveries, when they do not occur accidentally or as a consequence of trial-and-error procedures, are the product of scientific intuition. If the best statesmen are usually those with the best intuitions and judgments concerning politics, so the best scientists are often those whose scientific judgment or intuition is the best. There are cases in which scientists have been repeatedly right although the reasons they have given to support their theories have turned out to be faulty. The reasons for the superiority of intuition are not hard to find. The brain is more sophisticated and complicated than any computer we can construct. It can scan for variations in ways for which directions cannot yet be coded; it can reason below the level of consciousness in ways that neither numbers nor verbal logic can articulate. As John von Neumann pointed out in his posthumously published Silliman lectures, even if we used in its construction the smallest components available, and even if we knew (as we in fact do not) how to link the system up, it would require a housing 10^8 or 10^9 as large as the brain casing (or roughly as large as the Empire State Building) to house an analogue to the brain.[4] Even though miniaturization has made profound strides since von Neumann's death, this gives some indication of the scope of the problem.

The skill of a tea taster gives one indication of the capacity of the human brain to scan for "fits". Computer recognition is hopelessly primitive by comparison. Similarly, the human capacity to find parallels in history defies our ability to code or to articulate. The brain's coding apparently differs from that of mathematics and verbal logic.[5] Its code is apparently less precise but more reliable. And it apparently, along with the scanning capacity, plays a major role in intuition.

The humanist who wants to substitute in human events a verbal process called reason or understanding for a verbal and/or mathe-

[4]*The Computer and the Brain* (Yale University Press, 1958), 50.
[5]*Ibid.*, 90-92.

matical process called science has confused intuition with the articulation of communicable knowledge. The source of the confusion may
possibly lie in the Aristotelian distinction between science and art.
Science, according to Aristotle, must be certain, for it derives true
conclusions from necessary—not merely true—premises.[6] Thus hypothetical knowledge cannot be scientific, for its premises, even if true,
are not known to be necessary. One cannot intuit the necessity of the
premises in human events; therefore art rather than science governs
knowledge of human events. Modern science, however, insists upon
the hypothetical character of all empirical knowledge. The test for
communicable knowledge depends on replicability even if only in
principle. Thus there is no distinction between the physical and human
with respect to the need for confirmation and communication. There
is a distinction between subject matters with respect to the degree to
which theoretical knowledge is possible and to which warranted belief
or precision is possible.

Science requires an articulated secondary language that permits reasonable precision and replicability. Unless scientific procedures are
followed, to the extent the subject matter permits, intuitions cannot
be falsified and science cannot grow. Even intuition requires the techniques of science to prepare the base on which new intuitions develop.
If Einstein's intuition produced both the special and general theories
of relativity, that intuition operated within a framework of previous
discovery and research—e.g., non-Euclidean geometries and Lorentz
transformations (based on the Michelson-Morley experiment)—that
created an order within which the procedures of his unconscious mind
could generate the intuitions that led to relativity theory. Newton
could not have had Einstein's intuitions.

.   .   .   .

VII

Another major charge made by the traditionalist against the newer
methods is that since they use models, their practitioners are likely to
mistake the models for reality. If the causal connection were not insisted on, I would not lightly deny the charge. There is a human

[6]*Organon: Posterior Analytics, Topica* (Loeb Classical Library, 1960), 33-55.

tendency to reification. Surely the psychologists, sociologists, and anthropologists—and even the physicists, who know very little about politics—have a tendency to apply very simplified assumptions to very complex events. If, however, the traditionalist were to examine the propositions of the psychologists, for instance, he would find them no different from empirical generalizations—a category he likes. When a psychologist talks of projection or of a mirror image he is not, in the usual case, deriving these generalizations from an integrated theory, but is simply asserting an empirical generalization explicitly. The trouble with a generalization of this kind, apart from its general inapplicability, is that no context for its application is specified. Thus, as in the case of traditionalist arguments, it can be applied safely, for, in the form offered, it can never really be falsified.

On the other hand, it is natural to expect sophistication with respect to models from one who explicitly uses them. Only someone who has worked with models and the methodology of models knows how sensitive at least some models are to parameter adjustments. Thus a builder of models does not think of them as generally applicable. They are applicable only within a specified context; and it is extremely important to determine whether that context in fact exists. Moreover, the person who has worked with models usually has gone through the difficult task of trying to associate the parameters of the model with the real world. No one who has attempted this is likely to take it lightly.

I would argue that it is rather the traditionalist, whose assumptions are implicit rather than explicit and whose statements are made usually without reference to context, who is more likely to mistake his model for reality. Of course, even traditionalists are not likely to be as incautious as the historian Webster, who asserted that Castlereagh inherited his phlegmatic disposition from his mother who died when he was one year old. Yet the traditional literature of diplomatic history and international politics is filled with implicit assumptions as to motivation, interrelationships between variables, and so forth, that are implicit rather than specified, and the limits of application of which are never asserted. Even so careful and intelligent a traditionalist as George Kennan has made assertions about the likely effectiveness of United States aid in encouraging diversity and pluralism within the Soviet bloc which hardly seem to be sustained by the evidence.[23]

[7] "Polycentrism and Western Policy", *Foreign Affairs*, XLII (January 1964), 178.

Kennan did not explicitly articulate his model. He no doubt assumed that the provision of American aid provided the Polish government with an alternative to Soviet pressure. I would argue that had Kennan explicitly articulated his model, he might more likely have considered variables not included in his implicit model. Had he done so, he might have considered the possibility that the Polish government could argue to the Polish citizens that if the United States gave aid to Poland it must be a sign that the Polish regime was an acceptable regime. Therefore it would be unwise for the Polish citizen to oppose that regime or to expect even psychological aid from the United States in opposition. He also might have considered the hypothesis that the Polish leaders, as good Communists, and as a consequence of accepting American aid, might find it important to reassert at least some elements of Communist doctrine more strongly either to reassure themselves or to assure elements within the Polish Communist party whose support they needed that the leadership was not becoming a stooge for United States imperialism.

The probability that traditionalists will mistake their models for reality is further exemplified by Hedley Bull's criticisms of the new scientific approaches. Bull is so confident, on the basis of his premises, that those following the scientific method will engage largely in methodology both in their research and in their teaching, graduate and undergraduate, that he ignores the abundant evidence to the contrary. He himself admits that the other traditionalist critics of the new methods do not have adequate knowledge of these methods; yet he somehow fails to draw the inference from his own evidence that these critics have mistaken their implicit models for reality.

The traditional techniques with their inarticulated suppositions, their lack of specification of boundaries, and their almost necessary shifting of premises create a much greater danger that their implicit assumptions will automatically be applied to reality and a much greater sense of complacency than do scientific methods.

   .   .   .   .

3

SYSTEMS THEORY

The classic statement of systems theory occurs in W. Ross Ashby's, *Design For A Brain*. A brief and non-technical description of the objectives of systems analysis would include: the study of a set of interrelated variables, as distinguished from the environment of the set, and of the ways in which this set is maintained under the impact of environmental disturbances. This definition emphasizes the articulation of the system and of its components and the behaviors by means of which it maintains itself over time.

This orientation does not imply the actual or potential existence of a general theory of systems. We will later explain how and why systems theory implies the probability of comparative rather than general theory. Neither does systems theory imply the desirability or the actuality of system stability. It is true that the systems that do persist usually have the greatest importance for us; this reason would no doubt justify a concern with systems in equilibrium. There are, however, prior and theoretically more interesting reasons for concern with the problems of equilibrium. Differences in types of equilibrium are important in distinguish-

ing differences in types of systems. This important problem will also be
explored below. In addition, there is an important reason stemming from
the principle of economy. Many more systems fail to persist through
time than those that do persist. Although the parameter values that produce instability are large in number and differ in multifarious ways from
case to case, the conditions producing stability are much more limited in
number. Thus concern with stability, at least in the initial stages of inquiry, focuses attention on a relatively small number of systems, a limited
number of variables, and a limited range of variation. Although the
problem of inquiry may still be most difficult, it is much more focused
and manageable than is a concern with problems of instability. Moreover, to the extent that we can understand systems in equilibrium, we
have a fulcrum for the study of systems in disequilibrium. If we can
construct a theory for a sytem or type of system, as a system in equilibrium, we can then inquire how individual variations in the parameters
will produce deviant or unstable behavior. To know why a system
changes, develops, or breaks down it is surely helpful to know why the
conditions of change are inconsistent with the prior states of the system.
If we cannot answer this latter question, it is doubtful whether we have
correctly assigned the reasons for instability or change.

The systems theoretical approach is also chosen for the following
additional reasons: for explicitness of categories so that the framework
of reference will not shift as new "facts" are brought in; for the integration of variables that do not fall within a single discipline; for a degree of
explicitness that helps to reveal incompleteness; and for the generation
of hypotheses by indicating structural similarities to other subject
matters.

THE CONCEPT OF EQUILIBRIUM

The distinctions between equilibria are in some ways more important
than their similarities. Systems analysis is concerned with two basic
problems with respect to equilibrium. The first concerns the stability of
the equilibrium. It is important to recognize that the concept of stability
has meaning only in relation to the questions the investigator puts to his
data. The same system may be stable or unstable from two different
standpoints. The second question concerns the value of the concept of
equilibrium from the standpoint of explanation. Whereas the concept of

mechanical equilibrium provides an explanation of observed behavior, the concept of homeostatic equilibrium has a different role.

STABILITY

Equilibria may be regarded as unstable, static, or stable. Illustrations of the three types respectively would be a ball on a ridge, on a flat surface, and in a valley. Alternatively we can regard equilibria as locally stable or as generally stable. Locally stable equilibria are stable only in a favorable environment. A stable equilibrium, on the other hand, is capable of persisting through many large and unexpected environmental disturbances. The biological system of man, which persists unchanged through many different political and social systems, is an example of a system in stable equilibrium.

It is also important to distinguish between those cases where a system behaves differently because of an environmental disturbance but returns to its old behavior when the disturbance is removed and cases where the changed behavior persists even after the disturbance is removed. The disturbance that produces the latter form of change is called a *step function* and the system result is called *system change*. For instance, during wartime in England normal liberties were suspended and political suspects incarcerated without recourse to the courts. With the return of peace, normal liberties were restored. Thus only the state of the system but not the system itself had changed. In other cases, however, the removal of the disturbance that led to the new behavior does not lead to the restoration of the old pattern of behavior. The inflation and subsequent depression in Germany were among the factors making for the Nazi takeover. However, the restoration of the economy did not lead to the removal of the Nazi regime. If one is habituated to opiates, then the pupil will not contract when a flashlight is shined into it. These latter cases are called *system change*. Carthage was destroyed by the Romans. This is called *system destruction* or *dissolution*.

SYSTEM REFERENCE

In keeping with the explicitness of systems theory, we must be careful not to shift systems reference. Thus, for instance, one system may change while another system remains constant. Kennedy replaces Eisenhower and the Democrats the Republicans in the presidency, but the American constitutional system continues. Hitler replaces Hindenburg. The German political system changes but the social system continues. The Chinese Communists break up the extended family system and the Chinese social system has changed. The Chinese cultural system continues. Immigrants enter the United States and their cultural system is assimilated into the American cultural system. The biological system persists, however. The scientists of Huxley's *Brave New World* produce their alpha and beta types. Even the biological system has changed in this case. The examples are illustrative only. We are not stressing either a hierarchy in the systems illustrated or an absence of feedback between them. We stress here only the fact that nonsystematic discussions concerning system stability often cause confusion by failing to identify the system or systems about which statements are being made.

The preceding discussion also illustrates the fact that stability questions need to have reference to some research design. The concept of stability is meaningless until we specify, even if only imprecisely, the system, the variables whose equilibrium is of interest, the variation in values that will be considered to be consistent with equilibrium, and the length of time that has relevance. Thus the politician in a closely contested two-party district who is concerned with holding office will regard that situation as unstable. The party boss who selects the candidates may regard the system as quite stable, even though his candidates are elected alternatively with those of the opposite party and even though he may have to choose different candidates in different elections. Most Americans would find the American political system unchanged subsequent to the passage of the Communist Control Act. However, American Communists likely would not agree with this estimate. We would view the American and British political systems as stable. A visitor from Mars with a life span of 10,000 years might regard the changes in the two systems as kaleidoscopic. From the standpoint of an eternal observer, even the solar system is unstable, for eventually the sun will explode and destroy the solar system. The researcher cannot determine whether a system is stable or unstable until he establishes for himself the questions he desires to put to the subject matter. Stability always has reference to the framework of inquiries. There is no such thing as stability in and of itself.

MECHANICAL AND HOMEOSTATIC EQUILIBRIUM

The physicist usually deals with systems in mechanical equilibrium. When the physicist says that two weights are equal, he has available independent methods that can confirm this statement. Thus his balance scales can be confirmed by his spring scales. If the spring scales do not confirm the balances, and if the elasticity of the springs is not at fault, the physicist will predict that the balance is asymmetrical. When a physicist says that two equal forces will cancel each other, he does not merely assume their equality from the cancellation. He has an independent measure for the equality. Thus the use of the concept of equilibrium with respect to mechanical equilibria is not merely descriptive but is also explanatory and predictive.

The statement that a sytem is in equilibrium is neither explanatory nor predictive in the case of homeostatic equilibria. Yet social and political systems manifesting some degree of equilibrium represent some kind of homeostatic equilibrium rather than of mechanical equilibrium. There are many different homeostatic equilibrium systems. The physiological system is homeostatic. Thus the temperature of the human blood is maintained by processes that compensate for environmental disturbances. For instance, in cold weather, constriction of the blood vessels occurs, whereas in hot weather perspiration takes place. The thermostatic system that maintains room temperature is also homeostatic. When the mercury reaches the desired range, the furnace is turned off. When the mercury goes below the desired range, the furnace is turned on. In both illustrative systems there are underlying mechanical systems where the equalities of physics are observed. However, homeostatic systems are not systems of equality. The process of perspiration continues until the required temperature change occurs. If for some reason this process cannot occur, as would be the case if the human body were covered with paint, either sickness or death will occur. There is no independent measure that will establish the equality between the perspiration and the lowering of temperature. Therefore, although naming the biological system one of homeostatic equilibrium tells us something about the general type of equilibrating process that characterizes the system, the statement that the system is in equilibrium is itself neither of explanatory nor predictive value. In the case of the biological system, we still require an explanation of the processes that characterize, for example, the system of temperature control.

This may help to explain why systems theory is not a general theory of all systems. Although general systems theory does attempt to distinguish different types of systems and to establish a framework within which similarities between systems can be recognized despite differences of subject matter, different kinds of systems require different theories for explanatory purposes. Systems theory not only represents a step away from the general theory approach but also offers an explanation for why such efforts will likely fail. Thus the correct application of systems theory to politics would involve a move away from general theory toward comparative theory. That is, using systems theory one would search for different theories for the explanation of different types of systems.

TYPES OF HOMEOSTATIC EQUILIBRIUM

Discussion of the types of homeostatic equilibrium is important for several reasons. Knowledge of variations in homeostatic equilibria gives greater insight into the reasons why general theories are likely to fail in the social sciences. Political and social systems are variations of a particular type of homeostatic system, namely, the ultrastable or multistable type. Moreover, the definition of a political system will be linked specifically to the concept of ultrastable regulation.

Some systems are merely homeostatic whereas others are ultrastable or multistable. Consider an ordinary homeostatic system such as the automatic pilot in an airplane. If a plane deviates from level flight while on automatic pilot, the automatic pilot will sense this and, by the application of negative feedback, will adjust the flight pattern of the plane back to level. Consider, however, the case in which the automatic pilot has been incorrectly linked to the ailerons of the plane. If the plane now deviates from level flight, the automatic pilot mechanism will sense this. It will now make an adjustment, but the adjustment, instead of bringing the plane back to level flight, will throw it into a spin.

In principle it would be possible to build an ultrastable automatic pilot the behavior of which was not critically dependent on the linkages to the ailerons. That is, the automatic pilot could be so built that it would reject its own behavior patterns if these increased the deviation from level flight. It could then "search" for a set of behaviors that would restore the level character of the flight and, when it found it, continue to use it so long as it maintained the critical variable within the established critical limits for variation. Such an ultrastable system would have distinct advantages for survival over a merely stable homeostatic system. Even ultrastability, however, is not sufficient for complex biological survival. Ashby, therefore, applies the term "multistability" to those cases where the part functions of the system are themselves individually ultrastable and where they can therefore "search" relatively independently for those critical behaviors consistent with the maintenance of the system. It is obvious that complex social systems must also be multistable.

LEVELS OF EXPLANATION IN SYSTEMS THEORY

A completely general theory would lack explanatory power. It would enunciate only the most elementary truisms about social and political structures or alternatively mislead by appearing to convey information about specifics—for example, equalities—that in its nature it could not provide. On the other hand, extreme particularization in social and political theories, or models, should also be avoided. In the first place, we cannot construct models that faithfully copy the particularities of the real world. The detail is too fine for us and, in addition, many of our variables must vary in their structure from their real-world counterparts. For instance, in calculating military interchanges we use numbers for which there are no exact counterparts in the real world. In the second place, even if we could match the fineness of the structure of the real world, our verbal, mathematical, and computer tools would be inadequate from the standpoint of representing the complex interrelationships between them. In the third place, the more complex a model becomes, if it is a feedback model, the more sensitive it is to slight variations either in loop directions or rates of flow. Thus highly complex models run the serious risk of being artifacts. That is, slight variations that we could neither detect nor measure in the real world might—and highly likely would—produce major differences in outcomes and in behaviors. Such highly particularized models lack both generality and relevance to any specific problem of social science.

The most productive level for systems theorizing will in all likelihood be that middle level where comparative theories can be evolved. Thus, for instance, Kaplan attempted a comparative theory of international systems based upon the conception that if the numbers, types, capabilities, motivations, and behavioral styles of the international actors vary, there should be systematic interrelationships among these variations. If one desired a systems theory of national systems, one would look not for a general theory of all national systems, let alone of all political systems, but for a comparative theory of different types of national systems. In the same way, a comparative theory of foreign policy might possibly be developed. It would seem likely that differences in national political systems should also make for differences in the styles or objectives of foreign policy behavior.

Such middle-level comparative theories have sufficient generality to be of scientific interest. That is, we speak about a given class of cases rather than merely about an individual or particular case. On the other hand, these comparative middle-level theories are sufficiently specific so that they say different things about distinguishable systems rather than the same thing about every system. If the variables that are treated in the comparative systems theories have sufficient importance for selective aspects of real-world behavior, they should then constitute reasonable first-order approximations that are useful for exploring those realities. At this level of generality, the fact that analogs and even counterfactual assumptions are sometimes employed does not contraindicate the validity of the enterprise.

.   .   .   .

ALTERNATIVE APPROACHES

One may begin from different macrotheories—or first-order approximations—in order to explain the same microevents. Thus by suitable parameter adjustments, one may explain the events subsequent to 1870 either from the standpoint of a theory of international politics or from the standpoint of a theory of foreign policy. The different theories, however, will answer different sets of questions concerning these events. Thus, starting from the model or theory of international politics, we learn how public opinion produces behavior inconsistent with system stability and security optimization. If we start with a theory of foreign policy that explains how different types of polities produce different styles of external policy, we may learn how regime considerations under special circumstances produce variations in that style of behavior. In this case our primary focus is upon the foreign-policy process as a process within the national political system.

Whether we can use either or both levels of explanation depends upon the benignity of the data. Theories can be used only when their relevance is not swamped by external disturbances. There are cases where international behavior may be dominated by national considerations or, alternatively, where national regime considerations may be dominated by an international occurrence that overwhelms the actors. In the usual case, however, both sets of constraints operate and each first-order approximation serves as the best starting point to answer a particular set of questions.

One cannot build a theory of international relations, however, upon a theory of foreign policy; nor can one begin with a theory of international relations and derive theories of foreign policies from it. Either attempt would assume a general theory that encompasses both viewpoints. Either theory, however, may be useful in understanding the specific parameters to which the other theory needs to be adjusted.

There is still a third point of view which for some sets of questions may be the most productive. This is the cross-sectional or biographical slicing of history in order to delineate the dynamics of social change as a particular sequence of events unrolls and places inconsistent pressures upon actors holding critical role functions in several important systems. We are not speaking here of instability in the systems model, for presumably that would be revealed directly by the analysis of the model. Nor are we speaking of mere change, for every homeostatic system undergoes change in the process of maintaing the values of some critical variable. Thus the perspiration that supports the cooling function of the blood in summer is a change. We speak rather of those changes that are characterized by step functions—that is, by a basic alteration in the operation of the system. In the ultrastable systems designed by Ashby, disturbance of the system requires the system to "search" for some form of behavior that maintains the critical variables within the critical limits. If this cannot be done, then the system ceases to function.

Social and political systems differ from this example in at least one important respect. The actors are imbedded in social and political systems in such ways that it is a matter not merely of whether they tend to respond in the appropriate way but also of whether they will desire to. That is, in the usual case the actor can detach himself from any particular social system in which he is a participant. He must be motivated to act in ways consistent with the critical limits and the other actors must be motivated to induce him so to act.

The actors are imbedded in a web of systems. Thus John Jones has both nuclear and extended family relationships, a role in the business in which he is employed, a social and recreational role, and perhaps a religious role among many others. For some sets of environmental circumstances these roles may be not merely inconsistent but irreconcilable. Thus if Jones is a teller at a bank and if his wife desperately needs an operation and if he can get the money in no other way, he may have to choose between robbing the bank at the expense of his role as teller or failing his wife at this critical juncture. If Jones fails his wife, his family situation may be destabilized. It is unlikely that the failure of one clerk would destabilize the bank system. However, revolutions occur when critical numbers of key individuals respond to the demands of their other role functions at the expense of their functions in the state system. The conflicts that arise in cases of this kind are, along with the environmental changes that stimulate the problem, the cause of social change. This kind of cross-sectional problem can best be studied by examining how critical roles in different systems make critically inconsistent demands upon the critical actors who participate in the relevant set of systems. This is but another form of applied systems analysis or of engineering systems to the real world.

SYSTEM AND SUBSYSTEM DOMINANCE

An important category for examining the problem of system stability or change is that of system and subsystem dominance. A system is system dominant to the extent that the behavior of the system functions as a parametric given for the actors within it. That is, a system is system dominant if the impact of individual behavior upon the system is negligible. For instance, in a perfect market, any individual buyer or seller will act as if price is a parametric given for him—that is, as if his entry into or staying out of the market has no effect whatsoever upon price. Cultural systems are in general system dominant. Although particular individuals may in some cases be cultural innovators, even so, with respect to both the general character of the culture and specific cultural norms, no individual is likely to be able to make any significant impact upon the culture. At the other extreme, that is, the subsystem dominant extreme, we might consider the Communist dictatorship under Stalin at the height of his power. Within broad limits, Stalin had the capability to tear the social and political system apart and to restructure it. Popular resistance, as when the kulaks slaughtered their cattle, could be treated somewhat as are price inelasticities in economics. Somewhere in between we would have a system like the "balance of power" system of international politics which, although toward the subsystem dominant end of the continuum, is nowhere near as far toward it as was the Communist system under Stalin. In the "balance of power" system, in the usual case, deviant actors would be induced into conforming behavior by the constraining actions of the other actors. Nonetheless each of the essential actors has a visible impact upon the system and the equilibrium is different from what it would be either in the system dominant case or farther along toward the subsystem dominant pole.

THE POLITICAL SYSTEM

A political system,

like many other social systems, has recognizable interests which are not identical—though not necessarily opposed and perhaps complementary—with those of the members of the system and within which there are regularized agencies and methods for making decisions concerning those interests. The rules for decision-making, including the specification of the decision-making roles and the general constitutional rules governing the society, are enacted within the political system.[1]

This definition of the political system is related directly to the systems theoretical method of analysis and, in specific, to the concept of ultra-stability. The political system has the metatask capacity to act as the ultrastable regulator of the larger system in which it functions. It thus regulates the system by adapting it to environmental disturbances in

[1]Kaplan, *System and Process in International Politics* (Wiley, 1957), pp. 13-14.

such a way that the critical values of the system are maintained. In other words, it chooses the behaviors consistent with the critical values of the critical variables of the system. In the extreme subsystem dominant case —for example, Stalinist Russia—Stalin, and at most the Politburo, imposed decisions on the rest of the system.[2] In systems such as the British or American where the locus of the decision is in the governmental subsystem the decisions are modified by the activities of other actors within the overall national system. (The larger system tends toward political multistability.) In subsystem dominant systems such as the "balance of power" system political decision-making is decentralized onto the essential actors; the norms of the system are imposed by their equilibrating behavior. Thus politics occurs in this system but there is no specific political subsystem. If we were to think of an international system with perhaps 10,000 or even 100,000 competing actors within it, and without any specific political subsystem, we would have approached the system dominant extreme for political activity. That is, if such a system were stable, the stability would result from the independent decision-making of the individual units in a system in which the behavior of no individual actor had discernible impact upon the behavior of the larger system. (This system would be multistable from a political standpoint.) It is rather difficult to imagine this extreme case, but it is less difficult to imagine international systems that come closer to it than any historical system has.

We note several things about the foregoing definition of the political system. It specifies neither power nor the allocation of values as central to the definition of the political system. The free market allocates values decisively. Pressure groups and criminal gangs exercise power. The attempt by Max Weber to overcome this problem, by using the word "legitimate" before the word "power", only obscures the problem, for the essence of the political in his definition lies not in the monopoly of power but in the concept of legitimacy. The definition used here stems directly from systems theory. Politics is the regulation of the system. It involves action manifesting capabilities or "power"; it may involve restructuring the relationship of the roles in the system or creating or eliminating roles; and it also allocates goods or values. The essential characteristic, however, is linked to that of ultrastable regulation. Where

[2]We omit discussion of the influence of extranational actors for reasons of simplicity.

a distinctive subsystem (or actor) within the system fills this role, then the system is said to have a political subsystem. Its legitimacy or authority stems from its acceptance in this role by the other important actors in the system. Thus there may be nonlegitimate or illegitimate political systems. Where no such subsystem exists, or alternatively where the ultrastable regulation of the system occurs in a decentralized fashion, then we state that the system has no political subsystem but that politics occurs in it. Politics in this case consists of the efforts to influence those kinds of adjustments that the political subsystem (ultrastable regulator) would make if one existed. Some related definitions follow.

Revolutions occur when subsystems outside the political subsystem disrupt or substitute for its ultrastabilizing activities, restructure or reorient it, take it over, or replace it. Imperial conquest occurs when the political subsystems of one or more other systems are absorbed after conquest by the surviving system. Political amalgamation occurs when the ultrastable political subsystems of several independent systems independently coordinate their subsumption within an overarching system with a political subsystem. Revolutionary amalgamation occurs when subsystems other than the political subsystem independently coordinate the process of amalgamation.

We hypothesize that systems will behave quite differently, depending upon whether a specific political subsystem exists and depending upon the degree of system or subsystem dominance in the larger system. Thus, although the delineation of these characteristics does not in and of itself provide sufficient information concerning the differences that will ensue, it does direct attention to one of the significant problems of political analysis: those characteristics of the system making for either system or subsystem dominance.

A FINAL NOTE ON THE PROBLEM OF SYSTEM STABILITY

The duration of system and ultrastable regulator varies with our definitions of the systems. We can use definitions so broad that almost all changes including the replacement of one civilization by another will fit the definition. This does not seem useful. We will adopt the following constriction: when the system changes in such a way that a different theory is needed to account for its behavior, we will say that the system has changed. Thus the change from "balance of power" system to bipolar system will be called a system change. The change of a national system from democratic to authoritarian will be called a system change. For different research purposes, either broader or narrower definitions would be appropriate. In any case there is a limit to how much environmental disturbance any system can withstand. To state that an important characteristic of political and social systems is their ability to compensate for environmental disturbances and thus to persist through time is not to state that any system will persist regardless of the strength, duration, or multiplicity of environmental disturbances. An important difference between systems will be their capacity to overcome disturbances. And among the important research problems will be that of discovering which factors increase or decrease this capacity and how these factors vary with kinds of systems and kinds of environments.

4

SYSTEMS THEORY

AND

POLITICAL SCIENCE

Perhaps the first thing to be said about systems theory is that it is not a theory. It consists of a set of concepts. No propositions about the real world can be derived from it any more than propositions about physics can be derived from the infinitesimal calculus or from the methods of science in general. Advice to a political scientist to use systems theory to solve a problem, even when it is the appropriate methodology, would advance him as far but no farther than would advice to a physical scientist to use the methods of science.

When the concepts of systems theory are used to construct theory in the area of political science, they can be most helpful; when they are used to evade the problems of substantive theory, they can be misleading or harmful. There is no such thing as theory in general; there is only theory about some specific subject matter.

ORIGINS OF SYSTEMS THEORY

Systems theory, as a tool, was developed in neurology by scientists interested in brain behavior. The most concise and original account of systems theory occurs in W. Ross Ashby's book, *Design for a Brain*. Ashby and his colleague W. Grey Walter developed systems theory in order to explore analogues for certain aspects of the brain's functioning. Thus, for instance, Grey Walter designed a machine with a motor and headlights capable of plugging itself into a wall socket to recharge its battery when its headlights began to wear down and of plugging itself into a gas pump when its engine began to run out of fuel. By employing analogues of this kind, which Ashby and Walter did not mistake for the real brain system, they were able to explore how to produce simplified versions of certain observed behaviors. They used concepts previously employed but fused them into a coherent scheme of conceptions now called systems theory.

The reason for using a machine to study simple behaviors characteristic of only some of the brain's operations rather than more complex behaviors is transparent. It is very difficult to study exceptionally complex systems; the brain is a remarkably complex system with some ten billion or more cellular components and numerous and very poorly understood linkages among these components. Theoretical depth requires simplicity; many students of science would argue that Galileo's great breakthrough, which launched the growth of modern theoretical science, was the choice of a simple problem that the mathematics of his age was capable of solving. In any event it is well known that two-body problems are easy to solve, that multi-body problems are very difficult and extremely complicated to solve, and that the larger the number of bodies considered, the more *ad hoc* and the less general the solutions. Physicists are lucky because their simple problems can be found for the most part directly in the world of nature. Ashby and Grey Walter were not able to isolate within the brain structure the simple elements of the problem they desired to work with; they therefore built machines that were simple and that manifested some of the behaviors to be explored. The solutions achieved by such devices must be called heuristic in at least two senses: the machine model chosen may indeed manifest the behavior observed in reality but as the consequence of a different structure and a different set of operations. The machine model quite often employs components that have no exact counterpart in nature. Thus this kind of test for internal structure and system properties is indirect. Were it possible to study the system directly by repeatedly assembling and dissembling it, by testing the parts independently and in sequence; were it possible to use mathematical causal analysis; we would have more confidence in our conclusions about such systems. Where such methods are not available or at least not appropriate, model building may be quite useful. The simplicity of the model is not necessarily a shortcoming.[1]

.   .   .   .

Kaplan has distinguished between task and metatask system capacity.[2] Task capacity is the ability to reduce environmental disturbances. Metatask capacity is the ability to reorganize either oneself or the external environment in such a way that the disturbances do not arise, at least in the same form as before. All ultra- and multistable systems have at least some metatask capacity.

.   .   .   .

INSTITUTIONALISM

The systems approach is at least in some senses an institutional approach, if an informal one; and not merely formal institutional behavior is brought within that rubric. The emphasis on comparative systems, on styles of behavior, and on the framework in which the

[1]Mistakes are made more often when the model builder attempts to replicate the complexity of his subject matter. See Kaplan, "Strategy and International Politics", Vol. XIII, *World Politics*, July 1961, pp. 467-469, for an example of a case in which Schelling's introduction of commitments into a game theoretical example—a possibility that did not exist in reality—made the example less realistic than when the same example was employed by Luce and Raiffa, although they left commitments out of account. This case is important, because the easiest way to come closer to reality while adding complications is when one is dealing with a well-structured model thoroughly worked out in its most general and simplest aspects, as is the case with game theory. It is far easier to go wrong, and it is much more probable that one will go wrong, when one jumps into the middle level of complexity directly, as occurs, for instance, in simulation experiments. The well-chosen simple model may be both more realistic and much better understood than complex models.

[2]See *System and Process in International Politics* (Wiley, 1957), pp. 93-95.

behavior becomes manifest, is in many important respects institutional behavior. Where this approach differs from the usual institutional approach is in its restriction to an abstracted set of variables. Therefore, rather than merely attempting to describe institutional behavior, taking into account all the variables of a particular case, the systems approach attempts greater generality by its use of models that are first-order approximations of reality.

.   .   .   .

LIMITATIONS AND MISUSE OF SYSTEMS THEORY

Systems theory deals primarily with the macrostructure of political or social systems. It is not a tool for most policy problems, that is, for the microstructural problems of foreign policy, although it might shed light on some of them. Nor can it illuminate those areas where surprises may occur, where the situation is very different from anything that we have experienced. Thus if the pacifist argues not on the basis of values but on the basis of practical consequences, that one should give in to a Hitler because the regime would be ameliorated over time and because this act would do less damage than war, it is not possible to prove him wrong. Pacifism might have exactly the consequences he describes. It would no doubt be possible to give prudent reasons against accepting his judgment. Since there are so many more ways for things to go wrong than for them to work out right, the advocate of radical changes either in systemic structure or in type of behavior bears a heavy burden of argument and proof that his speculative arguments cannot support, except where the system is so patently unjust that it is offensive to humanity. Nonetheless, we do not know that he is wrong. And his intuitions, achieved through use of a computer, the human brain, which is capable of scanning for recognition patterns that we are incapable of translating into secondary or formally grammatic languages, may indeed have stumbled onto a truth that the rest of us are incapable of recognizing. Systems theory therefore is not a philosopher's stone for unlocking the secrets of the social and political universe or even of system macrostructures. It does not consist of a set of formulas from which we may deduce general truths for all social or political life. It is merely a tool for achieving a middle-level range of generalization about political or social system macrostructures.

Systems theory can be misused, sometimes even brilliantly misused, as in Chalmers Johnson's *Revolutionary Change*. Unfortunately operating within a Parsonian rather than an Ashbyan framework, Johnson is unaware that his theory of revolution is really a definition, and in particular a definition of a step function. He introduces three empirical causative factors that are not part of his definition. The first consists of those pressures caused by the disequilibrating social system, the most important of which is power deflation, the resort to force. The second is the quality of the purposive changes made within the system. Do they maintain confidence? If not, there is a loss of authority. The third empirical factor consists of the accelerators, the triggers that set off new sets of conditions, including those affecting the armed forces, ideological belief in the success of the revolutionary group, and special operations against the armed forces. If he had recognized that his concept of revolution was a definition, particularly of a step function, he would have been much less likely to attempt to discuss revolution apart from the characteristics of the system affected by the step function. If he had recognized that revolution was merely the equivalent of a step function, he would have more likely concluded that the effects of each of the indicators are so dependent upon the effects of each of the others and upon the kinds of systems in which they occur that the concept of general numerical indicators that cut across types of systems is questionable. His unsuccessful search for general indicators would then have appeared not as a failure but as a confirmation of what was more likely. His attention would likely have turned to a comparative study of systems. Within each system, he would then have turned his attention to the kinds of situations likely to give rise to revolution. The qualitative elements most likely would then have been much more strongly stressed. Thus, for instance, to understand the potentiality for revolution within a communist system, one should understand something about the nature of political organization that extends to the block and cell level.

It is the real emphasis upon the system—a revolution is not a system at all but only an occurrence within a system—that focuses attention upon the crucial element in the equation: the structural organization (whether formal or informal) within which events occur. When we forget this, it is a short step to the real truisms: the stress upon inputs and outputs in general, upon demands and supports in general, upon the functional prerequisites of systems in general. But there are no systems in general and there are no statements in general that tell us much about systems. The systems approach, properly understood, is a prescription for middle-level comparative theory. It is a prescription for dealing with the real world of politics, not for dealing with the free-floating world of metaphysical abstractions.

PART III

On Historical Explanations

This section includes my study on the Czechoslovak coup; a work on espionage and the Korean war, a selection from *Studies in Postwar Statecraft* (multilithed, University of Chicago Library, a work that was never readied for publication); and "The International Arena as a Source of Dysfunctional Tension".

Both historical studies deal empirically with problems of historical explanation. The study of the Czechoslovak coup analyzes two interpretations of the coup and demonstrates that it is not possible to prove either. Indeed both could be correct as could still other unexplored hypotheses. State motivation is often difficult to deal with, both because much of the decision process is unrecorded or tendentiously recorded, and because decisions are the product of the influence of many groups whose policy choices often converge for different reasons or of a policy process that may even produce a decision nobody wants.

To the extent that such studies are used to distinguish among nations on the basis of whether they will perform a given act, it is important to recognize that more often a better distinction rests on the purposes for which the act is done, the conditions under which it is done, the methods used in doing it, and its consequences.

If the Soviet Union sponsored a coup in Czechoslovakia, the United States sponsored coups in Iran and Guatemala. Quite often we do not know a nation's principles and the significant question consists not of whether it will or will not do something, but of the conditions under which it will do it. Quite often the answer to this question also is murky, and we are thrown back upon gross uncertainty with nothing more than strategic rules of prudence to guide us in our decisions—such as: What consequences will flow from acting upon a given hypothesis if we are wrong? Or if we are right? Does the other actor have an unusually good instrument ready to apply its policies capable of acting as a proxy and of relatively permanently installing itself in power, such as a Communist party? This ability might influence the disposition to act by creating opportunities that in turn give rise to motives to exploit these opportunities. Still other relevant questions of the same type can be asked.

One can reach at least some tentative conclusions about the disposition of a state to pursue given kinds of objectives under given kinds of conditions with given kinds of probable consequences and risks. Such an analysis should tell us something about the organizational purposes of the state. These organizational "purposes" are analytically distinct from the purposes of the role holders in the state although related to them and sometimes similar to them. Usually, however, statesmen are interested in the conscious motives of their opposite numbers. These motives are often difficult to discern with any confidence, and they might mislead by misdirecting attention from the organizational components of the decision process that in many cases may be the more important components.

It is true that one would like more assurance concerning the patterns of action and the objectives a state is likely to pursue than appears to be possible. This is particularly true because so much rests on the decisions that will be made, upon which the shape of the future depends in extremely important ways. It is not comforting to recognize that so much may depend upon intuition, guesswork, and a rule of prudence that may not "fit" the situation at all.

The second selection deals with a case where it is somewhat easier to negate a hypothesis. Here the weight of the available evidence comes down preponderantly in favor of one of the two conflicting hypotheses. Yet it remains possible that still further evidence, or a better interpretation of the evidence, would show General MacArthur to have been correct. In still other cases, it is possible to prove a hypothesis beyond any reasonable doubt.

Thus, contrary to widespread belief, General MacArthur did not act against orders when he crossed the Thirty-Eighth Parallel in Korea or when he sent American soldiers to the Yalu. Yet it is chastening to remember that Harry Truman said he did in his memoirs and so well-known a scholar as Robert E. Osgood agreed with him.

Whenever an inside dopester, or even a Yugoslav informant, tells us the truth about the conflicts within the Kremlin so that we can adapt American policy to their requirements, this example is worth remembering. Sometimes it is worth remembering even when the information comes from a responsible official of the state in question, as perhaps members of the Kennedy administration should have been aware when Khrushchev was passing them a series of messages through nonofficial channels.

"The International Arena as a Source of Dysfunctional Tension" examines some of the reasons why the international arena produces faulty generalizations. The same subject was treated in greater length in *System and Process*.

5

THE COMMUNIST COUP

IN CZECHOSLOVAKIA

The Communist coup in Czechoslovakia in February 1948 had considerable effect upon foreign policy and public opinion in the United States and other Western nations. By creating an image of a Soviet Union girding for war or carrying out an operation that had been planned since the close of World War Two, it eased the way for the ultimate coordination of Western military planning in NATO as well as for specific diplomatic initiatives. The coup, however, is interesting in terms other than those of its consequences. It was an extremely dramatic event. A study of the coup and of the events leading up to it sheds considerable light on Czechoslovak politics, the nature of the Communist party, the mechanics of Communist take-overs, the relationship between external events and local Communist politics in a bipolar world, and relations between satellite parties and the Soviet Union during the Stalinist regime.

Most of the matters just mentioned will be brought into outline, without need for further extensive analysis, by the case study of the

coup and the events leading up to it.* The case study, however, also
had significance for a general problem that it does not directly illuminate. Since the Soviet Union is considered a revolutionary nation
seriously challenging the present structure of world politics, analysis
of its motivation is important. Yet such analysis can be attempted only
inferentially on the basis of case materials. This has obvious consequences with respect to foreign policy determination. The important
set of questions that this problem raises will be treated briefly at the
conclusion of the case study.

In the meantime, we may note the significance of the problem. The
evidence on the Czechoslovak coup is largely in. Commentators in
general agree in their interpretation of Soviet motivation, as indeed
they have since early 1948. However, if the case study materials indicate
that alternative hypotheses are equally tenable—even eleven years after
the event—questions concerning the relationship of foreign policy
decisions to dogmatic interpretations of national motivation become
legitimate.[1]

A CASE STUDY OF THE COUP

The Communist coup in Czechoslovakia is often called the consequence
of Communist ideology. It is asserted that the Communists intended
the coup from the beginning, that it was just a matter of timing "a
stroke which completed Russian designs already laid during the negotiations in Moscow and Kosice in 1945 or even before the visit of
President Benes to Moscow in 1943".[2] Or it is said that the Communists "only gained what they had had already".[3]

These explanations are not very helpful. It is obvious that the
Communist party did not support Czech democracy as a matter of

*I want to thank Petr Zenkl and Pavel Korbel for useful comments on the
accuracy of the factual material in the case study. They were, however, not consulted
on and are not responsible for any of the interpretations of events.

[1]We will not discuss the questions that might be raised from the standpoint of a
formal theory of strategy, although these are impressive. These questions, however,
are discussed in my *System and Process in International Politics* (Wiley, 1957), Chapters
9, 10, and 11.

[2]Peter Calvocoressi, *Survey of International Affairs: 1947-1948* (Oxford University
Press, 1952), pp. 153-54.

[3]Franz Borkenau, *European Communism* (Faber and Faber, 1953), p. 536.

principle. But if it only took what it had, why shock world sensibilities by so overt a coup? And, if the coup had been planned as early as 1945, why wait until 1948? Would it not have been simpler and less risky to install a Communist regime with the advance of the Red Army? The Lublin Committee was transformed into the Polish government in that fashion. Is it not more likely that the Communist party of the Soviet Union was prepared to tolerate Czech democracy under certain conditions and that its capacity for tolerance was exhausted when these conditions no longer existed?

If so, the problem is to determine the condition or congeries of conditions that triggered the decision to subvert the democratic government. In short, what are the restraints that inhibit Soviet absorption of weak neighbors? If no restraints existed, the triggering of the coup would have occurred much earlier.

Soviet Policy toward Czechoslovakia

If one examines the genesis of Soviet policy toward Czechoslovakia during World War Two, it appears that the Soviet Union was never willing to trust entirely in the *laissez-faire* play of politics in Czechoslovakia. Czechoslovakia was an important military *glacis*. It was only 400 kilometers from France and it flanked Bavaria. The uranium deposits near Jachymov assumed a new importance by 1945.[4] Before the war Czechoslovakia had been the sixth largest industrial nation in Europe. Despite the postwar disorganization, Czechoslovakia could be expected to improve its position, since the Nazis, during the protectorate, had fostered the growth of capital industry in order to support their war efforts.

However, Czechoslovakia had followed a consistent policy of friendship with the Soviet Union. Its foreign policy was dependably antiGerman. The expulsion of collaborationist Germans—a goal of all Czech parties—would force the Czechs to depend upon the Soviet Union for protection.[5]

[4]According to a protocol of the Czechoslovak-Soviet treaty of November 23, 1945, the exploitation of all sources of radium and radioactive materials in Czechoslovak territory was transferred to Soviet control for twenty years.

[5]In a toast during March 1945 Stalin declared: "I hate Germans. Slavs footed the bill for the first world war and also the second world war is being solved at their

The Soviet Union has rarely relied upon good will alone for its protection. On December 12, 1943, the Soviet Union negotiated an alliance with Czechoslovakia directed against Germany and her associates, despite a Soviet agreement with Great Britain not to conclude an agreement with any of the small powers concerning frontiers or other postwar matters until the cessation of hostilities.[6] At the same time a form of pressure was maintained on the London government-in-exile by the refusal of the Communists in Moscow to participate in the London cabinet. They maintained that a new government would have to be formed when Czechoslovakia was liberated.

The question of the future status of Subcarpathian Ruthenia had been left open in the 1943 discussions between Benes and Stalin, although it was apparent that Benes was prepared to cede Subcarpathian Ruthenia to the Soviet Union if that country insisted. Therefore, it was particularly shocking to the government in London when the Red Army fostered a Ruthenian National Committee pledged to union with Russia.[7] Although the Soviet Union claimed it could not suppress a spontaneous nationalist movement, the ruse fooled no one. The unsuccessful attempt of the Soviet Union to negotiate a separatist agreement with the collaborationist Slovak regime was also disappointing to the London government.

During 1945 it was agreed that the Czech government should go first to Moscow and then return to Czechoslovakia in the wake of the Red Army. A new government, including Communists, would be formed in Moscow. In the meantime, Fierlinger, the Social Democratic Ambassador of the Czech government to Moscow, had been playing

---

expense. In the first world war the English and the French fought the Germans, but the Slavs paid dearly for that. And finally the Germans were put on their feet again to form the so-called European balance of power. . . . The Soviet Union wants nothing else than to gain allies who will always be prepared to resist the German danger. The Soviet Union will never interfere in the internal affairs of its allies." (Eduard Taborsky, "Benes and Stalin—Moscow, 1943 and 1945", *Journal of Central European Affairs*, XIII, No. 2, July 1953, p. 179.) While one need not believe everything Stalin said during a toast, the German problem evidently did preoccupy him.

[6]*Ibid.*, p. 157. Britain protested and delayed the agreement until after the Moscow Conference of Foreign Ministers that year. Britain was fearful that the pact might isolate the Poles. Roosevelt had approved the pact earlier. Fierlinger claimed that Benes had opposed the alliance in the form adopted. (*New York Times*, December 12, 1948.) There is no evidence to sustain his statement, however.

[7]Taborsky, *op. cit.*, p. 171.

the Communist game rather than representing his government. It had become clear from his behavior that considerable pressure was to be exercised by the Soviet Union.

In Moscow, it was agreed that the six parties having Allied approval and a few non-party technicians would organize a National Front government. Four of the parties were Czech: the Communist, Social Democratic, National Socialist, and People's. Two were Slovak: the Communist and Democratic. The Premier was to be Fierlinger, the fellow-traveling Social Democrat, although he had held no position of consequence in the party prior to the war. A Communist, Nosek, was named Minister of the Interior and was in charge of the police. Gottwald received one of the vice-premierships and several other important ministries. Thus, Communists and fellow-travelers had many of the key positions in the cabinet.[8] Slovakia received virtual autonomy as a result of Communist insistence. Since the collaborationist People's Party, the popular party in Slovakia, had been outlawed, the Communists hoped to be able to take over politically by posing as the champions of Slovak independence and by artificially restricting the parties in that nation.

The agreement formally reached in Kosice that formed the basis for the coalition government differed little from a mimeographed text prepared by Gottwald in Moscow and presented to the various parties in March in that city.[9] The Kosice Program provided for the "democratization" of the army and cooperation with officers of the Red Army. Partisan units, often of Communist persuasion, were incorporated into the army. The bulk of the postwar army had been organized in Soviet territory and many of its officers were Communists or pro-Communist.

A Provisional National Assembly was to be elected by "national committees" rather than by the population as a whole. This body was to prepare for the election of a Constituent National Assembly that was to draft a constitution for the country. Since the composition of the Provisional Assembly had been decided upon in advance by the parties and since firm party discipline existed, the peculiar form of election for the Assembly was not of major significance.

[8]Hubert Ripka, *Czechoslovakia Enslaved* (Gollancz, 1950), p. 29. The National Socialists held the important Ministry of Justice.

[9]Taborsky, *op. cit.*, p. 180.

However, the extensive powers of the self-appointed and often Communist-dominated national committees were used in the meantime to distribute land under the seizure program, thus placing many in the debt of the Communist party. These committees often arrested and tried collaborationists. It has been claimed that they often acted against those whose only crime was anti-communism, while exculpating genuine collaborationists who joined the Communist party.[10]

The Kosice Program called for land and labor reform. It extended to the fields of culture and education. German and Hungarian influence was to be minimized. Slavonic influence was to predominate and the special Slavonic Institute was to be re-established. All anti-Bolshevik remarks were to be removed from textbooks—raising an interesting question with respect to academic freedom; however, American occupation policy in defeated countries suffered from a similar ambivalence —and the study of Russian was to be encouraged.

After liberation, the Central Council of Trades Unions (URO and ROH), which had developed as part of the resistance movement during the war, proclaimed itself the only trade union organization in the Czech lands and adhered to the Kosice Program. It was the governing body of the Revolutionary Trades Unions Movement; a similar movement developed in Slovakia and the two united in mid-1946. The unions in this body were organized vertically and by 1946 included 2,100,000 workers, of whom 86 per cent were Czech. It was the largest organization in the nation.

The ROH had the right under law to represent all workers, to regulate its own organization, to create or dissolve any individual branches, to see that workers performed their functions as citizens, to see that the worker's right to work was protected and that he was employed to the best of his capacity. The ROH was given the right to participate in and make suggestions to all legislative and executive groups considering legislation or decrees affecting workers. It had a right to representation on all public bodies not popularly elected and the right to expect support from all public and private bodies in carrying out its objectives. The revolutionary guards of the labor organizations were later used as factory police.

The president of the ROH was a Communist, the secretary-general a

---

[10] Jan Stransky, *East Wind over Prague* (Hollis and Carter, 1950), p. 63.

Social Democrat, and the editor of its newspaper a National Socialist. Communists were reputed to dominate the Central Council,[77] although elections at the Workers' Council level in 1946 seemed to indicate a waning of Communist strength. The picture that emerges, however, is that of a labor organization with the power of livelihood over the individual worker, with the right to interfere in the exercise of his citizenship prerogatives, with the ability to paralyze the economy, and with an armed force upon which it could call.

Since the economic programs of the government were national objectives endorsed by all the parties, the ROH refused to use the strike to increase wages, although it also refused to give up the right to strike. However, as the president of the Central Council declared in September 1946, ". . . we would not hesitate to use this weapon [the strike] if anyone would try to revive the conditions of the First Republic after the working people have brought about order in production and economy."[78] The labor unions were one of the weapons used by the Communists in carrying out the coup of February 1948.[13]

Thus, the Communist party secured control of many areas of physical power in the state and was likely to be the most powerful political force. Even though the Soviet Union made some concessions to democratic procedures and the Czechoslovak Communist party was forced to compromise on certain issues, Czechoslovakia was not free to govern without the Communists or to conduct a foreign policy opposed to that of the Soviet Union.

Nevertheless, the Communists did make some concessions that they could have avoided if they had reduced the rules of the game to a matter of sheer physical force. Despite the sympathy of the Western Allies for Czechoslovakia, they gave no indication that they would intervene on her behalf any more effectively than they had done in the case of Poland. Had Czechoslovakia been converted into a "people's democracy" in 1945, it would have been just one more country in the list of those Communized by force in the immediate postwar period.

---

[11] William Diamond, *Czechoslovakia Between East and West* (Stevens & Sons, 1947), p. 122.

[12] *Ibid.*, p. 121.

[13] The strike had also been used before the coup to force the nationalization of industries not otherwise eligible under official government regulations.

Party and Nationality Problems

Although the Kosice Program had been agreed to by all parties, it soon became evident that the Marxist parties—i.e., the two Communist parties and the Social Democrats—split with the other parties on economic matters, while the other five parties split with the Slovak Democrats on the nationality issue.[14] Moreover, as 1946 wore on, the right wing of the Social Democratic Party gained in strength, thus weakening the Communist-Social Democratic bloc.

During 1946 two issues came to a head. One was settled by the organization of a Slovak Labor party[15] and a Slovak Freedom (Catholic) party, both of which adhered to the Kosice Program. The other issue centered on voting procedures. Voting in Czechoslovakia was compulsory. However, the right-wing parties had been outlawed on the grounds that they had collaborated w th the enemy, and their supporters therefore had no option other than to vote for one of the non-Marxist parties. The Communists proposed that the option of casting a blank ballot be provided so that dissatisfaction with the governing parties could be manifested. The non-Marxist parties thought that this maneuver would deprive them of many votes and consequently opposed it. When no agreement proved possible, the issue was finally placed before the Provisional Assembly and, on a straight party vote, the Marxist parties barely carried their position.[16]

In the elections of May, 1946, the Communists polled 38 per cent of all valid votes and the Social Democratic party 12.33 per cent, indicating that in Czechoslovakia, as in some other European countries, the Social Democratic party was caught in a vise as a result of its cooperation with the Communist party. Those who approved of its policies often preferred to vote Communist, and those who disapproved of its compromises with the Communists often seceded to one of the non-Marxist parties. Thus, the Social Democrats had suffered a considerable decline in strength since the end of the war.

The National Socialist party received 18.33 per cent of the vote; the People's party, 15.34 per cent; the Democratic party, 14.33 per cent;

[14]The Communist party opposed autonomy only after it lost the Slovak elections.
[15]The Slovak Labor party was the Slovak branch of the Czech Social Democratic party.
[16]Actually, only 0.45 per cent of all the votes cast were blanks. It is more difficult to estimate the effects of the disfranchisement of collaborators.

and the Freedom party, 1 per cent. The Slovak Labor party received 0.67 per cent, giving the Marxist parties a total of 51 per cent. The Communist party emerged as the strongest party, more than twice as strong as its nearest competitor. Moreover, the right-wing vote did not have to look for any place to go; there just was not very much of it.

However, one element in the situation disturbed the Communists greatly. In Slovakia alone, they polled only 30.37 per cent of the vote, while the Democratic party received 62 per cent. Since it had been agreed that the cabinet and other governing bodies would be divided according to the proportion of the vote rather than equally, as before the election, the Democratic party would dominate the Slovak National Council.

Although the Communist Klement Gottwald became Premier of Czechoslovakia, the most powerful post in the state, the Communists started to cast baleful glances at the situation in Slovakia. Moreover, since the Marxist parties had only a bare majority of the vote, they could not in combination carry a constitutional provision in the Constituent National Assembly, which, according to the 1920 Constitutional Charter, required a vote of 60 per cent of all the deputies.

Less than a week after the elections, a Czech football team defeated a Slovak team in Bratislava. A riot followed the game and accusations and counter-accusations were made. The Socialists stated that the riots indicated the growth of anti-Czech separatism in Slovakia, while the Communists alleged Catholic intimidation in the elections[17] and proof of an underground separatist plot.

A commission dispatched by the Communist Minister of the Interior to investigate the matter claimed to find documentary evidence of the plot, whereupon the Communists demanded the invalidation of the elections to the national committees and the subordination of the Slovak National Council to the central government.[18] The Slovak leaders

[17]The small vote of the Freedom (Catholic) party did constitute convincing evidence that a highly organized movement succeeded in swinging most anti-Communist votes to the stronger Democratic party; the Church organization had recommended to parishioners that they vote for the Slovak Democratic party. The prewar strength of the Catholic party had been such that a vote of 0.85 per cent was inevitably questioned; and it became known that the Democratic party had agreed to include among its candidates members of the outlawed Slovak People's party. This, however, establishes only that Slovak Catholics acted intelligently from a political point of view.

[18]Diamond, *op. cit.*, p. 52.

denied the charges, but a new agreement subjecting the existing powers of the Slovak National Council to more effective control by the central government was negotiated. It was agreed that the Council could legislate only on matters not affecting the whole of the republic; whether a matter did affect the whole of the republic was to be decided by the central government. Moreover, the executive powers of the Slovak Board of Commissioners, appointed by the National Council with the consent of the central government, were limited to decrees promulgated by the National Council. In all other matters, the executive power in Slovakia was to rest with the central government, particularly with respect to the economic integration of the country.

These changes could not be ascribed to Communist strength alone; the other Czech parties had always been opposed to Slovak autonomy and had agreed to the previous state of affairs only under strong Communist pressure. President Benes himself warned the Slovaks in February 1947 that there must be a definitive solution of their status, that the state could not survive another crisis on the issue, and that the Slovaks would not remain independent if they separated, for the Soviet Union would absorb them.

There were increasing indications toward the end of 1946 that strength within the Marxist bloc was flowing back from the Communists to the Social Democrats.[19] It is possible that this change in attitude stemmed partly from the more independent position being taken by members of the Social Democratic party as its middle and right-wing gained at the expense of the left. It may also have been related to that fact that many Czechs had joined the Communist party to save themselves from the depredations of the Red Army and that, by Soviet and American agreement, occupation forces had been withdrawn during November 1945. It has been claimed that the Czech Communists attempted to exploit this element of fear,[20] but its strength nevertheless began to decline. Evidence of this could be found in the press. Although no organization opposed to the principles of the National Front government was permitted to exist and, therefore, to publish a newspaper, the Soviet protests against alleged anti-Soviet remarks

[19]*Ibid.*, p. 45.
[20]According to J. Stransky (*op. cit.*, pp. 45-46), a secret order of the Czech Communist party contained the following instructions: "Never deny that the Republic is in a satellite position to the U.S.S.R. It is necessary that people should realize the position, and that our enemies should be afraid! "

in the official press of the People's party were successfully brushed aside.

The Economic Situation

Moreover, confidence was increasing as the economic situation improved. Shortly after the war, only $240 million of UNRRA aid prevented severe hardship. In addition to the food shortage, German economic measures in Bohemia and Moravia had changed the pattern of production and made the economy dependent upon raw materials that were lacking at the end of the war. German financial policy was responsible for a postwar inflation that pushed the prices of Czech goods beyond competitive world levels.

In 1945 Czech trade was only 3.9 per cent of 1937 exports and 5.5 per cent of 1937 imports in value (volume was much smaller in proportion). By the end of 1946, however, production had risen to 80 per cent of the 1937 level.[21] Because of the inflation elsewhere in the world, Czechoslovak products became competitive. By the end of 1946 the value of Czechoslovak exports slightly exceeded the 1937 total valuation, although imports fell just a bit short of the 1937 figure. The 1946 harvest was not far short of prewar standards and the number of livestock rose rapidly.

As the Communists lost strength politically, this loss was reflected in the Czechoslovak economic program. The nationalizations carried out in 1945 had represented a compromise. Sixty per cent of Czechoslovak industry had been nationalized. While this large program went further than the non-Marxists parties had desired, the Communists were dissatisfied also. The two-year plan which went into effect on January 1, 1947, specified that no further nationalizations were to take place while the plan was in progress; this was a victory for the right.

The plan was prepared in the General Secretariat of the Economic Council, in which all National Front parties, as well as non-party technicians, were represented. It was adopted by the National Assembly virtually without change. The plan had among its goals surpassing the

[21]Production in 1947 was only 96 per cent of the 1929 level. However, because of deaths and expulsions, the population was 19 per cent smaller in 1947 than in 1929.

1937 level of industrial production by 10 per cent; raising agricultural production to prewar levels; increasing the number of dwellings and of industrial and administrative buildings; improving water and sanitary facilities; reaching the 1937 level of transportation; raising the economic level of Slovakia to that of the Czech lands, and raising the level of backward areas in the Czech lands; and, after these tasks were completed, increasing the production of consumer goods.

The objective in the Czechoslovak plan of increasing productive capacity rather than the standard of living was more like the objectives of Soviet planning than those of the British Socialists. While there is no evidence of great political opposition so long as the standard of living was comparable to the prewar standard, there was a certain amount of consumer resistance to the lack of variety and quality imposed by the plan. Moreover, some difficulties were caused by the fact that a considerable proportion of industry remained outside the plan and that the economy was dependent to a great extent upon foreign trade which, in the case of the capitalist countries at least, could not be well integrated with the plan.

Foreign Policy Considerations

While in the political and economic sense Communist influence was waning in Czechoslovakia, the psychological pressure of the neighboring Soviet Union, the fear of Germany, and the large size of the Communist party and its control of effective points of physical power made it impossible to govern without the Communists. The arguments for a pro-Soviet orientation in Czechoslovak foreign policy were reinforced by American and British support for the Hungarian position at the Paris Peace Conference of 1946. More damaging to those favoring a bridge to the West was the early demobilization of the American army and the failure of the United States to counterbalance Soviet influence effectively in Eastern Europe.

The Czechoslovaks were, if anything, even more anti-German than the Russians. The speech of Secretary of State James Byrnes at Stuttgart in September 1946 therefore produced a profound shock in Czechoslovakia. If Russian efforts to woo the Germans were later to deflate the Soviet stock, the Stuttgart speech weakened the faith of the Czechoslovaks in the foreign policy of the Western powers.[22]

Winston Churchill's proposals in 1946 for a United Europe also caused dismay in Czechoslovakia. The Czechoslovaks desired a policy that ringed Germany with states obligated to unite in defense against possible German expansionism. A proposal calling for a European partnership including the Germans—with Germany as perhaps a major partner—and for cooperation between the Germans and French caused the Czechs to fear their own eventual isolation.

The Marshall Plan and the Treaty with France

Superficially Czechoslovakia had returned to a state of prosperity by early 1947. However, careful scrutiny of the trade ledgers revealed dangerous weak spots. Although Czechoslovakia ran large trade surpluses with the Soviet Union and Switzerland, its balances with the United States and Great Britain were negative.[23]

The growing inconvertibility of national currencies made it difficult to balance surpluses against deficits, particularly when dollars were needed. However, Czech imports from the United States and Great Britain had to be maintained at a high level if the goals of the two-year economic plan were to be met. Credits or loans were needed; imports from dollar areas and exports to non-dollar areas would have to be cut if the internal targets were to be met. Although no specific areas were mentioned, it was clear that some of the export cuts would have to be made in the shipments to the Soviet Union, thus embarrassing the internal economy of that country.

The announcement of the Marshall Plan Conference in Paris appeared to most Czechoslovaks as a last-minute lifesaver. A Polish delegation, including Hilary Minc, was in Prague at the time and this Communist delegation was even more enthusiastic than the Czechoslovak officials.

The announcement that Soviet Foreign Minister Molotov had quit

[22]In addition, the failure of the American army to come to the aid of Prague when it rose against the Germans in 1945 had caused many citizens of Czechoslovakia to believe that their country had been assigned to the Soviet sphere of influence by the great powers.

[23]New York Times, March 3, 1947.

the Paris Conference shattered the euphoria of the Polish-Czechoslovak talks. Minc said that Molotov must have had excellent reasons for his stand and that the Soviet Union had taken the proper course. However, he pointed out, the Soviet Union was a great country, while Poland and Czechoslovakia were small countries with all the problems of small countries. They needed the credits that the Marshall Plan offered. Minc said he was certain that the Soviet Union would not object if they went ahead and made arrangements to adhere to the Marshall Plan.[24]

The Poles proposed that the two countries send missions, headed by officers of cabinet rank, to the Paris discussions. Czechoslovak Foreign Minister Jan Masaryk urged greater caution and suggested that the ambassadors to France of the two countries be utilized. Masaryk further suggested that the ambassadors maintain a reserved attitude until they could understand the aim behind the Marshall Plan and the conditions attached to it.

The procedure suggested by Masaryk was discussed at a meeting of the Czech cabinet in July and adopted unanimously after the Communists[25] had been told by Masaryk that Bodrev, the Soviet *chargé*, had been informed of the pending decision and had raised no objections.

Meanwhile the Czechoslovak cabinet was debating the proposed Franco-Czechoslovak treaty. The Communists protested against the clause in the projected treaty that would make the alliance applicable only against Germany; they demanded that the treaty also apply against states associated with Germany. Although the democratic parties admitted the weakness of the treaty in this respect, they declared that it was desirable even without such a provision. The cabinet was unable to come to an agreement and, at the suggestion of Ripka, a National Socialist, it was decided to send a delegation to Moscow to discuss the treaty and general economic matters. Shortly thereafter Moscow requested an immediate conference. Since Ripka was ill, Masaryk, Gottwald, and Drtina were sent.

The delegation left for Moscow on July 8, the same day the Poles announced that they would not participate in the Marshall Plan.[26] After

---

[24]Ripka, *op. cit.*, pp. 52-53.

[25]Unlike the Polish Communists, the Czechs had been cool from the beginning.

[26]Ripka, *op. cit.*, p. 56. Before the Polish cabinet reached its decision, Moscow radio announced that Poland and Rumania would not participate. Rumania was still denying the Moscow report on July 8. *Ibid.*

the delegation arrived, Gottwald had a preliminary conference with Stalin without the knowledge of the other members of the delegation. Apparently all the important decisions were made at this preliminary conference. Gottwald informed the other members of the delegation, before the main conference, that Stalin was furious and demanded Czechoslovak withdrawal from the Marshall Plan.

At the conference Stalin declared that the aim of the Marshall Plan was to isolate the Soviet Union and that it held no immediate economic advantages for Czechoslovakia. He rejected Masaryk's request that Czechoslovakia participate in the Marshall Plan discussions and withdraw gracefully later. Stalin said that Sweden and Switzerland were hesitating and that such a move would influence their decision unfavorably. "In the Soviet Government no one doubts the friendship of Czechoslovakia for the Soviet Union. If you take part in the Conference you will prove by that act that you allow yourselves to be used as a tool against the Soviet Union. Neither the people nor the Government of the U.S.S.R. would tolerate that."[27]

When Stalin was informed by Masaryk and Drtina that Czechoslovakia depended on the Western countries for from 60 to 80 per cent of its raw materials, Stalin offered to purchase pipelines, electric motors, and other products that Czechoslovakia normally sold to the West, and to provide wheat in return. Although Czechoslovakia needed the wheat badly, the other elements of the plan involved an additional imbalance in trade with the West and a consequent reduction in the Czech standard of living. Masaryk privately drew the conclusion that the Soviets did not desire, and even feared, the recovery of Western Europe. He thought that Stalin expected war and was basing his strategy upon that expectation.[28]

The Czechoslovak delegation also consulted Stalin about the projected treaty with France. All the Czechoslovak parties would have preferred a more inclusive treaty—the democratic parties because they wanted the treaty to apply in case of trouble with Hungary, and the Communist party probably because it was thinking of the United States as a possible ally of the Germans. However, the primary object of the democratic parties was to create a contractual bridge with a

[27]Ibid., p. 68.

[28]Ibid., p. 70. Many informed Europeans felt in this period that war was drawing close.

Western power.[29] Therefore, they desired the treaty badly, even if it applied only against Germany. The Communists apparently feared just this contingency. Stalin denied that he opposed the treaty but declared that he wanted a really good treaty for Czechoslovakia, one that gave a guarantee of immediate aid in case of attack and that also applied to allies or satellites of Germany.[30]

Stalin pointed out that France had deserted Czechoslovakia at Munich and that it was necessary to have a strong treaty, that Czechoslovakia was not a country with great land space and would need aid fast. He mentioned that Great Britain, while offering to extend her alliance with the Soviet Union to fifty years, was also attempting to weaken it by eliminating the clause on immediate aid and the clause applying the treaty against the associates of Germany.

Stalin's apparent moderation must have disturbed Gottwald, who feared that the other delegates might conclude that Stalin did not forbid the completion of the treaty. Gottwald asked Stalin whether signing the treaty might not have an adverse effect upon the Anglo-Soviet negotiations.[31] Stalin answered that it certainly would, and the fate of the treaty was sealed. Although France later offered to modify it to apply to states that joined Germany in acts of aggression, the Czechoslovak Communists continued to find objections to the treaty and negotiations were never completed.

Onset of the Coup

All the signs pointed to an approaching crisis. During the spring of 1947 the Communist leaders, Gottwald and Slansky, had expressed the need for the Communist party to secure a majority of the votes in the coming elections in order to end the policy of compromise with the other parties.[32] The Communists evidently believed that it had

---

[29]Conversation with Petr Zenkl.   [30]Ripka, *op. cit.*, p. 91.   [31]*Ibid.*, p. 93.

[32]*Ibid.*, p. 96. Slansky apparently expressed himself more strongly than Gottwald. According to Douglas Hyde (*I Believed* (Heinemann, 1951), p. 234), William Rust, the editor of the *London Daily Worker*, had talked to Tito several months earlier and had been informed that Gottwald was out of favor. Tito said that the Czech Communist party had been arguing that, under the special conditions prevailing in Czechoslovakia, communism could be achieved by using democratic methods of organization. At the same time the other new democracies were imposing the

become necessary for them to gain firm control of the policies of the Czechoslovak nation. The democratic parties, while disposed to orient Czechoslovak foreign policy primarily toward the Soviet Union, desired to maintain a bridge to the West. Moreover, the economic needs of Czechoslovakia entailed relations with the West. After the Marshall Plan episode, Masaryk still expressed a hope of obtaining Western aid, at least in the form of "normal commercial loans for specific purposes".[33]

As the needs of the Czechs for foreign aid increased and as the negotiations with the Russians for a foreign trade pact were bogging down, the Communists began to make desperate efforts to consolidate their domestic political position. On September 5 bombs were sent through the mail to the offices of Zenkl, Drtina, and Masaryk. Although it was later proved, despite interference from the Communist-controlled Ministry of the Interior, that the plot had originated within a local unit of the Communist party, Slansky accused the National Socialist Party of staging this attempted assassination.[34]

On September 11, 1947, the Communist party reached an agreement with Social Democrats Fierlinger and Vilim that the Communist and Social Democratic parties were to follow a common line. The National Socialist party later rejected an invitation to join this united socialist front. Many Social Democrats were affronted by this agreement. Majer, the Social Democratic Minister of Food, handed in his resignation, but President Benes refused to accept it.

---

classical dictatorship of the proletariat. The Czechoslovak position was heretical, according to Tito, and was causing trouble elsewhere. He predicted that a showdown would occur soon. Although this may appear to confirm the speculation advanced by many writers regarding a split between Slansky and Gottwald, the evidence is very weak. Tito criticized Gottwald and the party and Slansky was secretary-general of the party. I am not familiar with any direct evidence that in the following months any major divergence in policy occurred between Slansky and Gottwald. Slansky did support Gomulka at the first Cominform meeting. Thus, contrary to the usual interpretation, Slansky and not Gottwald may have been the moderate. (V. Dedijer, *Tito Speaks* (Weidenfeld and Nicolson, 1953), p. 306.) On the other hand, there is some indirect evidence that the Czech Communist party was under pressure from Moscow, possibly for ideological and strategic reasons. As the international situation grew more serious, the need to secure tight control of Czechoslovak production and of the strategic *glacis* became of paramount importance to the Communist cause.

[33] *Christian Science Monitor*, August 4, 1947.

[34] He claimed that only the employees who opened the packages—rather than Zenkl, Drtina, or Masaryk—would have been injured had the bombs exploded.

In late September the Cominform was established. In its announcement, the Cominform vigorously attacked the Socialist parties and
accused them of betraying the cause of the working class. This charge
increased the resentment felt within the Social Democratic party toward
the pact with the Communist party. During November complicated
maneuvering by Vilim led to a Social Democratic party congress in
which Fierlinger[35] was replaced as party president by Bohumil Lausman, an opportunist who had been won temporarily to an anti-
Communist position.[36]

In October, the Communist party engaged in new efforts to reshape
the Slovak Board of Commissioners more to Communist liking. The
Communists accused the Democratic party of conspiring with the outlawed Slovak People's party and with maintaining relations with
Durcansky, an *émigré* Axis collaborator, to plot against the republic.
These changes were not entirely without foundation and there were
indications of linkages between some Democratic party deputies and
Karol Sidor and Ferdinand Durcansky.[37] However, leaders of the
National Socialist party thought that the charges went far beyond the
available evidence and that they were spread in this form by the Communists in order to destroy the Democratic party and to take over
Slovakia. There was evidence that the Communist-controlled police
had inspired denunciations of Slovak Democrats by *agents provocateurs*.

By November the Communists demanded the right to include representatives of the ROH within the Slovak Board of Commissioners—in
effect, to "pack" it. They also demanded the right to include representatives of the ROH and other "non-political" groups in the Czechoslovak National Front. They were effectively resisted by the other
parties. The Slovak National Council was reorganized, however, the

[35]Mikoyan asked Ripka whether Fierlinger's fall did not indicate that Czechoslovakia was detaching herself from her Soviet alliance. (Ripka, *op. cit.*, p. 124.)
Similar complaints came from representatives of satellite states. It is difficult to
judge the extent to which these statements represented fears and the extent to which
they constituted attempts to intimidate the Czechs.

[36]Majer supported Lausman, since he was the candidate most likely to defeat
Fierlinger. (*Ibd.*, p. 121.) Lausman had received Communist support in the past
and in 1945 he had favored a merger of the Communist and Social Democratic
parties. During the coup, he returned to a policy of cooperating with the Communists. Later he fled from Czechoslovakia, only to return in 1954 when he betrayed
many who had participated in resistance activities against the Communist regime.

[37]*Ibid.*, p. 112.

Democratic party losing three seats. One of these went to the Freedom party, another to the Labor (Social Democratic) party, and the third to a pro-Communist non-party technician.

During November, President Benes informed Valerian Zorin, the retiring Soviet ambassador to Prague, that the Communist party would lose the forthcoming elections. He reported the impression that Zorin also expected this result.[38] In Moscow, in this period, suspicions were expressed concerning Czech foreign policy. Lebediev accused the Czechs of desiring to throw the Communists out of the cabinet as the French had done. Mikoyan ominously informed Czech representatives, "Your disagreements and your internal struggles are your own business; what interests us is your relations with the U.S.S.R.; we will trust you if you remain our allies."[39]

During the autumn a series of purges was initiated in the Soviet satellites, and the Petkov affair came to a head when despite American protests Petkov was put to death by the Bulgarians. Moreover, the alarming information spread that at a meeting of the executive committee of the Communist party Gottwald warned of a reactionary coup against the government and announced that the Communist party might be forced to take drastic measures to protect its position.

During November, shortly after the execution of Petkov in Bulgaria, Petr Zenkl and some others called on American Ambassador Lawrence Steinhardt in Prague to discuss the Czechoslovak situation with him. Mr. Zenkl expressed fear that the Communists were preparing to destroy the democratic system and doubted that a fair election could be held while the Communists controlled the police. Mr. Steinhardt replied that he knew Stalin and was sure that Stalin wanted to maintain Czechoslovakia as a display of cooperation between East and West.

Mr. Zenkl referred to the execution of Petkov and the ineffective American protests. Steinhardt replied that Bulgaria had been a defeated enemy country. The situation in Czechoslovakia was quite different, he said. Czechoslovakia was an ally for whom the United States had great regard. Moreover, American troops were in Bavaria on the Czechoslovak border.[40] The United States, he said, would take an active

[38]Ibid., p. 136.   [39]Ibid., p. 134.

[40]According to General Wedemeyer's testimony at the Inquiry into the Military Situation in the Far East (p. 2329), the United States had only one division in Europe in 1948 and five understrength divisions in the United States, in addition to four divisions in the Far East. According to a statement by General Marshall, during

interest in anything that happened in Czechoslovakia, and added that
he himself would be there to represent the United States if anything
were attempted. Mr. Zenkl replied that he did not doubt the friendship
of the United States or of Mr. Steinhardt for Czechoslovakia.[41]

During November and December Nosek, the Communist Minister
of the Interior, began a purge inside the intelligence service and the
SNB, the mobile security police. Although Nosek was forced to dismiss
the Communist Porkony as head of Intelligence because he falsified
evidence in the bombing plot, he was able to retain Porkony within the
service and to intensify the replacement of non-Communist technicians
by Communists. Weapons, including submachine guns, were discovered in the home of a Communist deputy. The Communists were
forced to disavow the deputy and they were clearly embarrassed by the
disclosure.

During December the Czechoslovak-Bulgarian treaty negotiations
bogged down because of cabinet disagreements. The Bulgars wanted
the treaty to apply to any aggressor, not just to Germany and her
associates, and were evidently concerned about their neighbors, Greece
and Turkey. Although Gottwald stated that such a wording of the
treaty had the approval of Stalin, President Benes personally opposed
such terms. Jan Masaryk wrote to Moscow that Czechoslovakia would
sign such a treaty if the Soviet Union would be a party to it, whereupon
Moscow replied that the terms of the treaty concerned only Czechoslovakia and Bulgaria.[42]

---

the period of the Conference of Foreign Ministers in 1947 only one and one-third
divisions in the United States were useful for transfer to combat abroad. (See John C.
Sparrow, *History of Personnel Demobilization in the United States Army*, Department
of the Army, 1951, p. 282.) These were hardly effective military forces. They were
quite unlikely to deter the Czechoslovak Communists.

[41]Conversation with Mr. Zenkl. According to Pavel Korbel, it is reliably reported
that Mr. Steinhardt informed President Benes in the late fall that Czechoslovakia
could expect no American assistance in the event of an attempted Communist coup.

[42]Ripka, *op. cit.*, pp. 139-40. The treaty was signed after the coup as the Czech
democrats had specified. Ripka speculated that this was a response to American
hints of trouble if the rebel Markos government in Greece were recognized. There
is no evidence that the United States took so strong a stand or that a threat of this
kind had any bearing on the terms of a satellite treaty. On February 10, 1948, during
discussions of the Yugoslav-Bulgarian treaty, which had a similar clause, Stalin
referred to it as "Comsomolist"—i.e., childish—and as advocating a "preventive
war" course of action. He opposed the treaty on those grounds, although it specified
action "linked to the United Nations". Dedijer, *Tito Speaks*, p. 329.

Meanwhile the economic crisis continued. During November 1947 it was reported that Czechoslovakia was in dire need of American loans or credits because of Soviet demands that practically exhausted Czechoslovak export capacities in heavy goods. These were the products, moreover, that Czechoslovakia traditionally traded to the West. Instead of decreasing, the Russian demands were increasing.[43]

By the middle of November the terms of a five-year trade pact between the Soviet Union and Czechoslovakia were being completed in the Moscow negotiations. At the same time the United States was growing more doubtful about advancing credit to Czechoslovakia.[44] Although Ambassador Steinhardt intervened energetically to secure credits for Czechoslovakia,[45] some American officials thought that American credits would serve only to advance the integration of the Czechoslovak economy with that of the Soviet Union. On the other hand, the failure of the United States to act reduced the alternatives available to the democratic parties and strengthened the arguments of the Communists.

Toward the end of November reports circulated that the trade negotiations were lagging. It was noted that the failure of the Soviet Union to deliver promised grain had resulted in a serious shortage as a result of the great drought in Czechoslovakia and that the Czechs were unsuccessfully attempting to get grain elsewhere.[46] In an effort to secure good will for the Communist party, Premier Gottwald, without the knowledge of the cabinet,[47] appealed to Stalin to increase scheduled grain deliveries by 150,000 tons. Stalin responded by promising 200,000 additional tons of grain and also promised to grant credits to Czechoslovakia.[48] Although many observers doubted that the transportation system between the Soviet Union and Czechoslovakia would permit the fulfilment of Stalin's promise, early deliveries were made with great publicity. Gottwald also delivered a personal attack upon Majer, the anti-Communist Minister of Food, accusing him of failure to solve the food situation.

By the middle of December the negotiations for a five-year trade pact were concluded successfully. The agreement provided for the ex-

[43]*New York Times*, November 2, 1947.   [44]*Ibid.*, November 23, 1947.
[45]Ripka, *op. cit.*, p. 311.   [46]*The Times* (London), November 29, 1947.
[47]Or of Ripka, the Czech negotiator. *Christian Science Monitor*, December 17, 1947.
[48]*New York Times*, December 2, 1947.

change of $500 million in goods. The Czechs were to get food, fodder, cotton, fertilizer, oil products, ore, and other materials. The Russians were to get oil piping, rails, machinery for generating power, general industrial machinery, sugar, textiles, and chemicals, among other products. The pact accounted for 16 per cent of Czechoslovakia's foreign trade, 40 per cent of her grain requirements, and 25 per cent of her cotton requirements.[49]

Hubert Ripka, the Czech trade negotiator, states that the pact was on the whole advantageous for Czechoslovakia. The Soviet Union cut back its demands for industrial products and increased its delivery schedule for food products. However, to pay for the increased grain, Czechoslovakia had to step up its deliveries of consumer goods to the Soviet Union. This would require the Czech worker to tighten his belt over the next several years.[50]

Later in December Premier Klement Gottwald urged a new five-year plan designed to increase Czechoslovak heavy industry by 80 per cent. To carry out this program, 30 per cent of current production would have to be diverted to the production of capital goods.[51] Taken in conjunction with the trade pact, the plan required a considerable reduction in the Czech standard of living. While the effects of the plan would not be felt quickly enough to influence the forthcoming elections, the long-term effect would probably be politically disastrous for the parties that proposed it. Even so, the Social Democratic party was disposed to support the Communist party on these economic objectives.[52] As a result, many right-wing Social Democrats left the party, thus decreasing the influence of its anti-Communist wing.

The Coup Is Organized

During January 1948 the situation built up to a climax. Early in January the case of the bomb plot was brought into Parliament when

[49]*The Times* (London), December 16, 1947.

[50]Ripka, *op. cit.*, p. 131. At the same time the Soviet currency was deflated, rationing was ended amid great fanfare, and prices of foodstuffs and some other goods were lowered. To fulfil the promises made to the Russians, it was necessary for the Soviet Union to step up its purchases of civilian goods. Therefore, the agreement seemed to meet internal Soviet needs that were serious and possibly of crisis proportion. See *World Dispatch*, December 23, 1947.

[51]*Ibid.*   [52]Ripka, *op. cit.*, p. 145.

Drtina demanded the dismissal of the police who destroyed the evidence of Communist complicity. The Communists responded with threats and accused the National Socialists of intending to start a "Reichstag fire trial".

Toward the end of the month, Hubert Ripka was visited by an unnamed Communist deputy who informed him that he feared the worst unless thoughtful persons on both sides could agree upon a compromise. This deputy then suggested a confidential meeting between Gottwald and Slansky on one side and Ripka and Zenkl on the other. Since Ripka viewed the suggestion as an effort to intimidate the National Socialists and cause them to accept the Communist reorganization of the Ministry of the Interior, he refused to consent.[53]

When Ripka met Gottwald on ministerial business, Gottwald accused the National Socialist of attempting to make a Van der Lubbe[54] out of him. He charged the National Socialists with fostering reaction and with raising the trouble about the police only to enable them to claim that the elections were rigged after they lost. Ripka retorted that he was aware of the survey of public opinion carried out by Communist Minister of Information Kopecky, according to which the Communists were going to lose from 8 to 10 per cent of their previous vote.[55]

This was ominous, as the Communists had no intention of permitting such a reduction of their power in the state. Moreover, before the interview was broken off, Gottwald asserted strongly that the Communists would never give way on the issue of the security police. Since, as later events confirmed, they could not count upon the support of the Social Democratic party on this issue, this could only mean that they were prepared, or wished others to believe them prepared, to resort to force to maintain their control of the police.

By February it was evident that the drama was coming to a close. Word came back to Czechoslovakia that Hungarian Communists were predicting the emergence of the Communists as the masters of Czechoslovakia by the end of the month.[56]

[53]Ripka, *op. cit.*, pp. 180-81.

[54]The insane Dutchman who, unlike Dimitrov, received no assistance and was convicted of the Reichstag fire that the Nazis themselves had staged.

[55]*Ibid.*, pp. 182-83. That would mean a reduction of the Communist vote from 38 to 28 or 30 per cent of the total vote. See also *Manchester Guardian*, April 29, 1948.

[56]Ripka, *op. cit.*, p. 185.

The next issue that arose seemed to be a minor one from a superficial standpoint. It concerned a proposed 25 per cent increase in pay for civil servants. The URO and the Communist party opposed the increase on the ground that it would lead to inflation. They warned that they would have to resort to strikes to secure increases for workers generally if the increase for civil servants went through. Since the civil servants were underpaid, the specific Communist objections were not too pertinent. However, if they intended to depress living standards generally as a consequence of the projected five-year plan, this was hardly the time to increase wages.

Even more important was the possibility that the Communists could split the Social Democratic party away from the other democratic parties on this issue. Thus, if they could bring matters to a head on the economic issue rather than on the police issue, they had a good chance of carrying a majority with them.

The democratic leaders understood this as well as the Communists. Therefore, the anti-Communist Social Democrat Majer introduced a compromise before the cabinet that was much closer to the Communist than to the National Socialist position. The National Socialists, however, accepted this compromise as soon as their proposal was beaten. The wavering Social Democrats were kept in line despite the threats of Zapotocky and the URO delegation. Majer's resolution was then passed over the Communist opposition. Zapotocky said the URO would not accept the decision and that the unions would answer the government through the congress of unit committees—i.e., of shop committees or works councils. He accused the Soviet Democrats of joining the "reactionary" forces, and Gottwald shouted at them, "You will pay us back for that!"[57] The vehemence of the Communists was indicative of the pressure under which they were acting[58] and of the seriousness of the situation. Time was very short indeed.

Before the meeting of the Czechoslovak cabinet on February 13, it was learned that Minister of the Interior Nosek had dismissed eight non-Communist police commissioners in Prague and had ordered their replacement by Communists.[59] Since the commissioners had control of

[57]Ripka, *op. cit.*, p. 191.
[58]Presumably, from the Cominform and Moscow. If the decision had already been made, they would pay for blunders in carrying it out.
[59]*Ibid.*, p. 196.

the arms used by the police, this seemed an obvious preparation for a coup. The matter was introduced at the cabinet meeting and the representatives of all parties except the Communist party voted for a resolution ordering Nosek to reinstate the dismissed police commissioners.

The unity of the non-Communist parties interfered with the plans of the Communists and they sought to provide another issue on which to force a cabinet split. According to reports circulating on February 16, the secretariat of the Communist party had worked out a plan of radical socialism that the National Socialists and the bourgeois parties would be forced to oppose and that the Social Democrats would support. As these reports had it, the Communists hoped that rejection of this proposal by the bourgeois parties would precipitate a cabinet crisis permitting Gottwald to form a new cabinet from Communist, Social Democratic, and URO elements. This cabinet would stage an election in which the Communists would win more than 50 per cent of the votes. According to the informant, Slansky assured the secretariat of the party that everything had been cleared with the Cominform and Zhdanov.[60]

Ripka, Zenkl, and other leaders of the National Socialist party thought it dangerous to permit the Communists to choose the issue on which the break would come. Since Nosek had not carried out the resolution of the cabinet with respect to reinstating the Prague police commissioners, they saw an opportunity to parry the Communist gambit by handing in their resignations on this issue if Nosek continued to disregard the cabinet decision. The democratic leaders hoped in this fashion to demonstrate to the public that the regime was in danger. Then, if a cabinet crisis was provoked, they hoped to be able to advance the elections to an earlier date, before the police had a chance to rig them.

Gottwald abruptly adjourned a cabinet meeting when the other parties refused to discuss any other issue unless he would force Nosek to comply with the cabinet resolution. The People's and Slovak Democratic parties agreed to act in unison with the National Socialist plan to cause a cabinet crisis over this issue if Nosek did not comply. Majer, the Social Democrat, promised to go along with the anti-Communist grouping. Representatives of the democratic parties then proceeded to

[60]*Ibid.*, p. 200. The formulation is peculiar. The information that the Soviet Union backed the move might have been used to intimidate the non-Communists, but why did the Communists need assurance? Was there a substantial bloc that opposed the move and that had to be told that the plan was both indigenous in origin and supported in the highest party circles?

inform President Benes of their plans. He advised them to hold firm to the course they had chosen and agreed that it was necessary to insist upon the cabinet resolution regarding the police.

Benes also told them that Premier Gottwald had conferred with him and had accused the National Socialists of plotting to install a cabinet of technicians, thus eliminating Communist participation in the cabinet. Benes said he replied that he would never accept a cabinet that did not include representatives of all the parties of the National Front or that did include representatives of non-parliamentary groups.[61] In effect, he was warning Gottwald that he would not approve a cabinet including URO elements or excluding the democratic parties at the same time that he was assuring him of continued Communist participation in the cabinet.

The Coup Takes Place

Soviet troop movements were reported on the Czech periphery. On February 19 Valerian Zorin, the Soviet Deputy Minister of Foreign Affairs and ex-ambassador to Czechoslovakia, arrived in Prague ostensibly to check on the deliveries of Russian wheat and to participate in a scheduled celebration of Soviet-Czechoslovak friendship. The mission was quite minor for so important an official.[62]

Coincidentally, on the same day that Zorin reached Prague from Moscow, Ambassador Steinhardt arrived from the United States. Shortly after his arrival, he received a visit from Mr. Zenkl. The Ambassador informed Mr. Zenkl that the United States was in no position to aid the Czechoslovak democrats other than by expressions of sympathy or moral support. Ambassador Steinhardt asked whether the democratic parties would take any steps to prevent a coup. Mr. Zenkl noted the difficulties of the situation. The democratic parties had no arms with which to defend themselves, while the Communists had caches of arms and controlled the police. He was not sanguine about the situation.[63]

[61] *Ibid.*, p. 215.

[62] It may be questioned whether he was present to impress the Czechs with the interest of the Soviet Union in impending events or whether he was present to make sure that the Czech Communist party carried out its mission. On February 10 Zorin had been present at the Moscow Conference in which Stalin had attempted to bring the Yugoslav and Bulgarian Communists into line.

[63] Conversation with Mr. Zenkl.

In the meantime the Social Democratic ministers attempted to persuade the Communists to give way on the police issue. Gottwald shouted at them, "If you do not march with us, you will be liquidated like the others."[64] The National Socialists, Democrats, and People's party agreed not to participate in the cabinet meeting of February 20 unless they were first informed that the cabinet decision of February 13 had been executed. The Social Democrats also agreed to abstain from cabinet meetings until that issue had been settled satisfactorily. When the Communist reply was unsatisfactory, the three parties decided that their ministers would hand in their resignations that afternoon. The Social Democratic party promised to convoke a meeting of its executive committee to determine its position.

At four o'clock the twelve ministers belonging to the three parties handed their resignations to Benes, who congratulated them on the course they had chosen and promised not to accept the resignations. He said that he would not compromise on the issue and that the important thing was to hurry the elections. The Communists' losses would exceed all their forecasts.[65]

That same day the state radio service, which was under the control of the Communist Minister of the Interior, Kopecky, attacked the twelve "reactionary" ministers. The radio urged all workers to meet in the Old City Square on Saturday morning, February 21. Communist squads took physical reprisals against those workers who refused to participate in the rally. Gottwald spoke at the rally and accused his opponents of being agents of foreign reaction. The formation of Committees of Action was urged by the Premier.

According to plan, Committees of Action, supposedly representing the people but actually set up through Communist channels, came into being throughout the country. Later that day Gottwald called on the President and demanded that he accept the resignations of the ministers. Benes refused. Later factory committee representatives called on Benes and repeated the demand. He again refused and had his position printed in the newspapers.[66] Benes declared that he would not accept a cabinet of technicians, a cabinet that excluded the Communists, or one that excluded any other party.

[64]Ripka, *op. cit.*, p. 225.
[65]*Ibid.*, p. 227.
[66]Still published independently by the parties.

The democratic parties would have preferred that Benes insist upon the resignation of the entire cabinet. They were disturbed by the fact that their requests to see the President on the 21st had been refused, although he had received several Communist delegations. Meanwhile Benes was deluged by a flood of Communist-inspired telegrams and messages. Also the police were required to take oaths to support the government of Klement Gottwald and to take orders from Minister of the Interior Nosek.

On Sunday, the 22nd, the Communists staged a packed congress of union unit committees. The democratic parties staged counter-demonstrations throughout the state against a background of increasing Communist violence and intimidation. That day the Communists began to arrest some of those who took part in the demonstrations.

Later that day word arrived from Jina, Chief of the Political Division in the Office of the President, that President Benes was depressed by the brutal methods of the Communists. Benes requested the democratic parties to agree to his appeasing the Communists. He wanted to accept the resignations of the democratic ministers and then to persuade the Communists to accept a cabinet of all the parties.[67] Although the parties could not prevent the President from accepting the resignations of their ministers, they refused to approve such an action.

Even later that night, SNB mobile police units occupied Prague and several secretaries of the National Socialist party were arrested. Gendarmes with submachine guns were stationed at the homes of leading members of the democratic parties.

During the afternoon of the 23rd, President Benes, who had received Gottwald and Nosek that morning, conferred with the leaders of the National Socialist party. He said he had informed Gottwald that he would not permit him to make a putsch. Then he called Gottwald's demands the equivalent of Munich and said, ". . . I will act no different from what I did then. I want to have no part in this second Munich you are engaged in preparing."[68] This was ominous, inasmuch as Benes had acceded to the Nazi demands at Munich without accepting responsibility for them. In effect, Benes was stating that, if he would not participate in the Communist plans, neither would he oppose them. Nevertheless, he informed Gottwald that he would not accept a cabinet list obtained by intimidation or by an artificial splitting of parties.

[67]*Ibid.*, p. 245.   [68]*Ibid.*, p. 251.

But Benes qualified this posture of opposition: "If the Communists persist in their threatening attitude, and if they insist that I bow to their demands, I shall refuse, and I shall resign myself rather than comply."[69] Benes was very worried about the massing of the Red Army. "I think as you [Ripka] do," he said, "that Moscow will not run the risks which an armed intervention would involve. However, I cannot rule out the possibility of seeing their troops cross our frontiers. In that case, what could we do?" He ruled out Ripka's demand that they fight, even if it meant defeat. "No one will help us. Moscow knows that. . . . They take themselves for realists; at bottom they are only fanatics. Their whole policy is a provocation to war."[70]

On the 21st, one of the leaders of the Slovak Democratic party had been arrested, and Communist printers refused to print its newspaper. On the 23rd, the secretariats of the three anti-Communist parties were raided and their files seized. That day the Minister of the Interior announced discovery of a plot against the republic. Unofficial Communist charges were circulated that the American embassy was involved in the plot. Newsprint deliveries to the papers of the democratic parties ceased. General Bocek, Chief of Staff of the army, announced his resolution to oppose "all tendencies which hide a desire to provoke a reactionary reversal of our foreign policy."[71] Thus, Bocek blossomed out as a collaborator of the Communists.

Meanwhile the Social Democrats were following a hesitant policy. On the 20th, Lausman had promised not to participate in a government from which the other parties were excluded. He claimed to have refused all Communist offers. However, Lausman refused to accede to the request of his party comrade, Majer, that the Social Democratic ministers resign immediately.

A meeting of the central executive committee of the Social Democratic party was scheduled for Monday, February 23. During the crisis, the Social Democratic paper, *Pravo Lidu*, followed an unhesitating anti-Communist line. As late as the night of February 22 Lausman had promised not to participate in a cabinet that did not include the other parties.

On the 23rd, when the Communists were already resorting to direct action, the central executive committee of the Social Democratic party met. The Fierlinger wing of the party, with the help of Lausman,

[69]*Ibid.*, p. 253.   [70]*Ibid.*, pp. 256, 257.   [71]*Ibid.*, p. 267.

defeated the motion of Majer stipulating the resignation of the Social Democratic ministers. It then passed a resolution calling for talks with the Communists and participation with the URO in a conference designed to create a Central Committee of Action to set up a new National Front. That evening Lausman and Vilim were received by Benes. On the 24th, Fierlinger's men, aided by a Communist mob and the police, occupied the editorial offices of *Pravo Lidu*, in the face of resistance by Majer.[72] The secretariat of the party was also seized by force.

That same day, Minister of National Defense Svoboda made a speech pledging fidelity to the revolutionary cause. Although Majer was still an accredited minister in the cabinet, a Communist mob forcibly ejected him from his government office, despite appeals for aid to the Minister of the Interior. The renegade People's party deputies, Petr and Plojhar, took over the offices of *Lidova Democracie*, the People's party newspaper, by force. The independent liberal daily, *Svobodne Noviny*, was also seized by force, as was Melantrich, the publishing house of the National Socialist party, and its paper, *Svobodne Slovo*. Several editors were arrested and the general manager was prevented from occupying the premises. *Mlade Fronta*, the Young Communist publication, hailed with joy "these measures which, at last, have freed our Press from traitors to the nation."[73]

On the 23rd the Communists created a new National Front, consisting of Communists, Social Democrats, URO elements, and some renegades from the other parties. On the 24th Alois Neumann and Emanuel Slechta, two National Socialists, agreed to participate in a Gottwald cabinet without the knowledge or approval of their party. Benes was informed by the party, when it learned of this, that the action of the two National Socialist deputies was unauthorized. On the 24th Benes made an appeal by letter to Gottwald again to "discuss the matter of a new and lasting cooperation . . . reasonable agreement is possible because it is absolutely necessary."[74]

The Communists replied that they refused to cooperate with the three parties.[75] *Rude Pravo* threatened a general strike unless Gottwald's

---

[72]*Ibid.*, p. 275.   [73]*Ibid.*, p. 285.   [74]*Ibid.*, p. 292.

[75]*New York Times*, February, 26, 1948. Benes said he "insist[ed] on parliamentary democracy and parliamentary government as it limited democracy." The presidium of the Communist party said that the other parties had gotten in touch with "hostile foreign circles" and had aimed at a *putsch*.

demands were satisfied. At noon on the 25th the radio announced that Benes had accepted the resignations of the twelve ministers. In response to a telephone inquiry, however, the chancellory maintained that no decision had yet been reached. But by four o'clock Benes had approved the new ministerial list submitted by Gottwald.[76] The Communist coup had been carried out successfully.

TESTING THE HYPOTHESES

It is clear that the case material is not sufficient to confirm outright either the hypothesis that the Czechoslovak coup had been planned from the very beginning or the hypothesis that it had not. The alternative hypotheses will now be tested and a case built for rejection of the first.

The First Hypothesis Rejected

One factor alone would seem to have been sufficient to necessitate the coup. That factor was the five-year plan advocated by Klement Gottwald in December 1947. A plan calling for an 80 per cent increase in heavy industrial capacity, and for that objective to be accomplished by diverting 30 per cent of the productive facilities from production to consumption, would be so unpopular that it could be carried out only under a dictatorial regime. No free people will tighten its belt to that extent unless there is a clear and present danger.[77]

Although the Czechoslovaks desired to cooperate with the Soviet Union, their image of the West differed greatly from that broadcast by the Kremlin. Therefore, that clear and present danger did not exist for the Czechs. Moreover, the National Socialist, People's, and Democratic parties were sure to exploit the issue. The agreement of 1946 that cabinet posts were to be distributed according to strength in Parliament signified that over a period of years the Communist party would lose its key

---

[76]Ripka, *op. cit.*, p. 293.

[77]Particularly at a time when conditions were just approaching those of prewar. According to Slansky, wages (1939= 100) were indexed at 397 in 1947 and prices at 286. (*For a Lasting Peace; For a People's Democracy*, December 1947.) Slansky's figures are subject to doubt but that does not change the general picture.

positions in the government and thus its ability to veto policies to which it objected.

Although the Communist party was making propaganda use of the five-year trade agreement with the Soviet Union and although the economic terms of that agreement were not completely unfavorable to Czechoslovakia, the agreement would produce a further decline in the level of consumption, thus driving an additional nail into the coffin of the Communist party.

In addition, the failure of Czechoslovakia to join the Marshall Plan was unpopular because the plan promised to mitigate Czechoslovakia's economic problems. Yet this may have been the very reason why the Czechs, as well as the Poles and the Rumanians, were not permitted to join. Had they joined, their trade and production schedules would have been tied to Western credits and Western needs rather than to Soviet needs.[78] As a member of the Marshall Plan Council, Czechoslovakia automatically would have negotiated with the West; the very bridge the Russians desired to deny them would have been created in aggravated form. The iron curtain would have been pierced. As the organization of the West increased, disorganization would have appeared in the Soviet bloc. The stability and viability of the Soviet bloc were in question and that involved the vital security interests of the Soviet Union.

The monolithic unity of the Soviet sphere has been asserted so frequently that the cracks in that monolithic structure are often overlooked. However, it was just those cracks, those symptoms of impending disorganization, that the Soviet Union desired to repair.

The series of purges in the satellites that began in 1947 constitute evidence of a "nationalist" opposition to Moscow policy. The Balkan federation proposed by Dimitrov infuriated Stalin because it appeared to envisage a bloc of Communist states combining to act as a counterweight to the Soviet Union.

It is significant that on February 10, 1948, Stalin demanded that three federations be formed immediately and that his suggested federations grouped those states between whom serious friction existed. The federations he proposed included Yugoslavia and Bulgaria, in dispute over Macedonia; Hungary and Rumania, in dispute over Transylvania; and

[78]For a distinct statement of this fear, see Zhdanov's statement to the Cominform conference, printed in *For a Lasting Peace; For a People's Democracy*, November 10, 1947.

Czechoslovakia and Poland, in dispute over the Teschen region.[79] Federations of this character would have weakened the Communist parties in the satellites by permitting Stalin to play off not only the parties within each federation but one federation against the others. Stalin's plan would have hardened the organizations along the most divisive lines.

Stalin had definite problems of leadership. Gomulka opposed the formation of the Cominform and also opposed Zhdanov's policy of collectivization and forced industrialization.[80] Moreover, it is apparent from Rumanian and Czech responses to the Marshall Plan that others were in opposition even if their positions were not as overt as those of Gomulka. Kostov argued economic policy with Stalin during the February 1948 meetings in Moscow and had to be shouted down. At the Cominform meetings Slansky supported Gomulka on the partisan issue against Zhdanov.[81]

As late as April 1949 Czechoslovakia maintained its trade pattern with Yugoslavia despite the Cominform boycott. It was only after Hungary refused to tranship goods to Czechoslovakia,[82] and after Mikoyan made a trip to Prague, that Czechoslovakia broke off her trade relations with Yugoslavia.

Was the Cominform itself an attempt to get the various Communist parties into face-to-face relations with the Moscow bosses, and to play the party organizations against each other to assure Moscow's leadership? Even if this were not so, the problems of maintaining unity in program and action were apparently becoming formidable.

Why could not Moscow have played down the industrialization program, thus reducing the friction resulting from the economic problems of Czechoslovakia and the satellites?[83] No categorical answer can be

[79]Dedijer, op. cit., p. 330. The conclusion, however, is mine rather than Dedijer's.
[80]Ibid., p. 306.
[81]According to Douglas Hyde, op. cit., Tito reported that Gottwald had got into trouble for advocating democratic methods of achieving communism. However, Hyde's alleged source, Rust, is dead, and while Hyde seems to be an honest reporter, he lacks acuity.
[82]See New York Times, May 15, 1949.
[83]The Soviet Union's five-year plan was designed to achieve prewar conditions by 1948. See Malenkov's statement in For a Lasting Peace; For a People's Democracy, December 1, 1947. The Soviet Union had nationalist economic objectives as well as nationalist strategic objectives. The satellites were being milked for the Soviet Union, particularly for the Great Russians who, according to Malenkov, led all the rest.

given to this question. The sharp dispute with respect to this issue between Zhdanov and Gomulka at the sessions establishing the Cominform would indicate that the imposition of industrialization on the satellite bloc was an important reason for establishing the Cominform.

Gottwald advocated the five-year plan shortly after the Cominform meeting. According to reports, a twelve-year plan for Poland and a five-year plan for Czechoslovakia were formulated at the Cominform meeting. These plans called for an abnormally high level of investment, forced savings to be accomplished by reducing consumption, the direction of labor to specific jobs, and other harsh measures.[84]

According to an escaped Czech civil servant, the Communists were using Czechoslovakia as a source of materials for the economic reconstruction of the Soviet Union and as a source of military supplies. He reported that the Communists were attempting to build an eastern Ruhr in Czechoslovakia and Poland and to integrate the economies of Eastern Europe and East Germany.[85]

It is necessary now to turn back to the German problem. The plans for Anglo-American bizonal fusion in Germany had been viewed gravely by the Soviet Union. Increases in the level of permitted production in the Western zones were matched by planned increases of from 200 to 300 per cent in the Soviet zone. The failure of the Moscow meeting of Foreign Ministers in March-April 1947, the Truman Doctrine, the Brussels Pact, French adherence to the Anglo-American program with respect to Germany, and the veto of the Soviet proposal for four-power control of the Ruhr must have confronted the masterminds of the Kremlin with a nightmare,[86] especially when during the summer JCS 1067, providing for the dismantling of German heavy industry, was formally revoked. Moscow envisaged the enlistment of the Ruhr productive capacity in the service of the Western powers. The Soviet leaders

[84]*The Times* (London), January 10, 1948. The Polish plan was not put into outline form until late 1948 and was not set in operation until 1950. It was a six-year plan. The other satellite powers also adopted plans emphasizing heavy industry in this period.

[85]Arnost Heidrich, who was secretary-general of the Czechoslovak foreign office until he escaped just before Christmas 1948. *New York Times*, January 16, 1949.

[86]Zhdanov particularly referred to the German problem and the Ruhr and the American effort to bring "under its sway the major sources of coal, iron, and steel". (*For a Lasting Peace; For a People's Democracy*, December 10, 1947.) James Byrnes felt the Russians would give up almost anything to get an accord on the Ruhr. Walter Millis, ed., *The Forrestal Diaries* (Viking, 1951), p. 347.

had no hope of matching this productive capacity, but may well have believed that Draconic measures were necessary in order to achieve a situation approaching parity.

Rejection of the Marshall Plan and insistence upon forced industrialization produced convulsions in the Soviet sphere of Europe. The difficulties they caused within the various Communist parties and the harsh measures required to keep the various populations in check involved great material—if not moral—costs for the Kremlin. Moreover, this crisis occurred when unrest was evidently so great within the Soviet Union that increases in the standard of living had to be promised the Russian people. It is doubtful that these steps were taken for purely ideological reasons. Stalin generally was able to subordinate ideology to the consolidation and maintenance of Soviet power.

If the reasons stated above are valid, the Soviet leaders thought it necessary to impose the five-year plan on Czechoslovakia because of its great industrial capacity. From that standpoint, Czechoslovakia was the key European satellite. Therefore, the coup clearly was required at approximately the time that it was carried out. However, to say that this consideration would have been sufficient to produce the result is not equivalent to stating that it did produce the result.

A hypothesis must account for all the evidence, and some pieces of evidence presented in the body of this memorandum have not yet been accounted for. Gottwald and Slansky were speaking of the necessity of winning a majority in the election as early as the spring of 1947, roughly half a year before the Cominform meeting and the order to force through the five-year industrialization program.

No totally convincing answer can be offered if that fact is presented as an objection to the hypothesis, because sufficient information is not available. However, there is evidence that many programs of the Soviet Union are in the consideration and planning stages for months before the orders for their execution are issued. The developing cold war would undoubtedly have given rise to talk in top Communist circles of certain strategic needs, including firm control of such strategic areas as Czechoslovakia. Moreover, the resolution to win a majority in the elections in order to have that type of firm control does not of itself imply an intention to dispense with parliamentary devices or to resort to force.

It must also be remembered that these statements by Gottwald and Slansky were made just after the announcement of the Truman Doctrine.

While the efforts of the democratic parties to build a bridge to the West were both justified and intelligent from the standpoint of Czechoslovakia, there is no gainsaying the fact that their purpose in building such a bridge was to weaken the dependence of Czechoslovakia upon the Soviet Union. However, this is just what the Soviet Union could not afford, for it required that Czechoslovakia become firmly organized in its bloc of nations.

Although the Soviet Union had secured relatively easy victories in Czechoslovakia in regard to the Marshall Plan and the French alliance, the remarks made by Mikoyan and Lebediev reveal growing suspicion of the motivation of the democratic parties. Although the democratic parties had every reason to resent the brutal methods of the Soviet Union and the Czech Communist party, it is undeniable that the rift between the parties was widening as conditions returned to normal within the country. The position of the Communist party was correspondingly weakened.

Even if the democratic parties had no intentions of forcing the Communist party out of the cabinet, one wonders whether they might not have developed such an intention had their position become sufficiently strong at the elections. Certainly the Communists feared this and they were probably correct in fearing it; but in any case the mobilization of the Czech economy in the service of Soviet objectives could not have been achieved if the democratic parties had won.

There is no evidence that the coup had been planned as early as the spring of 1947. But there is reason to believe that the Communists were cognizant of the importance of controlling the government and that they therefore were beginning to consider the possibility of a coup. The Czech Communists were probably under pressure from Moscow, and certainly were under pressure from Belgrade, where the Tito forces disliked the moderate methods of the Czech Communists. It is even possible that the Czech Communists made efforts to avoid this eventuality and that their requests to confer with the democratic parties were not merely attempts to intimidate them. I express no firm conviction on this point.

The point to be emphasized is that the coup was not a mere exercise of the power of the Communist party. That power could have been exercised with greater ease and less risk in 1945 or 1946. It represented a decision based on Soviet estimates of the international situation and of the Soviet Union's security requirements in that situation. It also reflected the suspicion with which the Soviet Union views the external world and the relatively high priority given to security considerations when the international situation worsens.

There is a Soviet syndrome: danger leads to industrialization program leads to rigid political controls and purges.[87] The syndrome continues to operate until external factors change or internal correctives come into force.

Soviet policy was responding to American policy just as American had responded to Soviet. If the Soviet Union, given its estimates of its security requirements and of the political reliability of non-Communist Poles or Bulgarians, saw fit to destroy democracy in those areas, this did not imply a decision to destroy it everywhere the Red Army went, regardless of security and reliability.

If, on the other hand, the Americans were shocked by the brutality of the action and feared that it portended other action requiring defensive measures, this did not imply a decision to attack the Soviet Union. But the very fact that the United States took these measures and the fact that the Soviet Union had suspicions led to changes in the calculus of security and reliability invoked by the Soviet Union.

In other words, suspicion and force kept feeding themselves—particularly so because of the low tolerance of the Soviet Union for restraint where the opposition is very weak. It is unlikely that there was a master plan to take over Czechoslovakia from the very beginning.

On the other hand, evidence strongly indicates that the Soviet Union has no intrinsic regard for democratic government. If Stalin permitted Czechoslovak democracy to survive in the period from 1945 to 1948, this indicated only that he was not prepared to risk the displeasure of the West or to increase the risk of war under the international conditions then existing. There may also have been a desire to secure the cooperation of non-Communists in the economic reconstruction of Czechoslovakia.

If the Communists resorted to force in 1948, it would seem to indicate only that they considered cooperation with the West less likely than in 1945, that their need for heavy industry had increased since 1945, or that they considered war a present danger.

[87] 1927, 1937, and 1947 were all years in which purges were organized.

In all likelihood, the Soviet Union viewed the Truman Doctrine and changes in Allied German policy as indications of belligerent motivation. This interpretation, as all Westerners know, had no foundation in fact. However, the American fears that the Czechoslovak coup indicated a Soviet intention to wage major war may have been lacking in foundation also. Nevertheless, those fears did *exist*, as the war scare of March 1948 demonstrates.[88]

The First Hypothesis Defended

If we examine still other evidence, it is possible to resurrect the first hypothesis, to the effect that the coup had been planned from the beginning. Rakosi, Revai, and Geroe, leaders of the Stalinist wing of the Hungarian Communist party, all stressed the "salami" theory of Communist control—that is, the stage-by-stage take-over. According to this theory, in the first stages of the Communist take-over, because of the ravages of war, the Communists required the cooperation of the other parties and of their supporters to re-establish the satellite economies. In this period a semblance of freedom could be maintained, provided that the Communists controlled the key Ministry of the Interior and, even better, that the Soviet army was in evidence to intimidate potential opposition.

That this "salami" procedure was put into operation can be supported by the composition of the satellite governments after World War Two. Indeed in Hungary in particular a relatively free election produced a landslide majority for the non-Communist Smallholders' party. The way in which police pressure was used to purge and to control the non-Communist parties in the satellites other than Czechoslovakia is too well known to require exposition.

Clearly the process of tightening the Communist reins occurred in the other satellites in the 1947-48 period—that is, roughly at the time of the Czechoslovak coup. In this sense, the coup may be viewed as part of a larger and more general plan for the consolidation of Communist rule in the satellites. One can view slight differences in the speed and

[88]See *Forrestal Diaries, op. cit.*, p. 15, for Clay's "*Eyes Only*" telegram on the danger of war, and p. 359 for the C.I.A. estimate on March 16 that war was not probable for the next "sixty days".

the style of the take-overs as responses to local conditions and international pressures. Czechoslovakia was an Allied nation, whereas
Rumania, Hungary, and Bulgaria had fought the Soviet Union. Poland
was also an Allied nation, but the hostility between the London government and the Soviet Union set off the Polish situation from the Czechoslovak. Moreover, Poland was overrun by the Soviet Army while the
war was in progress, whereas Czechoslovakia was entered by Soviet
forces only at the time of German collapse. Even so, Western sympathies for Poland forced compromises that were not made in the case
of Hungary, Rumania, and Bulgaria. In addition, the Czechs were the
most westernized of the satellite peoples in terms of customs and
sympathies.

Thus it is possible to interpret all variations in the treatment of the
satellites as functions of different internal conditions, differences in the
mode and timing of occupation, and differences in Western support.
From this standpoint, the similarities of the take-overs, in terms both
of style and of timing, may seem more striking than the differences. The
take-overs may thus be viewed as part of a master plan set in advance—
at least in broad outline if not in detail. Yet one may reverse the explanation. It may have been the requirements of the cold war—in particular,
the need for economic expansion—that forced the imposition of tight
political controls in the satellites. Seen as a response to world conditions,
differences in timing and styling then become related to internal obstacles to the imposition of political control.

SUMMARY REMARKS

The case study is sufficiently clear with respect to the mechanics of the
coup and the role played by the various Czechoslovak parties as not to
require additional comment. The interplay of domestic and international
factors is also evident. The difficulty of assessing motivation has been
demonstrated in the preceding sections. Perhaps a further remark or
two concerning this difficulty and its significance are in order.

It is obvious that any assertions concerning Soviet objectives and
motivations with respect to the Communist coup in Czechoslovakia
must be hedged about with serious reservations. Perhaps if we had
documentary evidence concerning the actual meetings of the Com-

munist high command at which the decisions on Czechoslovakia were
made, we might feel an assurance that is presently lacking. But even the
most convincing evidence that the precipitating cause of the coup was
the need to institute the Soviet industrialization program would not
exclude the hypothesis that the coup would have been staged even in
the absence of any Soviet need for Czechoslovak industrial productivity.

If motivations are so obscure in a case documented as well as the
Czechoslovak coup—at least with respect to circumstantial evidence—
considerable caution should be employed in orienting foreign policy to
estimates of national motivation. This does not mean that such estimates
should be excluded completely from consideration. Certainly the willingness of the Soviet Union to use force, subversion, and local Communist movements to implement its foreign policies ought to be taken
into account in determining American foreign policy. But the organizational characteristics of the Communist bloc, together with the military
capabilities of that bloc, provide far stronger grounds for the policy
that led to the formation of NATO than the factors which precipitated
the coup. Even had the coup been a purely defensive move by the
Soviet Union, the strategic considerations which ought to have formed
the foundation for Western policy would still have applied. These
strategic considerations, after all, had been understood very clearly by
Winston Churchill, as his Fulton speech demonstrated.

If the area of motivational analysis is subject to great uncertainties,
national policies—particularly those upon which vital national interests
are dependent—clearly ought not to be tied dogmatically to particular
interpretations of motivation. Obviously, this does not mean that no
interpretations should be made. A policy insensitive to variations in
motivation probably would not serve any realistic purpose. For instance,
NATO planning is based upon the assumption that Britain and France
will not join the Soviet Union in an attack upon the United States. We
could not make any useful plans at all if we made no assumptions about
the potential behavior of other states. This is not the place to explore
this theoretical consideration in detail. But it is fairly obvious that the
Soviet Union is powerful and hostile to the United States; at any rate,
this is certainly a desirably conservative assumption. The Czechoslovak
coup does give strong evidence that the Soviet Union is willing to
countenance the use of force under some circumstances; Hungary has
given even stronger evidence since then.

But within these limitations we do not know with even a high degree of reliability, let alone for sure, what objectives the Soviet Union was attempting to implement at the time of the Czechoslovak coup. Moreover, the Soviet Union has some freedom either to change its objectives or to change its plans in order to take advantage of too rigid a dedication on our part to particular interpretations of Soviet motivation. Such rigid interpretations further prevent us from exploring a situation and from finding out, perhaps to our advantage, that our hypothesis concerning Soviet motivation is incorrect. Therefore, particularly with respect to large and powerful but hostile states—but in other cases also —it is desirable to develop policies that are sensitive to variations in assumptions concerning motivation and that permit us to explore whether or not these assumptions are wrong.

Ranges of policy decisions may be excluded from consideration on the basis of evidence concerning motivation. We do not consider joint military blocs with the Soviet Union under present world conditions. We do not expect betrayal by Great Britain. Short of a major change in internal political alignments, Italy can be considered a loyal member of NATO. On the basis of good evidence, some ranges of response are judged to be highly improbable and are excluded from the considerations that govern policy choices. Within the range of reasonably probable behavior, however, and to the extent to which our policy is sensitive to variations in motivation, it is important not to tie policy exclusively to hypotheses that may be disproved. For instance, we may be right to count on missile bases in Italy, but we should attempt to develop a policy on missile bases that will still be good if Italy lets us down. This is even more true in the case of a hostile state like the Soviet Union that might take advantage of a mistake on our part to injure us severely. We should neither leave ourselves too open to a hostile move by the Soviet Union nor exclude the possibility of a mutually desirable accommodation. Nor should we exclude the possibility of exploiting some unexpected Soviet weaknesses. We must remember that our assessment of Soviet motivation may be wrong, and that for any number of reasons the Soviet Union may change its objectives.

6

ESPIONAGE

AND THE KOREAN WAR

General MacArthur has asserted that intelligence received from espion-
age sources precipitated the entry of the Chinese Communists into the
Korean war. The general has charged that two Communist spies—
Burgess and MacLean—informed the Communists that the United
States would not extend the hostilities to Manchuria.

Thus assured of a "privileged sanctuary" the Chinese could enter the
Korean war with little risk. Under other circumstances, General
MacArthur charged, the Chinese Communists would not have dared to
run the risk of American retaliation. Coming from a less responsible or
less respected source than General MacArthur, the charge that espionage
was the major factor in the Chinese intervention in the Korean war
would be dismissed by most specialists in international politics. Major
nations rarely take major decisions on such a basis. They cannot know
whether the information is correct or whether the decision will be
changed.

The Communists had been led to believe that the United States would
not defend Korea. Many feel that this belief precipitated the original

North Korean attack. If that was an important precipitating factor in the North Korean decision to attack, the Communists should have learned that the United States might change its mind and fight once war starts.

Major states usually run great risks only when they have important strategic objectives. The hydroelectric installations on the Yalu River constituted one highly important strategic objective. Keeping anti-Communist forces away from the Manchurian border was another vital strategic objective for the Chinese Communists. These strategic objectives seem reason enough for Chinese intervention.

However, when a man as brilliant as General MacArthur makes a claim that espionage was the prime factor in Chinese intervention, the charge must be given a degree of serious consideration. Moreover, there can be little doubt that Burgess and MacLean were acting as spies and passing along whatever intelligence they could get. This gives some plausibility to the charge.

There are a number of difficulties in investigating this kind of charge. First, one does not know for sure what information Burgess and MacLean got hold of. Nor does one know how quickly information was passed along to the Chinese Communists.

Red intelligence has not always been the world's most efficient organization. In July 1945 Red intelligence sent an urgent message to the Canadian spy ring to discover the name of the American occupation commander in Germany. If Red intelligence had taken the trouble to get an American newspaper, it would have discovered that General Eisenhower was the retiring American occupation commander and that General McNarny was his successor. The information was public; a phone call to the American forces in Germany or even to the local Red forces in Germany would have uncovered this information. If Red intelligence occasionally is this inefficient, who knows what happened to the information passed along by Burgess and MacLean, or when the information got to the Chinese Communists, if ever?

Nevertheless, Red intelligence is often effective. So possibly some pertinent information got to China. Therefore, the only way to put the charge into perspective is to discover what information may have been available. Even then, it must be pointed out, we do not know how the Chinese evaluated the information or how it influenced their decisions.

The first critical information which might have led to either Chinese or Russian intervention became available shortly before September 15, 1950. On that date the Joint Chiefs cabled to General MacArthur [paraphrased]:

(d) General MacArthur should undertake no ground operations north of the thirty-eighth parallel in event of occupation of North Korea by Soviet or Chinese Communist forces. In this event, air and naval operations north of the parallel should not be discontinued; and

(e) In the event of employment of major Chinese Communist units south of the thirty-eighth parallel, the United States would (1) not permit itself to become engaged in a general war with Communist China; (2) authorize General MacArthur to continue military action as long as it offered a reasonable chance of successful resistance.

Had this information got to the Communists, they would have had reason to believe that they could have prevented American ground movement beyond the Thirty-Eighth Parallel simply by moving Communist troops in. In other words, no ground warfare would have been involved and air and naval warfare would have been confined to Korea.

Moreover, the Communists were apparently being told, if they had this information, that the United States did not think it could offer effective military resistance if the Communists wanted to extend the war south of the Thirty-Eighth Parallel. Thus, the Communists would run practically no risk by intervening.

Did the Communists get this information? In all likelihood the British were informed of the American decision. If they were informed, MacLean and Burgess (or, more likely, Kim Philby, as we now know) were probably in a position to pass it along. But possibly the information did not get passed along to the Communist powers or perhaps the Soviet Union did not forward the information to China.

Or possibly the Communists did not want to take the chance that the United States would change its mind again. In any case, the Chinese did not openly intervene while such intervention was still virtually riskless.

Shortly thereafter General MacArthur asked for permission from the Joint Chiefs to cross the Thirty-Eighth Parallel. Permission was granted on September 29, the same day a resolution to the same effect was submitted to the United Nations.

On October 3 the substance of an interview between Indian Ambassador Panikkar and Chinese Premier Chou En-lai was revealed. Premier

Chou informed Panikkar that China would intervene in the Korean war if American forces crossed the Thirty-Eighth Parallel but not if South Korean forces crossed the parallel. Evidently Chou did not know that American intervention north of the parallel could be halted by a token Chinese occupation. In any event, the Chinese did not occupy North Korea openly.

At this time, there was no reason to consider any action against China. Bombing Manchuria would have constituted aggressive action against a peaceful power. There were no Chinese planes in Korea to be pursued across the Korean border. Therefore, the one Chinese decision that espionage might have accounted for—namely, open occupation of North Korea—did not take place.

However, on October 8, one or two days after American forces crossed the Thirty-Eighth Parallel, American intelligence reported the presence of some Chinese forces. It seems likely, then, that a secret build-up had been taking place. If the Chinese had proceeded on the basis of espionage information, the build-up would have been publicly announced to forestall American crossing of the Parallel (unless the Chinese wanted a direct confrontation with the United States—a scarcely plausible hypothesis). Instead, it was secret and should have portended to American authorities Chinese intervention in the Korean war.

American intelligence agencies were apparently also operating at somewhat less than full efficiency. Events later in November proved that the Chinese build-up was much larger than the United States had been given any reason to believe.

In the meantime, American planes strafed a military airfield in Siberia and American forces raced toward the Manchurian border.

On the first of November, enemy jet aircraft were encountered for the first time. Evidently these aircraft were Chinese, although this was not yet certain. Thus the first act which might have led to an American decision to engage in "hot pursuit" took place.

On November 5, General MacArthur announced publicly that "elements of alien Communist forces" had moved into Korea from across the Yalu River. On November 14 these Chinese forces were seriously underestimated at 60,000 to 70,000 men.

On November 5, the day the Chinese intervention was announced by General MacArthur, he called it a "grave matter". The next day General

MacArthur called Chinese intervention to the attention of the United Nations. General MacArthur informed Washington that his forces were handicapped by an inability to pursue Chinese planes across the border. He asked permission to engage in "hot pursuit" but not to bomb across the Manchurain border.[1]

By November 13 President Truman, the Joint Chiefs of Staff, and Secretary of State Acheson had approved "hot pursuit". On that day six allied nations were informed: "We are not asking the concurrence of [your] government because we believe the highly limited application of hot pursuit doctrine in this situation would turn upon military necessity and elementary principles of self-defense, but we think it important that the government be notified of the problem." The message said in addition that "hot pursuit" would not provoke the Chinese but would serve as a "warning". A warning of what? That the United States would bomb Chinese Manchurian bases if the Chinese intervened? The Joint Chiefs had already authorized the bombing of the bridges across the Yalu River. What other reprisals could the United States consider? A naval blockade, perhaps, or even the use of atomic weapons but China could not be sure.

By this time the Chinese build-up was virtually completed. In the meantime, the consulted allied governments protested. These protests were called to the attention of the United States on November 23 and on November 24. The authorization to engage in "hot pursuit" was then revoked.

Why was the authorization revoked? Because of allied protests? Or because the Chinese build-up was now so great that "hot pursuit" would no longer serve as a warning? The chances are that the answer to this question will never be known. It is unlikely that those who made the decision can in retrospect select out the precise factors that led to the decision.

The exact date of the revocation is not known. However, November 24 was the earliest possible date. Assume November 24 was the date. The Chinese attacked on November 25, one day later. Even upon this assumption, there was not time for information concerning the revoca-

---

[1]See testimony of General Collins, Chief of Staff, United States Army, *Military Situation in the Far East*, p. 1260. Hearings before the Committee on Armed Forces and the Committee on Foreign Relations, United States Senate, United States, Government Printing Office 1951.

tion to reach China, let alone for the information to trigger the military decision to attack. The decision to attack must have been made considerably earlier. The build-up had taken several months. It would have taken several days at least to reverse the decision to attack.

Even if Burgess and MacLean or, more likely, Kim Philby got the information the day the decision was made, how could they code it and get it to Communist sources in one day? What courier could have got the information to Red intelligence the same day? Then how would the information have been got to China, evaluated, and turned into a battle-field decision? Even a week would not have provided time enough for all this.[2]

General MacArthur at the time stated flatly that the Chinese attack had been planned in advance. "It now appears to have been the enemy's intent, in breaking off contact with our forces two weeks ago, to secure the time necessary surreptitiously to build up for a later surprise assault upon our lines in overwhelming force. . . . This plan has been disrupted by our own offensive action, which forced upon the enemy a premature engagement." According to General MacArthur, the Chinese attack had been planned during the time when the United States still intended to engage in "hot pursuit". Therefore, whatever led to the decision, the information that the United States would not engage in "hot pursuit" could hardly have been one of the factors.

It had been claimed that the Chinese would not have dared to attack had not they known their "privileged sanctuary in Manchuria" was safe. They did not know the sanctuary was safe when they attacked. But it is doubtful that any information about "hot pursuit" would have influenced their decision to attack. General Hoyt Vandenberg, Chief of Staff of the Air Force testified: "Hot pursuit in my opinion would have been of morale value to our Air Force . . . but would not have been decisive in my opinion".[3] General Vandenberg did not believe that bombing the Yalu power dams would have been of much help either. Russia, he felt, would keep China supplied with war material.

The inability of the air force to halt Chinese supply operations in Korea indicates that bombing Manchurian bases might have helped the

[2]Some place the origin of the Chinese counter-offensive on November 26 rather than November 25. But, even if this date were chosen, November 26 in Korea— because of the international date line—would be November 25 in the United States.

[3]*Far East Hearings*, p. 1388.

American efforts, but that it would not have been decisive. Nor would such bombing have appreciably dampened the flow of material to the Chinese forces. Actually, neither the Americans nor the Chinese thought that Chinese forces were particularly vulnerable or that the Chinese attack was a desperate measure. A strong China would not have been deterred by the threat of air reprisals against Manchuria. And China did seem strong in relation to available American forces. Both Chinese and Americans evaluated highly Chinese prospects for victory in Korea.

The Chinese armies split the American armies and nearly drove them off the peninsula. As late as January 12, General MacArthur thought that American forces would have to evacuate Korea and fight a long-distance war. The Joint Chiefs of Staff concurred in this pessimistic belief.

Nor would the bombing of Manchuria have been without its costs. As General Wedemeyer pointed out there was a "gentlemen's agreement" whereby the Chinese did not bomb American bases in Japan as long as Chinese bases in Manchuria were not bombed. Who would have lost more if that agreement had been broken?

General Vandenberg testified that full-scale bombing of China would have used all the resources of the American Air Force. The Air Force, he said, was operating on a "shoe string" basis. If all its planes were used in China, there would have been no protection for American vital interests elsewhere on the globe. Russia would have had a free hand in Europe.

We may never know how much espionage information China got from Burgess and MacLean (or from Philby)—or how China evaluated that information. But it seems scarcely plausible that this information led to the Chinese decision to attack. The information that the United States would not engage in "hot pursuit"—if it came at all—came too late to influence that decision. Moreover, in this period, General MacArthur had not yet asked for permission to bomb Chinese bases in Manchuria.

7

THE

INTERNATIONAL ARENA

AS A SOURCE OF

DYSFUNCTIONAL TENSION

Tension is not of itself an evil. Indeed, certain levels of tension are necessary if either life or social processes are to occur. Therefore, tensions may be either functional or dysfunctional. Dysfunctional tensions produce an inaccurate orientation to reality, impede or prevent the attainment of desired goals, or permit their realization at an unnecessarily high cost. Dysfunctional tension is, in general, undesirable, although it may at times be an appropriate instrument of policy. It should not be assumed that international tension is a cause of war, at least in a simple or direct fashion. Dysfunctional international tension is, however, usually productive of undesired consequences.

Of course, the extent and kind of dysfunctional tension which develops depends partly upon the specific social structures of the individual actors within the international arena, i.e., the nation states.[1] However, it is necessary to restrict our attention to one special phase of the problem, namely, the dysfunctional tension that the social structure of the international arena tends to produce.[2]

An interesting feature of the international arena is that it is a social structure containing a very small number of actors and is not subsumed in a larger social system that includes the members of the international arena directly. This fact has serious consequences for the action which occurs within the system. The statistical averaging-out which forms the basis of actuarial systems cannot be a feature of the play of the game in this system. The importance to the system of some individual members or actors looms so large that individual changes in membership or relative power may alter both the form of the social system and the play of the game in a decisive and radical fashion. For confirmation of this point, one has only to consider the consequences of the change in the international situation from the nineteenth century to the interwar period, or to the present essentially bipolar structure. Again, one may consider the shift from the wartime dictatorship of the "Big Three" to a situation in which smaller powers can upset the policy calculations of the major powers. In addition, a player's gambit may change the rules of the game, and, if a contestant loses, he may not be able to reenter the game by acquiring a new set of chips. The stakes are very high in such a game and, therefore, the cathectic significance of action increases and dysfunctional "swings" of behavior are facilitated. This situation is exacerbated if the important actors are oriented to fundamentally different types of goals.

Since the number of actors is small, behavior in the international arena tends to be non-repeatable. In some aspects of the domestic economy, one anonymous actor leaves the market and another enters it, but the same game continues. The international game produces much greater novelty. Korea and Indo-China are different gambits. Their origins, importances, and characteristics differ. Should an agreement be reached with regard to Korea, a new act of aggression would be essentially different from the first act. Knowledge that the aggression would

---

[1]Nation states do not exhaust the membership, but we cannot examine the matter further in this article.

[2]The inference that a different form of international social structure would be less productive of dysfunctional tension is a possible rather than necessary conclusion.

be opposed introduces a different calculus. The non-repeatability of precisely commensurable situations in the game entails an indetermined-ness or ambiguity for which the human agents of the actors have a limited tolerance. The lack of clear-cut and ready-made solutions imposes a strain toward such solutions. And frequently they are of the fish-or-cut-bait variety and therefore more definite than the circumstances warrant. The agents, in the effort to give structure to the situations confronting them, tend to reduce the alternatives available to them. Various amend-ments to foreign aid bills passed by the United States Congress fall within this category.

Behavior, then, is relatively non-repeatable and the actors are more highly particularized than are actors within the domestic arena. How-ever, the behavior pattern of the actors changes within limits. Consider, for instance, the change of Great Britain's behavior after the shift from Chamberlain to Churchill. On the other hand, contrast the continuity of foreign policy from Conservative to Labor to Conservative govern-ment in Great Britain. It is no good to construct a typology as the sales-man may construct a typology of customers, for here it is a specific actor whose behavior is important and the specific determinants of that behavior are not going to be evened-out by the law of averages.[3] This frustrates the abstract generalizing tendency of the human mind and introduces an uncertainty which can paralyze action in indecisiveness or release tension by abrupt and inappropriate action.

The inability to abstract produces an overreaction in the direction of abstraction and the literature relating to the international arena is there-fore singularly poor in descriptive power. "Nationalism" explains the behavior of modern states. States are "aggressive" or "peace-loving", "imperialistic" or "conservative", "aggression unpunished will raise its ugly head again". Literally, the variety of decisive experiences and their very failure to reduce themselves to a typology are responsible for the overly abstract nature of descriptive generalizations, which, in their turn, reflect a dysfunctional and inaccurate orientation to reality. Like-wise, historians tend to fit the policies of states into a rigid framework and to introduce an artificial consistency into them. An artificial ration-ality is also introduced into these policies. One cannot fail to be struck by the fact that international decisions seem to be made first and the

[3]For this to follow, we require only the additional assumptions that the actors are structured complexly and that their four-dimensional environments are variegated.

reasons found later. But this, strictly speaking, is not a function of the international social structure except to the extent that the irrationality is induced by the inability of the agents to orient themselves accurately because of the small number situation or some other element of the social structure.

The small number situation is also partly responsible for the failure of expectations to be fulfilled. To an extent, this is a corollary of our previous conclusions, i.e., the changing character of the game, the non-repeatability of the items in the game, and the highly individualistic characteristics of the actors. On the other hand, one element responsible for reliability of action is an expectation by the actors that *this* is what "ought" to be done. As Wolfgang Kohler says, when something happens often enough, it acquires a "rightness". People become used to it and it is accepted as given. Yet the relative variety of decisive international experiences precludes, or at least makes more difficult, the development of a standardized system of expectations. In addition to external factors, therefore, there is also a problem of motivation, which, while related to or even the result of these external factors, nevertheless becomes a separate and distinct source of dysfunctional tension. One actor cannot depend upon the action of other actors. Such a situation can be expected to facilitate paranoid interpretations of reality and pathological behavior, although the degree to which this would be true would depend upon the thresholds of individual agents for such behavior and the extent to which the state's social structure stabilizes their response patterns.

The failure, so to speak, of a "collective" superego to develop can be traced partly to other elements in the international social structure. The mediation of selected agents of actors, i.e., of diplomatic agents, between the actors means that for the mass of individuals, who in their social relations constitute the state actor, the play of the international game lacks reality, although certain consequences of the game—for instance, war—have immediate consequences of a heroic order. Thus commitments entered into in the playing of the game acquire an alien cast and diminish in binding quality, viz., public and Congressional reaction to our Yalta commitments.

The indirect nature of the consequences of the playing of the international game is also at issue. The game, after all, is not played with either recognizable or uniform counters and the chain between action and consequence may be both attenuated and confused by the multiple nature of the action pattern. In the first place, the game is not played with monetary coins of given weight and composition. The medium of exchange is power, which is relative rather than absolute, which is instrumental rather than thinglike, and which is composed of incommensurables like guns, standards of living, morals and morale, etc., these items being related in a highly complex and, as yet, at least partly unresolved fashion. Since the means, or the medium of exchange, is not necessarily the end—the means is power relative to others; the end is power to live in a certain fashion—the means-end problems become quite acute and the game itself acquires a non-zero-sum character. In other words, the supply of goods is not a constant; one state's gain is not necessarily another state's loss. In fact, all may gain or all may lose in the playing of the game.

In addition, the effects of policy are remote. What are the effects of President Eisenhower's address upon the European policy of the Soviet Union? The chain of consequences is neither unilinear nor direct. While the means-end problem confuses the goal of action, the indirection of effect confuses the penalties and rewards of actions. These conditions minimize the development of superego rules of behavior regulating action in the international arena, or at least the absorption by agents of international problems within a system of normative rules according to conscious or unconscious analogy. At a non-psychological level, they tend to reduce restraints upon the agents by making it difficult to fix responsibility for consequences upon them. The indeterminacy effect in the international arena reinforces this, i.e., the tendency of expectations underlying policy to produce certain of the effects predicted for them. When an attempt is made to fix responsibility—as with our China policy —the net result may be a refusal of agents to make any decisions, since the "ability" to fix responsibility varies directly with the difficulty of fixing responsibility.

Another factor contributing to unreliability in the international arena is the degree to which action in the arena is instrumental. That is, the other actors are evaluated according to the ability of the actor to use them for his ends, regardless of whether this also facilitates the attainment of ends which they value highly. While this state of affairs is not a necessary one, the reasons for its existence are quite strong. Among them are the smallness of the number of actors involved in the play of the arena, the variability of the situations confronting the actors, and the difficulties of predicting the behavior of actors. In addition, the mediation of the relationships among the actors permits the internal structure of the actors to develop along different lines, and to be oriented to ends which are different—perhaps fundamentally different. These effects may be modified somewhat by the growth of supranational organizations which acquire the status of actors with respect to certain areas or types of actions.

These remarks do not exhaust the list of factors leading to dysfunctional tension within the international arena, even if attention be restricted to those factors produced by the specifically international features of the social system. Should their existence be deemed important, however—even when stated at this high level of generality—it may prove desirable to orient policy, at least in part, to take them into account, for it is quite conceivable that certain actions, by increasing the dysfunctional orientation of other actors, may produce undesired reactions. It is not possible to think of therapeutic policies in the same sense in which the social worker may consider them and we cannot dwell on either the gross or subtle differences in the problem, but the conception may be worth not overlooking.

PART IV

On Values

This section includes the two appendices from *System and Process* that deal with the mechanisms of regulation and the realm of values, the chapter from *System and Process* on the national interest, an article on utilitarianism and its addendum published later, and a revision of one of the "nightmares" from *The Year 2000* (Macmillan, 1967) by Herman Kahn and Anthony J. Wiener. I wrote the original draft of the "nightmare" and it then underwent a number of revisions both by myself and by Kahn and Wiener. In the form in which it appears here, I am ready to accept responsibility for the text but not credit for each item of the whole. There is no reason to draft it entirely afresh as it raises the important issues in the form in which I desire to raise them.

The nightmare represents an attempt to show how society can drift into a dehumanized situation imperceptibly by decomposed, or incremental, decisions, even when each specific decision may be beneficial on balance. It also attempts to raise ethical questions not merely about manufactured biological beings or transformed men but also about machines that have some of the important systems characteristics of humans. It might be morally wrong to mistreat such machines and it might also turn out to be dangerous. If the machines differ from humans in some important respects, they might also turn out to be dangerous regardless of how we treat them. I do not doubt that these concepts may seem fantastic to some; although it will likely be generations before such machines are created, it is perhaps not too early to begin to think about them.

The article on utilitarianism makes three basic points. There are some kinds of social relations for which utilitarian calculations are dysfunctional. There are some kinds of social circumstances in which even altruistic calculations will do harm to the community unless at least an abstract quasi-Kantian moral rule is adopted. Although my calculation is not formally complete, it is demonstrable that some acts that do no measurable harm to society in the single case—and that have some good side effects—do harm if performed by large numbers of people. If the individual calculates that his performance of the act will not encourage other people to perform it, then the social effects of widespread performance should not deter him. Yet large numbers of people might make this very same calculation. There are numerous such possible acts, including, among others, using excess water for a good purpose in a large city during a drought, or driving someone somewhere in one's automobile and thereby contributing to air pollution. The case is possibly even stronger if we remove the restriction to altruistic acts that most act utilitarians make, although if there were universal altruism this might generate even more conflict than does selfishness. Finally, the point is made that even if these undesirable consequences did not follow, the consequences for the human psyche would be dysfunctional.

In the selection on mechanisms of regulation, the examples used are always examples of actors within systems. The term "system" in this usage refers to the internal systems of the actors, that is, to subsystems of the more inclusive system.

8

THE MECHANISMS OF

REGULATION

Such things as learning and repression are generally treated as psychological mechanisms. If, however, the specific action content is removed and they are treated in terms of the routing of information within the system, the various psychological mechanisms are isomorphic with mechanisms manifested in the behavior of social organizations.

At this stage of the discussion, a general account of regulation is required. Regulation is the process which maintains a system. However, given rules of behavior are imbedded in the system's structure and change as the system adapts its structure to circumstances. These laws of change which specify the form of adaptation are the system transformation rules.

Without structure of some sort needs could not be satisfied, nor could they even exist. However, part of the structure is an adaptation—whether functional or not—to present circumstances and may be viewed as less "basic" for some purposes. Within the structure there is a hierarchy of instrumentality. This hierarchy determines which elements of the system's structure and goal orientation must be adapted to changed circumstances or changed information. For instance, with respect to the human organism, various inhibitions which are built into the super-ego permit the individual to adjust to a particular society. However, in a different society these restraints may prove to be unnecessary and uneconomical.

If a being from another planet had visited Great Britain during World War Two, he would have discovered many restrictions on the movement of labor. Had he looked no farther, he would have assumed that freedom of labor was not valued in the British system. However, had he examined how the British system operated earlier and had he heard speeches by leaders of both parties stating war aims, and so forth, he might have concluded that these restrictions were temporary and that they would be removed if the war came to a successful conclusion.

One of the regulatory tasks of the British system was to fight the war in such a way that earlier essential rules of the system could be restored if the war terminated successfully. The task of regulation is to satisfy the needs of the system both with respect to immediate instrumental priority and also with respect to long-range needs.

The needs of a social system are in part a function of the needs of its subsystems, including both social subsystems and personality and biological systems. The needs of the system are in part a function of subsidiary needs which are derived from the integrative functions of the social system. An integrated system cannot provide for the needs of the subsystems unless there are agencies that act for the system. These agencies have housekeeping or instrumental needs. They generate values which serve to maintain these instrumental functions.

These housekeeping functions, although originally instrumental, generate autonomous structures and autonomous need subsystems. By increasing specialization and by making metatask regulation possible, these functions permit more efficient satisfaction of needs, although transforming many of the needs in the process. If the system is a well integrated system, the needs of all system levels can be satisfied simultaneously. However, there may be parameter values for which this is not the case even if a system is normally well integrated.

Moreover, if the larger system becomes dominant over its subsystems —and this is the case in most hierarchical systems—its needs will be satisfied independently of the needs of the subsystems. In this situation, dysfunctional and disintegrative processes may take place in the subsystems. If, on the other hand, the needs of the system can be satisfied only within a wider or a more highly organized framework, integrative processes may be operative.

Needs provide motivation. A social system is motivated as truly as an individual human being. Social needs will be acted upon if the system is so structured that the need of the social system establishes a need for some individual(s) to act in conformity with the need, just as human bodily needs are satisfied only when the system operates upon its parts in such a way that they act in conformity with the needs of the body.

On occasion the body malfunctions and improper signals are sent. Drunken behavior is an illustration of this. Cancer is another illustration. Treason and profit making at the expense of production during war represent analogous cases in the social system.

If a goal, as defined by the needs of the system, cannot be obtained, the system has a number of ways of resolving the problem. It may seek some similar goal or objective. It may attempt to eliminate the need. It may attempt to compensate for the need by some sort of substitute activity.

The choice the system makes determines the way in which information will be received, processed, and used. In every instance, the environment will be redefined in terms which permit the system to scan for the information it perceives to be relevant to the choices it has made. In turn, this will require the creation of institutional pathways appropriate for receiving and transmitting this information.

For instance, if a decision is made to prevent fluctuations in prices, it becomes necessary to establish bureaus which study these fluctuations and which attempt to locate the factors responsible for them. The objectives determine to some extent the kind of information the system will seek. The set of objectives will determine the ways in which the information is routed through the structure of the system.

If, for instance, another bureau exists to satisfy an objective of increasing production regardless of price structure, it will look for information consonant with its objective. Moreover, it will define the importance of information in terms of its objective. If the price control bureau must pass its information through the production control bureau, there may be occasions on which the information will fail to be transmitted further either because it is not regarded as important or because it is even regarded as dangerous.

In this case, conflict will take place between the bureaus. The price control bureau will attempt to find ways to by-pass the production control bureau. If the bureaus are coordinate, the larger system may manifest erratic behavior as, first, one set of information is passed along and operated upon and, later, a second and conflicting set of information is transmitted and utilized.

A system can act to satisfy needs only by employing a mechanism which scans for, transmits, and utilizes information. Every mechanism has the function of satisfying system needs. Mechanisms become pathological only when they produce structural changes in the system which later filter out needed information and thereby prevent successful adaptation by the system to its environment. Mechanisms are not in themselves pathological. Pathologies occur only when the mechanisms inhibit adaptation. To study this, consideration of specific mechanisms will be useful.

SPECIFIC REGULATORY MECHANISMS

Catharsis

Catharsis occurs when a need is satisfied. The information element is very important here. Psychological investigation has revealed cases in which the release of energy generates positive feedback. Some neurotics are aggressive because of a desire to destroy an ambivalent object. This need becomes stronger the more feelings of guilt are built up, but aggression increases the feeling of guilt. Thus, rather than reducing the need for aggression, the expression of aggression increases it.

There is a social analog to this process. Suppose, for instance, that external territory is acquired by force in order to meet economic needs. If the needs actually are satisfied, the action may be cathartic. If, however, new subsidiary needs are engendered, a positive feedback cycle may originate. For example, attempts to compensate for inflationary high prices by printing money produce positive feedback. Such action is not cathartic even though it is in response to a need.

Cathexis and Anti-Cathexis

Cathexis represents the direction of regulatory capacity toward the satisfaction of a basic need of a system, that is, of a need which, if not satisfied, will produce internal system disturbances. Anti-cathexis, that is, anti-cathectic activity, is the direction of regulatory capacity toward the inhibition of activity which is dangerous in a particular environment.

Infants have no knowledge of danger. Therefore, there may be an initial period in the life development of humans when they have feelings of omnipotence. National actor systems, on the other hand, are unlikely to manifest an initial belief in omnipotence. If they should manifest such a belief at all, it would be more akin to pathological megalomania.

Organized political forms are represented by adults—in particular, by adults who are highly manipulative in character and who have a firm sense of the objective limits of the social and physical world. Adults have already learned that the world is a place in which not all objectives can be satisfied.

Just as men must adjust to the demands of their neighbors, so must political systems adjust to the demands of their neighbors. An infant may rely upon the concern of its parents to protect it from the consequences of its own excessive demands. A political system will be destroyed by its neighbors if it makes excessive demands it is not strong enough to enforce.

Therefore, if a political system has leaders with delusions of omnipotence, this is likely to represent a breakdown of the reality function rather than an aboriginal stage in development. This breakdown is most likely to occur in the subsystem dominant, directive type of system, that is, in the system which has greatest control over internal factors. When subject to great stress, it represses in a manner which focuses attention on ends rather than upon means. Therefore, it may pursue these ends almost regardless of reality considerations.

There is no guarantee that such a system will not succeed simply because it is pathological or aberrant. A madman may shoot and kill a stranger on the street. The most flexible systems may be quite unprepared for this kind of disturbance. Indeed, were they prepared for this sort of unexpected occurrence, they would hardly be flexible in expected and important areas of control or regulation.

Although the madman may shoot down a sane man, he is hardly likely to destroy a sane society. Before his activity can continue, agencies of social regulation will bring him under control. However, the international system is a system in which only small numbers of actors participate. Whereas the actors in this system are more likely to prepare

for aberrant behavior and to be able to discover it since military prepara-
tions take time and are hard to hide entirely, it is possible that pathological behavior in this area may either succeed in its objective of control
or destroy the international system itself.

When anti-cathectic activity becomes pathological in the form of
things like continued repression, aberrant activity begins. Maintenance
of a proper ratio between cathectic and anti-cathectic activity is the
proper objective of metatask regulation.

Learning

Learning occurs whenever a system modifies its characteristic response
to a stimulus. Since no external change occurs, learning must involve an
internal modification of the system. This change includes a change in
the information state of the system. Information concerning the stimulus
places the stimulus in a new or different relationship to the other
information of the system.

What is learned may not be true objectively. Learning involves only
change in meaning or significance. Consider the case of a society where
leaders pray for rain whenever there is a drought. Suppose that they
cease to pray in the event of drought. The system's behavior has then
been modified and its information placed in a new context. The society
may have learned that no relationship between prayer and meteoro-
logical conditions exists. Or it may have learned more generally that
propitiatory religious practices do not work—or even more generally
that religion is untrue. Or it may even have learned that prayers will be
acted upon by malevolent demons who will put a spell on the crops. In
the last case prayer may be regarded as positively dangerous.

Learning always involves a change in meaning, or at least an addition
to meaning. Even learning the names of cities involves behavior that
associates the name of a city with "city". If a child learns the names of
cities, the name of each particular city he learns acquires new meaning
for him. Previously, if the stimulus "Detroit" occurred, his behavior
may have been random or incorrect. Later, after learning, the child gives
the response appropriate for the name of a city.

Changes in information involve changes in relationships between
items of information. These changes—even when social learning is

involved—may occur simply as the result of alteration in the psychological state of human individuals. They may have no further structural consequences. Or changes in information may require changes in the ways in which information is stored in such places as libraries and files. Or they may involve changes in the circuits of computing machines.

Changed information may also have as a consequence changes in the structures of the political bureaucracy. The priest may be assigned to new duties and a meteorologist hired to predict the weather. A new bureau which scans for particular kinds of information in a new manner may come into being. The information for which it looks will be different from that desired by the priest. Weather planes may be sent over the ocean to chart wind currents, for example. Thus a whole train of associated consequences may be set off.

One change in information state may set off many others, some of which meet resistance. The introduction of modern medical practice is often resisted by priests and witch doctors in savage tribes, for instance. Assimilation by society of all the associated consequences of change may be a long and difficult process. If it is too difficult, learned information may be lost or destroyed.

Displacement

Displacement occurs whenever an activity is blocked and the regulatory capacity previously assigned to it is diverted to some other activity. The system in which displacement occurs, however, remains ready to pursue the previous activity whenever circumstances are favorable. For instance, during war economic activity may be displaced from consumers' goods production to capital and military goods production. As long as the information states of the system maintain the appropriate ordering of parameter value and economic activity, the displacement will tend to give way to the old state of affairs when peace returns.

Because, however, such a change-over in activity only rarely can be made without special administrative or bureaucratic modifications, displacement will involve some inertia or some difficulty in returning to the previous activity whenever the specific factor which produced the change ceases to be operative.

Repression

Repression occurs whenever an activity is viewed as dangerous to the system *and* when activity is displaced from that activity *and* when future information concerning the possible desirability of that activity is not transmitted to the centers of regulatory control of the system.

Repression, unlike displacement, involves the active suppression of information because of its danger. This may occur whenever one national actor is dependent upon the good will of another and its leaders scan out information which does not indicate satisfaction of this need. When repression occurs, systems deny the relevance or even the existence of information disproving the assumptions upon which policy is based.

If repression involves the denial of an important need of a system, the need will remain active, and internal conflict or disturbance will become manifest. If, for instance, in a social system sexually oriented social activities are repressed because of a puritan ethic, the repressed needs may find substitute expression in religious ceremonies. If the system represses consumers' goods production because of external danger, sickness and low individual production may occur.

If there is a continuing systemic need for certain things, repression will give rise to derivatives or distortions of these needs. These derivatives may be similar to the need or quite different depending upon the strength of the need which is repressed and the strength of the repression.

Repression is not necessarily dysfunctional. The system may need to engage in full-scale production of war materials for purposes of defense. If the emergency is sufficiently acute, scanning for information to see whether the emergency has passed may itself become a secondary source of danger to the system. In a social system at war, the system may have to remain deaf to contentions that the emergency is not acute and that more can be spared for civilian consumption.

During the emergency this blockage of information is quite functional. However, if information itself becomes so dangerous that it is ignored and transmitters of it punished, the system loses in long-term adaptability. It is no longer able to acquire information which places its decisions in proper context. If the blockage of information is reinforced by denial of the need—so that the temporary is stated as permanent or the conditional as absolute—adaptability is further decreased.

The mechanism of repression is perhaps the most fundamental in all social and psychological activity. All systems tend to cut off information about needs which are irrelevant or dangerous. So long as their environments do not undergo fundamental alteration, this is quite functional.

However necessary the slaughter of children may be in societies living on the verge of starvation, the practice could hardly be continued if it were advocated in purely utilitarian terms. In fact, just that kind of sanction would probably be sufficient to produce deviance and instability in the society. Either the society will fail or it will reify its conditional practice.

Repression is dysfunctional only if the environment changes or if the environment has been misinterpreted. In these cases, the investment in the repression is so great in terms of institutional practices and structures that the system does not adapt. The information necessary to adaptation is not transmitted.

Even where repression is functional, pathological symptoms will appear if an important system need is repressed. Only when the environment is so favorable that no important system need is repressed, will pathological symptoms be entirely absent.

Frustration

Frustration occurs when a system is blocked in its efforts to obtain important objectives and to satisfy important needs. Frustration therefore is a state in which activity is held back by various kinds of blockages.

How a system responds to frustration depends upon how its leaders interpret information. If the system cuts off information concerning the means of action and focuses only upon the goal of action, it will make stronger and stronger efforts to obtain the contraindicated objects. If it focuses upon the means and excludes information concerning the goal, it will divert or displace activity. Its actions may then appear irrelevant to an external observer.

If it interprets all action as dangerous, a system will become passive. The major share of its activity will be expended upon inhibitory processes. Controls will be erected against activity. If this mechanism is adopted, people will seem to lack energy. They will lack strong ideals and will dissociate their actions and the affective "emotions" which ordinarily invest important goal-directed activity. Means will be important, but they will be emptied of content. Avoidance of conflict will be the major goal of the system.

If the mechanism employed focuses attention on means in general, that is, on means which reconcile conflicting interests, the system will be vaguely optimistic and will ignore system needs. It will focus attention on actions or policies which "work" regardless of whether "workability" has any function in terms of system needs. Such systems, if social systems, will be "liberal" and humanitarian without conviction.

In areas where activity is regarded as dangerous, the cultural values which correlate with focusing upon means alone are cynicism, worldliness, and indifference or contempt for pleasure or gratification. Particular forms are more important than substance. Efforts are devoted to the support of restrictive forms which prevent action, particularly changeful action. This is a conservative mechanism.

If the mechanism is one which focuses attention exclusively on ends, radical behavior will be the likely product. Ends will be invested with tremendous affect, and they will be pursued regardless of consequences or external conditions.

Although this type of generalization is extremely hazardous and should be made only with grave reservations, system dominant, directive systems tend to be conservative and cynical. Spain is an example. For some purposes the European monarchies of the nineteenth century also fall into this category.

Subsystem dominant, directive systems tend to be radical in manner and careless in their means. Soviet Russia and Nazi Germany are examples of this type. Such systems produce convulsions among their subsystems when doing this appears necessary to the pursuit of some important objective.

System dominant, non-directive systems focus attention on means. These systems are vaguely optimistic and rather insensitive to important system needs. The United States is a good example of this type. Great Britain is drifting in this direction. These systems focus attention on means in general rather than on a particular set of means. Subsystem dominant, non-directive systems, of which Great Britain used to be an example, tend to use displacement rather than repression and therefore tend to minimize frustration and its effects. They are more resistant to disturbances. But, if disturbances are sufficiently severe, they may use any of the mechanisms.

Sublimation

Sublimation occurs when a system need is satisfied by a means which conflicts with other system needs *and* a new means which does not conflict with other system needs is found to satisfy the need *and* the apparatus which satisfied the old means has its aim transformed. Why is not the old apparatus simply dismantled? The apparatus may be too specialized to fit in elsewhere, or it may resist and search for a new function. In either case, if some functional outlet is not provided, disturbance may result.

Children may sublimate their pre-genital sexual drives by means of artistic endeavor. This activity may later become an autonomous need of the personality system. Many social needs involve the transformation of efforts which were previously directed toward other ends. American consumption of luxuries is an example. These luxuries may constitute very real needs although they were not originally present in society.

Sublimation is usually functional. However, if society faces an emergency, the existence of such autonomous or sublimated needs may interfere with the pursuit of needs which are more important from the standpoint of survival.

Projection

Projection occurs when the system has information which leads it to believe that a lethal danger threatens it. The system then devotes its regulatory capacity and its attention to the area of danger. However, it scans for a limited class of information, namely, information concerning that danger or concerning possible aid.

Projection does not involve a simple outward projection of internal motivations. The system readies itself for an appropriate response to a significant disturbance. To prepare an appropriate response in the area of sensitivity is an important mode of regulation. If danger is expected, a hostile response is in readiness; if aid, a friendly response. The situation may even be tested by an initial signaling response of the appropriate kind which stops short of final action. This signaling response has the function of informing others that, if they take certain actions, a particular kind of response will be forthcoming.

There is still another element to projection. Since the system scans for the information which threatens it or which it needs, it tends to be inattentive to information which does not come within this category. Therefore its leaders tend to acquire a partial and misrepresentative picture of the external world. This is functional when the initial expectation was accurate but dysfunctional when it was false. Moreover, this selective scanning tends to inhibit the receipt of information that signals changes in the environment.

The preparatory responses may produce in the environment the very response which was anticipated. In the area of personal relations, it is a commonplace observation that some people create the very hostility they fear and that others arouse friendly responses where previously a friendly disposition may not have been present.

Projection may occur also when a system's leaders have hostile intentions against another actor in the environment. In this case, the leaders may anticipate the appropriate response from that actor. If this information concerning the response of alter signals danger, the system may repress either information concerning the response or information concerning its own intentions. In this latter case, sensitivity in the dangerous task area may still be so great that the system continues to scan for evidence of a hostile response. This latter case, therefore, also constitutes projection.

When the information of a system indicates the presence of potentially lethal environmental disturbances or great internal stress, projection may be anticipated. Leaders of systems using projection as a characteristic mechanism may display great flexibility in interpreting information in conformity with anticipations. They may construct vast delusional systems designed to explain items of behavior which do not readily fit into the anticipated pattern.

Since, however, virtually all the regulatory capacity of such systems is devoted to task regulation in response to the great strain and danger confronting these systems, there is little capacity to scan for information which would permit a rebuilding of their information states. In short, projection is a sign that—at least in the area where projection occurs—the metatask regulatory capacity of the system is minimal. These systems are always "shoring up the levee" one bag at a time. Their hypotheses concerning the world are "one-bag" *ad hoc* hypotheses which add additional postulates for each new item of information because these systems lack the metatask regulatory capacity to construct economical hypotheses.

Introjection

Introjection occurs when some goals or values of another system are adopted in order to ward off some threat to the first system. Introjection may in fact accomplish this purpose. But it is difficult to assimilate alien values and the institutions or social structures necessary to implement them.

Somewhere in the system strains will appear as a result of faulty assimilation. If information of these strains is repressed, only that information indicating satisfactory assimilation will be processed. When this is true, the new goals or structures will be highly and favorably cathected. However, the unfavorable information will tend to build up as the strains between the two sets of needs and institutions become more severe.

When the divergence becomes too great, the adopted goals will cease to be cathected, and the old values will be restored. However, if the need to continue in favor with the external system is still operative, this need will have to be repressed. Thus introjection involves ambivalence in attitude and "swings" in belief and behavior.

Japanese assimilation of American political institutions after the close of the war illustrates introjective behavior.

Identification

Identification involves introjection. The source of the introjected goals or institutions becomes itself an object of cathexis. Information concerning the disadvantages of cooperation is first repressed; later it breaks through and leads to discord. Should this situation become dangerous, the information is repressed again. Cyclic behavior is characteristic of identification, but the course of this behavior depends upon the strength of the various stimuli.

Western Germany has identified itself with the West, particularly with the United States. There is a genuine community of interests. However, this very community of interests has so far prevented the unification of Germany. The stresses arising from this situation also produce an underlying current of hostility, which, under some para-meter conditions, may replace the present solidarity and produce anti-Western activity in Germany.

Except for the fact that Western German political parties and indus-tries would lose heavily in the Communization of Germany, this under-lying hostility would have received even greater expression by this time. This possibility would be even greater were it not true that there remain some aspects of the German social and cultural pattern with which democracy remains congruent.

Apathy and Isolation

Social apathy and psychological isolation are isomorphic mechanisms. Isolation involves a dissociation of action and affect. When failure is expected, leaders of systems defend themselves against the consequence of failure by refusing to invest their efforts with affect. Attention is diverted from information demonstrating the importance of the need and the cost of failure.

In political systems in which stress is concentrated upon the individual citizen, he may become apathetic by dissociating his activities in the political system from his personal and social needs. The inter-connection is denied, and affect is focused purely on social relations. Such citizens are apathetic toward the political system. They have no affective involve-ment in its fate.

The political system may then have a need to attempt to inhibit close personal relations between citizens which might arise as a com-pensation for the affective barrenness of the life of the citizen. Mass participation in events serves this end primarily rather than the more obvious end of fortifying loyalty to the political system.

REGULATORY SYNDROMES

Syndromes, unlike mechanisms, refer to substantive patterns of action of systems although they also include the use of information routing mechanisms. The discussion of syndromes makes more use of analogs than of isomorphisms and thus must be regarded as rather speculative.

However, the discussion of syndromes, speculative though it may be, has heuristic importance. In the first place, many remarkable analogs to psychological behavior can be found. In the second place, there is a major difference between the ways in which the personality system and the political system use syndromes. The human individual usually remains within the confines of a single syndrome for most of his life because of the relationship between his behavior, childhood experiences, and possibilities of change within his physiological and psychological structures. As different subsystems of the international actor systems rise to predominance within the system—or sometimes even without a change in the dominant subsystem—the political system can swing from one syndrome to another. In particular, when external circumstances block successful use of one syndrome, it becomes possible to resort to the inverse syndrome.

Compulsive and Psychopathic Syndromes

The compulsive and psychopathic syndromes are inverse patterns. The compulsive pattern is characterized by the avoidance of dangerous internal problems. Attention or regulatory capacity is directed to external problems. Since the object of such regulation, however, is to avoid rather than to come to grips with internal problems, the action patterns are routinized and lack "depth". Some objectives acquire positive cathexis—compulsion or obsession—apart from their relevance for the solution of internal problems, and others acquire a negative cathexis—phobia.

The psychopathic syndrome is characterized by exclusive attention to internal problems. External objectives are pursued because of their immediate relevance without consideration of long-term needs and therefore without reference to the needs of alters or to the responses of alters. Things are taken by force.

With respect to personality systems, these syndromes are well explored. The relation between them has not been clear, however. The fact that one syndrome will typically turn into the other if the direction of regulatory effort is changed has been somewhat obscured by physiological and psychological factors which make just this shift of regulatory attention unlikely, or perhaps impossible.

In terms of personality, the compulsive type is given to dry and logical thought. Attention is focused upon those aspects of the environment which keep the individual from making contact with his own biological needs. This type is compulsively independent or even aloof. Actions are governed by principle. But these principles tend to be rigid. Insufficient attention is given to factors in the environment which make the principles inapplicable or which make their modification advisable.

The psychopathic personality, on the other hand, is concerned exclusively with personal gratification. It is completely unable to understand other individuals as personalities who have aims and desires of their own. This type of personality flees from thought, refuses to consider the complex pattern of relationships which join individuals in the external world, and is uninhibited by any moral standards or principles. The psychopath is warm, friendly—and vicious.

Since the superego is formed at an early age or not at all, the structural factors preventing the transformation of the psychopathic syndrome into the compulsive syndrome are overwhelming despite the intimate relationship between the two syndromes.

To apply these syndromes directly to the behavior of organized social and political systems is hazardous. In the first place, national actor systems in particular lack the strong need for external intercourse (through the mediation of leaders) which is found in the human personality system. Most needs can be satisfied internally. In the second place, social systems lack affective and reproductive subsystems.

Nevertheless analogs can be found if the previous qualifications are remembered. The subsystems of the Japanese "feudal" system were compulsive in character. The samurai were unconditionally loyal to the daimyo. This system was characterized by high tension, however, because loyalty often conflicted with personal needs. Therefore, the values of the system were introjected and the samurai identified themselves with the daimyo. However, when the position of a particular daimyo weakened, the samurai were likely to give vent to their accumulated grievances. They would forsake their allegiance to the lord and betray him to his enemies.

Characteristically, when released from tight compulsive controls, such systems manifest uncontrolled behavior. Moderation is foreign to them. Moreover, characteristically, they return under new lords to the old system relationships.

Japanese prisoners of war tend either to kill themselves or to transfer their allegiance to a conqueror. They can control their own destructive tendencies only by submitting to authority.

"Tight" social systems like the Japanese cannot be modified gradually. The system is so directive and the needs of the system so conflicting with the needs of its subsystems that the least loosening of the bonds is likely to produce anarchic behavior. Such systems can be entirely replaced by alternative directive systems. However, the substitution must be complete. Otherwise the subsystems will continually test the limits of control and act in a "lawless" manner. The internal controls are dependent upon external controls.

If the old social order breaks down, convulsive disorders may be precipitated by conflicting efforts to establish new directive orders or systems. Social disorder may occur when very "tight" directive systems are weakened either because disorder is precipitated by individuals who lack internal compulsive controls; or because it is precipitated by individuals who find the existing social order in conflict with strong internal needs which must be pursued compulsively; or because the system suffers a breakdown from its own internal strains, in which case complete disorganization may set in.

German behavior also has been characterized by compulsive-psychopathic "swings". Extreme and even picayune insistence upon formal legality is replaced, when controls are removed, by the most violent kind of ruleless and ruthless behavior. Sentimentality and brutality alternate.

The Schizoid and Paranoid Syndromes

These syndromes represent more severe pathologies than the compulsive and psychopathic set but have an intimate relationship to that set. The paranoid is a compulsive who lacks the capacity to relate his behavior to the external world. He thus constructs tight and internally consistent delusional systems which serve as a substitute for reality.

The schizoid is a psychopathic type who is unable to secure gratification for internal needs from external sources. He may make fitful efforts toward external gratification, as in the hebephrenic type, or he may completely withdraw cathexis from the external world and enter into a catatonic state. Deterioration of his mental processes indicates a withdrawal of affect from thought since most thought deals with external relationships. Thought then is used, if at all, only as a means for internal gratification rather than for purposes of reality testing.

Personalities who are psychotic are highly disorganized. Social systems cannot easily attain such a state of disorganization and continue to persist. Therefore analogs of this behavior will be found in mobs, poorly organized or disorganized social groups, and in riots. National actors will only rarely exhibit such behavior. Even then it will not be exhibited for long—possibly at the end of a long, hard, and losing war.

The Manic and Depressive Syndromes

Manic and depressive syndromes have in common an orientation to the outside world for the satisfaction of internal system needs. Satisfaction is not expected primarily to rest upon self-help. In individual personality systems, these phases cycle depending upon whether aid from alters is or is not expected. If aid is expected, the manic phase is dominant. If not, the depressive. Megalomania occurs in the extreme manic phase; suicidal tendencies tend to occur in the extreme depressive phase.

The so-called manic-depressive psychosis will not be duplicated in organized social systems for the same reasons applying to paranoid and schizoid psychoses. Such systems cannot persist.

However, just as milder manic-depressive cycles occur in normal or less than psychotic personality systems, mild degrees of these syndromes can be detected in organized social systems. These syndromes occur most often in the behavior of inessential national actors who, in fact, are often satellites of essential actors or dependent upon the protection and good will of essential actors. Underdeveloped areas may behave in this way and may come to expect aid as a right.

To some extent these syndromes may also become manifest in the behavior of subsystems of essential national actors that are of the system dominant, non-directive type. The system can act only if the goals of the subsystems are compromised. Agreement and compromise lead to optimism and affective solidarity.

Since, however, internal compromises have determined what the decision of the system is, internal considerations are more important than external. For this reason, the action most effective with respect to overcoming external disturbance is not taken. This information must be repressed to some extent. But it breaks through as a recognition that the system is not master of its fate. Therefore, system dominant, non-directive systems tend to have cyclic moods of optimism and pessimism.

Such systems tend toward compliancy. They focus regulatory attention upon means. However, they do not attempt to maintain a particular set of highly integrated means but rather to avoid conflict over ends. Thus the attention to means serves not to maintain a system with distinctive characteristics, but to force attention away from conflicts over ends which would bring the subsystems of the system into conflict and lessen the possibility of gratification.

CONCLUSIONS

The fact that a mechanism operates at one system level does not indicate that it also operates at a different level. Normal personalities, for instance, may operate within a pathological social system. Just those personalities which adjust to the pathological tendencies of the social system may manifest non-pathological behavior. Those who are unable to adapt will be brought into conflict with the social system and will develop, as a consequence of this conflict, personality pathologies.

Some social systems may be adaptive because they displace strains to personality systems. "Normal" personalities in this system may be personalities which in one way or another manage to isolate themselves either physically or affectively from the fate of the regime.

Most systems will manifest various mechanisms depending upon the strengths of various stimuli. And, depending upon conditions, these systems may not only manifest given syndromes in given task areas but also may swing from syndrome to syndrome within a task area.

The major task facing social science is not to describe the mechanisms and syndromes. Rather it is to locate and describe the stimuli which will evoke the various mechanisms and syndromes in different systems. Until this is done, it will not be possible to predict how a system will regulate its activities or how it will behave in various task areas.

Although some conclusions can be reached concerning regulatory processes, they will remain general, abstract, and difficult to apply until more is known about the ways in which specific actors regulate in given task areas when confronted by specific disturbances or tasks. All international actors, moreover, make use of all mechanisms to varying degrees.

The use of references to system responses and motivations—a use that is deliberate—seems to violate common sense because in interpreting social and human behavior we ordinarily reason as if the individual human were the only focus of action. But there are other relevant explanatory frameworks for explaining action. To explain how a human arrives at a decision, we must look inside him to the micro-events that produce the decision. To explain how his decisions affect a system, human interactions constitute the web of microevents. To explain how systems interact, their actions become the relevant microevents. Myopia on this issue is the product of an egocentric frame of reference. Our usage here is not a fallacy, "organic" or otherwise.[1]

[1] See pp. 8 and 28–34 above and 236–237 below for a discussion of some elements of this problem. It is true, however, for the reasons given on p. 8 that often some microreferences are essential to macroexplanations in social systems, and also *vice versa*.

9

THE REALM OF VALUES

Philosophers have raised many questions concerning the valuable. These questions will not be considered directly because they are largely irrelevant to the present inquiry. They will be considered indirectly inasmuch as the discussion of the empirical value problem will elucidate the source of many of the difficulties concerning the formulation of the philosophical questions.

The following definitions will serve as the framework for the present inquiry. System needs arise from system structure. Needs are the source of objectives. Objectives satisfying needs are valuable. Objectives that seem to satisfy needs are valued.

Under some circumstances continued existence may not be valuable to a system. It may be structured (according to its transformation rules) to die rather than to endure a given set of circumstances. At least the avoidance of death is not an axiom of the systems approach. Life may be a necessary but not a sufficient condition, if considered only as physical survival? The real question is: What is it that survives? Death may be preferable to certain kinds of survival.

The behavior of a system is not direct evidence either of the objectives of a system or of the needs of a system. These may be inferred from behavior but may not be revealed directly by behavior.

VALUES AND FACTS

Objectivity and Subjectivity

Are values objective or subjective, conditional or unconditional? Many disputes have raged over this question. Unless one desires to risk misunderstanding, it is important to define carefully objectivity and subjectivity.

A proposition is objective if the sentence asserting it can be confirmed by others using the methods of science. If Mr. X believes and states, "The leaning tower of Pisa is in Florence", the denoted object of the proposition is subjective, but the statement of belief is objective. Anyone who wishes to discover whether Mr. X believes that the leaning tower of Pisa is in Florence may find out merely by asking him.

Consider a man who sees two vases on a table although other people see only one. Even the individual who sees two vases may find evidence for only one vase if he uses his hands to feel the objects on the table. Perhaps the individual has a brain tumor. His experience is objective. In fact, he cannot change it by any act of will. Each time he looks the experience will be confirmed. Moreover, depending upon the development of medical science, it may be possible to predict, after X-raying the head of this man, that he will see double. Thus others may predict what this man will experience. This prediction, theoretically at least, may be confirmed by the ordinary methods of science. The assertion by the man that there are two vases on the table is subjective. The assertion that he sees two vases is a statement of objective fact.

What does it mean to state that a value is objective or subjective? Obviously, as defined, valuations occur just as cognitive experiences occur. In the case of double vision, observers can determine whether the reported experiences refer correctly to events external to the reporter.

Difficulties arise when attempts are made to determine whether the report is a true report of what is experienced. No direct means of testing such assertions are available. Therefore, if such reports are to be meaningful in an empirical sense, indirect means of testing such assertions have to be employed.

There are two senses in which reports of valuational experiences have to be tested. First, it must be determined whether the report is a true report of what the individual believes he values. Second, it must be determined whether it is an accurate report of what is valuable to him.

The question of honest reporting of belief poses difficult practical problems but no theoretical problems. It is possible, at least in theory, to discover discrepancies between reports and beliefs. In many areas of life, these discrepancies become obvious to external observers. In other cases, complicated inferences must be made. In these cases, the possibility of error becomes high. However, the possibility of error raises no problems concerning the principle of distinguishing between reports and the truth value of reports.

The distinction between a person's beliefs concerning his values and the valuable raises more difficult problems. Even so, most individuals are familiar with some common sources of error. First, an individual may err in reasoning from premises to conclusions. Thus he may believe he values something although closer examination would reveal his inconsistent reasoning and consequently would lead to a change in belief. In the second place, an individual may err in his cognition of the world. He may believe erroneously that someone has done something or that certain resources are available. In the third place, an individual may err in estimating the consequences of an action. He may believe that he prefers a given action. However, if he were aware of the consequences of that action, he might prefer a different action or a different instrumental object.

Therefore, in principle, valuational experiences are amenable to the application of objective or public and scientific criteria. In this sense, they are objective rather than subjective.

Since what is valuable depends upon the state of the evaluator—that is, upon the needs of the evaluator—and upon environmental circumstances, values are conditional. What is valuable functions with circumstances. The statement that something is valuable for someone under specific circumstances is, however, an unconditional statement.

Many difficult questions are still to be answered. However, first attention will be turned to philosophical objections to the position taken so far, namely, that values have an objective character.

Philosophic Objections.   Some will grant that it is possible to determine whether an objective satisfies a goal. They maintain, nevertheless, that values are not objectively factual. They deny that any examination of facts will suffice to permit value judgments. From the statement "man breathes", they will say, it is impossible to derive the conclusion "man ought to breathe". Since any statement of the "ought" type can be derived only from another statement of the same type, the search for a final link in the chain of "ought" statements will be fruitless.[1]

The critics are quite correct when they state that "man ought to breathe" cannot be derived logically from "man breathes". On the other hand, they have begged the question. The statement that "man values breathing" is a perfectly proper inference from observations which indicate that he will attempt to overcome obstacles in order to escape suffocation. Whether escaping suffocation is more important than other values can be determined only with the greatest difficulty. But that a particular man values breathing can be determined with ease. That breathing is at least conditionally valuable for man may be established by its necessity for life.

Scientific method in value inquiries is not different from scientific method in the area of physics. The statement that "a caused b" implies that a was caused by something, and so on. Philosophers have been hunting in vain for first or prime causes. However, no good physicist will attempt to solve any problem of physics by posing the problem in this manner. Scientific statements are implicational. They take the form "If, if a, then b and a, then b". Logical statements take the same form.

A scientific model is a system of related assertions. The model makes certain predictions about its variables. This permits the model to be tested. Values may be tested in the same manner. A prediction that something is valuable for a person constitutes a prediction that it will satisfy his needs under given conditions. Thus value theories may also be tested by the methods of science.

Action or belief concerning the valuable is not the ultimate criterion. In some cases, an external observer may know better than the person himself what is valuable for that person.

"Ought" statements are usually uttered as elliptical sentences. "X ought to do g" may be elliptical for "X ought to do g because g has the consequence h, which is valuable for X", or for "X ought to do g because g has the consequence j which is valuable for Y". If the first

---

[1] I have also used this argument—which now seems mistaken—in "An Introduction to the Strategy of Statecraft", *World Politics*, July 1952, p. 552.

statement is correct concerning the valuable for X, then X ought in fact to do g. If the second statement is correct concerning the valuable for Y, then it is still an open question whether X ought to do g. If Y's being satisfied is valuable for X and nothing else conflicts with this value, then X ought to do g; otherwise there is no implicational necessity.

"Ought" implies that which is necessary to accomplish an objective. "Two plus two equals four" and "one ought to add two to two to get four" are equivalent statements, as Morris R. Cohen has cogently demonstrated.

It is incorrect to state that disagreement concerning the valuable is not in any sense amenable to normal methods of science. Whether the contending parties accept the results of scientific demonstration is a separate question. Many individuals reject the findings of science in the areas of physics. Some believe that the earth is flat or that it stands on an elephant. The fact that some individuals resist or fail to understand scientific demonstration is no more a proper refutation of the findings of science in the area of values than in the area of physics.

THE FOUNDATION OF VALUES

Values and Pathologies

Systems can maintain themselves if they can satisfy their needs. Under unfavorable conditions, that is, under conditions which prevent the satisfaction of some needs, the system may be maintained by pathological mechanisms of regulation. Such systems protect themselves by focusing attention on given classes of information and by screening out or distorting other classes of information.

Neuroses are often pathological regulatory mechanisms. They then represent less than the optimal adjustment of the organism. Nevertheless, neuroses may satisfy both primary and secondary system needs. In many cases, it is costly to restructure the system to eliminate the neuroses—and in some cases it is too costly.

It is necessary to give a precise definition of "pathology". Is illness pathological? It may be considered pathological if resources are available to the ill person that will restore the previous state of health, for instance, if medicine is available which can be purchased at the drug store. Information concerning the availability of the medicine supplied to the ill person may set off a chain of events leading to the purchase of the medicine and the restoration of the state of health.

However, consider the case where the medicine is not available. Is the condition pathological? It may be regarded as pathological in the sense that the morbid condition would be subject to correction if the medicine *were* available. This definition, however, is different from the first. In the first case, the input of information is sufficient to correct the condition. In the second, information is insufficient. In either case, medicine has value for the system.

It may be objected that illness is pathological regardless of the availability of medical aid. However, from the standpoint of regulation, the system may be regulating optimally under given conditions. Consider still a third case, namely the physiological state of brain damage resulting from carbon monoxide poisoning. Is this state pathological? Obviously the system cannot regulate itself to correct this condition. Was the dodo bird pathological because it was inadequate for purposes of survival?

The dodo bird was the victim of poor heredity. Carbon monoxide poisoning is not hereditary. But the consequences of carbon monoxide poisoning are as irreversible as those of hereditary endowment. Any non-pathological system, however, will attempt to avoid carbon monoxide poisoning.

Thus, from the standpoint of the regulatory mechanisms, a mechanism is pathological only if it is not optimal under the existing or probable future conditions. The neurosis is pathological only if it regulates the personality system inefficiently.

Consider the case of an individual who is a quadruple amputee and ugly. Such an individual might do well to repress information concerning his biological needs and the happiness other people receive from certain kinds of affective and social relationships. This defective individual cannot cognize information of this character without becoming subject to other disturbances. He has not eliminated his needs by means of neurotic repression but he has found the best adjustment to his situation. Although his adjustment is not pathological, his state is undesirable.

Some changes in the biological system are irreversible, and others are very costly to correct. The personality system must adapt to these changes in some way. Once the adaptation is made, it becomes difficult to reverse or change it even if the circumstances which made it necessary are eliminated.

In the first place, a neurotic adaptation involves the withdrawal of regulatory capacity from the metatask regulatory system. Repression is a task oriented mechanism. Therefore, the capacity necessary to recognize and to adapt to changed circumstances is weakened. Moreover, the adaptation—once acquired—works, even if inefficiently. It permits some dangers to the system to be avoided. It uses automatic ready-at-hand responses which free the limited capacity of the regulatory system for other necessary life functions.

A changed system of responses involves many unknowns. Particularly given the great tension of the neurotic system and the implicit, although not always conscious, recognition of its own inadequacies, it must fear and resist efforts to change it or information indicating the desirability of change.

Often information of which the individual has no conscious awareness is most influential in leading to action. Thus there are times when the individual feels compelled to act by forces over which he lacks conscious control. At still other times, beliefs are influenced by factors of which the individual lacks conscious awareness.

The last qualification clears up a considerable difficulty. Since it also makes some sense to say that the valuable is something which is valued, the discrepancy between a person's belief concerning his values and the valuable impugns the pragmatic adequacy of a definition based upon system needs. If, however, beliefs will correspond with needs under conditions of complete information—and this is a theoretically testable hypothesis—the discrepancy ceases to be disturbing.

Moreover, if in cases in which conscious awareness of information concerning system needs does not eliminate the discrepancy a pathological regulatory mechanism can be demonstrated—again a theoretically testable proposition—the last stronghold of subjectivism in value theory will have been conquered. Pathological regulatory mechanisms will become manifest in one way or another, perhaps in an abnormally high state of tension, in parapraxes, or in inaccurate reporting of the social or physical environment.

Accommodation and Conflict

Much conflict stems from imperfect information. But accommodation between individuals may also result from imperfect information. Some individuals misjudge their interests in a situation and therefore come to agreement in violation of those interests.

Whether individuals have interests in common depends upon their internal states and the states of nature. Therefore, the fact that disputes concerning the valuable are, in theory at least, amenable to scientific decision does not imply that different interests can be reconciled.

Nevertheless, some general observations may be made. In the first place, there is no *a priori* reason why individuals cannot have psychological needs which are best satisfied if other individuals lead happy and useful lives. Such needs would reflect interdependent utility schedules. There is as much evidence that such interdependences exist as for the contrary hypothesis.

Whether the hypothesis of interdependence is correct and, if correct, whether it applies to all other individuals, to some only, or differentially to others cannot be answered with any reasonable degree of assurance. Nevertheless, to the extent that interdependence exists, it tends to increase the possibility of accommodation of interests, particularly if all pertinent information is available.

Secondly, whether interdependence of utility or happiness is an original need of human beings may not be important if the need is an autonomous need of individuals in society.

Consider love as a need of the individual. In this context love is instrumental to his well-being and therefore has value. If, however, the object of love is neglected and treated instrumentally, the relationship with the loved object will be destroyed. For instance, suppose a man selects his wife for transient characteristics like beauty, wealth, and health. If he makes his choice on this basis, he will destroy his own capacity for love and, therefore, for the satisfaction he gains from the relationship. What is in its nature a diffuse and affective relationship will be turned into a specific and instrumental relationship.

Moreover, if the wife is aware of this, that knowledge will undermine the value of the relationship for her by denying her the security and affective support she needs. Therefore, though love is instrumentally valuable, attitudes toward love cannot be instrumental without under-mining the relationship of love.

In short, the relationship of love can be maintained successfully only if it is viewed attitudinally as intrinsically rather than instrumentally valuable. Many relationships within society which are valuable instru-mentally—that is, valuable because they fill other needs and thus have a derived status—can be sustained only if they are treated as intrinsically valuable relationships. Their instrumentally valuable status gives rise to an autonomous and intrinsically valuable status.

Thus, whatever the ultimate origin of some interdependent needs, their value status may be independent of those origins. For this reason, there are many occasions in society when one individual intrinsically values the happiness of other individuals. Such interdependences reduce the area of conflict and increase the area of accommodation in society.

The Good and the Just

The range of accommodation within society is also increased by com-municative factors which are peculiar to the physiological organization of human beings. In the first place, apparently unless humans communi-cate with each other and cathect social relations, mental deterioration takes place.[2] Thus adequate regulation is dependent upon continued communication. The work of Hebb and others indicates that insulation from external stimuli generally produces pathological regulatory pheno-mena.

The concept of the self emerges only through communication with other men. Without an integrated concept of the self, higher mental processes and control of the environment to satisfy system needs would become more difficult, if not impossible. When society becomes ex-cessively mobile, men lose their integrated concept of the self and anomie becomes characteristic of personality systems.

George Mead has described, in *Mind and Society*, how the concept of the self develops through the "generalized other". Freud has described the processes which lead to formation of a superego. Thus the commu-

[2] See Martin Whiteman, "The Performance of Schizophrenics on Social Con-cepts", *Journal of Abnormal and Social Psychology*, Vol. 49, pp. 266-271.

nicative process develops within man attitudes recognizing the needs of other men as internal needs of the self. These needs for the happiness of at least some others have an autonomous status as intrinsic valuables. Only pathologically regulating individuals lack these needs.

Man is thus torn between two sets of sometimes conflicting needs which he must in some way reconcile. Man must adjust to his personal needs in the natural and social environment which is individual to him. But man must also adjust to the needs of generalized man in the environment which is general to man or to a given community of men.

The general concept of man involves an abstraction from the circumstances that individualize specific men and from the environments which set specific problems for individual men. However, at a more pragmatic level appeals for cooperation will fail if they are phrased in an exclusively instrumental fashion. And individual men who think in such terms will become unfit for society—as Aristotle said, either beasts or gods. Even if such men are biologically possible, natural selection will tend to breed them out.

All societies are based upon a concept of justice. Justice or fairness depends upon rules that are independent of particular personalities. *Noblesse oblige* is an obligation of all nobles. Decorum and restraint are expected of all judges in Great Britain, not just of Judge Jones. All veterans wounded in war have the right to free medical treatment, not just Private Smith.

Social systems can maintain themselves only if the rules according to which they operate are independent of labeling. Society—which men need to survive—constrains men to communicate, even to think, in terms of just relations. Those who cannot conform tend to be eliminated. Others adapt to the concept of justice, and it becomes an intrinsic and autonomous need of their personality systems.

The very stuff of tragedy occurs when vital needs of the particular individual are in irreconcilable conflict with the needs of society. Must life be sacrificed for honor? Should one commit treason to save one's life? Secondary or unimportant conflicts may be resolved one way or another and forgot. But the great conflicts are inherently insoluble.

If a particular man represses his most basic psychological or biological needs, his regulatory mechanisms will become pathological. If he neglects basic social needs, he destroys his identity as an actor in society. To repress this unacceptable information, since his needs for solidary relations with others are still vital, he must again employ pathological regulatory mechanisms.

There is only one escape from this dilemma. That escape is to modify the environment in such a way that the two sets of needs cease to be irreconcilable. Thus, in most social situations, there is an underlying strain toward social change. But as change occurs, the society itself changes. As society changes, statuses, roles, and social values change. The ways in which man and his needs are viewed change also.

To the extent that change reduces or eliminates irreconcilable cleavages of interest between some men and society or between some men and some other men, individual interests converge and become compatible. What is good for individual men becomes good also for society. The society becomes so regulated that it produces good for all men.

10

THE NATIONAL INTEREST

AND OTHER INTERESTS

A debate has raged concerning whether the national interest is objective. Those who regard the national interest as objective usually.regard national interests as permanent, unchanging, and related to power. Those who regard the national interests as subjective usually affirm that it includes values other than power. They also cite disagreement between individuals and groups of individuals concerning the national interest as proof that it is subjective. Objectivists reply by making a distinction between interests and passions or between interests and opinions.

The interest of a system is to obtain the valuable. The interests of a nation is to satisfy national needs. Thus national interests are objective, and there are as many national interests as national needs.

However, what lies behind the distinction between "passion" and "interest" which historically has been commonplace in discussions of statecraft? Does a sharp distinction between analytic levels of action permit a more precise analysis of the problem of the national interest?

PASSIONS AND INTERESTS

National interests have been identified as objective although related to the national level of action and to the structure of the system of action at the national level. However, this does not account for the historic distinction between "interest" and "passion". Does this distinction reflect simply a dispute concerning the national interest? Or is some more basic issue involved?

Many times policies have been opposed as based on passion or sentiment rather than on interest. Somehow this use of "passion" and "interest" implies that some objectives are more ephemeral or less real than other objectives. Although the distinction between "passion" and "interest" rarely is precisely explained, it appears to rest upon the belief that national actors are concrete physical entities. Somehow this physical substratum appears to be the most important element is national life. Therefore national power is the supreme goal of national action. National power is both the means and the objective of statecraft. The more power a nation has, the more secure its life. Other objectives are regarded as ephemeral, or even as dangerous to the life of the nation.

This position has been argued as if it constituted an eternal law of nature rather than a prescription for action within a particular international system of action. The "interest" formulation constitutes both a description of what has occurred and a prescription for national policy.

The "interest" doctrine is a reasonably adequate description of the "balance of power" international system, although, at times, sentiment or "passion" did seem to outweight "interest", for example, Palmerston's support for Greece and British neutrality in the American Civil War after Lincoln's Emancipation Proclamation.

As a prescription for action, the "interest" doctrine accords reasonably well with the essential rules of the "balance of power" international system, although it does not take proper account of the possible dangers arising from deviant national actors. As interest is understood in this volume, Palmerston may have been wise in running some risks to encourage non-directive national actors. Such action may have had long-term value for stabilizing the "balance of power" system by inhibiting deviancy.

The "interest" doctrine also neglects the consideration that external policy has the function of maintaining a given social structure within the national system as well as the function of preserving the security of the national system against potential enemies. If there really were a sharp separation between domestic and foreign policy, conditions in the international system would be inconsequential for the internal life of the national system—provided only that the system were secure against enemies.

However, efforts to protect national systems externally affect the internal life of the national system. Things like the draft, industrial mobilization, and problems of security affect the national system. In an age when small professional armies waged war, when conscription affected only the poor and the rootless, these consequences may have been obscure.

The policy best adapted to maintaining external security may not be the best policy from the standpoint of maintaining internal values. Likewise, an external policy that would be best if supported internally may be poor if it arouses opposition within the nation or if it creates economic hardships which lead to apathy and indifference.

If the "interest" doctrine, based upon the concept of national power, is correct, it should be confirmed by the permanency of national policy regardless of changes in government within national actors. Proponents of the "interest" doctrine long have used the striking continuity of foreign policy and the abandonment by incoming governments of positions on foreign affairs taken while out of office as confirmation that the national interest rests on solid realities rather than on "ideas", "opinions", or "passions".

In part, the proof is an artifact. In non-directive systems governments usually rest upon center-based majorities. The majority is usually provided by the great "middle mass" of citizens. A radical break with past policy most often would condemn a party to the status of a permanent minority. Therefore, from a political point of view alone, great changes in foreign policy cannot often be expected simply because one party rather than another comes to office.

However, it must be admitted, some parties out of power, particularly socialist parties, have miscalculated the extent to which foreign policy can be independent of the instrumental means of implementation. At times, popular policies are espoused out of office only to be forsaken when office is attained.

National actors in a "balance of power" or bipolar system require for their defense and also for the effectiveness of policy allies, bases, access to raw materials, and so forth. These needs, although they may be implemented in different ways, cannot well be eliminated by changing office holders.

Moreover, a number of factors may reinforce the specific objectives or means of implementation chosen by preceding governments. In the first place, enunciated objectives tend to become imbedded in the information states of the decision makers who choose them and also in the information states of those decision makers who come to office later. In the second place, once an objective or means of implementation is pursued, the investment in that objective is lost if a change is made. Other actors have already pledged their cooperation. Claims have publicly been made. Reversals would cloud the entire issue and make policies appear arbitrary. Besides, time, money, and personnel have already been expended. Moreover, the organization is structured to scan for information which seems consonant with the given objective and to ignore information which appears to conflict. This is particularly true at non-political levels in the administration. Furthermore, these levels in the administration brief political appointees and play a large role in directing their attention toward given courses of action and away from other equally plausible courses of action.

Alliances and blocs in particular represent large investments of effort and resources. New administrations may intend to make changes, but it is difficult to make changes at a single point without touching off a ramified series of consequences. It is much easier to maintain existing agreements than to negotiate new sets of agreements.

The Republican administration in 1953—even had it wanted to—was in a poor position to renegotiate the role of national forces in NATO or to take a position quite different from the position of the Truman administration with respect to German rearmament. The Republican administration was free to suggest minor modifications, but it would have raised the wrath of its treaty partners had it claimed that it was not bound or committed by the agreements of the government that was its predecessor. Indeed, such a position would have set a most undesirable precedent. Would even a more conservative Republican group have been willing to pay the cost of reassessment each time the French, Italian, or Belgian cabinet changed?

Generally, only when internal changes within a national system lead to radical changes in the political system of that nation may a change of alignment become a matter of necessity rather than convenience. Obviously, if Italy were to acquire a Communist government, both the United States and Italy would desire to examine the role of Italy in NATO.

Logistic considerations also predispose nations to some objectives rather than others which—apart from logistic considerations—may be equally desirable. Thus air fields in Patagonia may serve as well to service bombing missions as those in Libya except that they are farther from potential targets. Raw materials may be as cheap to acquire in one place as another, except that the transportation route may be safer, and so on.

For these reasons, and perhaps for some others also, it is rare that the foreign policy objectives of a national system change radically. If the Communists, for instance, were to take over Italy, the foreign objectives of Italy would change radically. But most governmental changes are not that sweeping. Particularly in non-directive national systems, the changes rest upon a framework of national consensus.

The replacement of a Labour government in Great Britain by a Conservative government may change national values somewhat. But the place to look for the consequences of the change is not in a vast and sweeping replacement of previous national policies. Rather changes in the priorities accorded alternative objectives or the speed or willingness with which given policies are carried out may characterize the change in governmental policy. The Labour government probably gave India and Burma their freedom faster than a Conservative government would have. But a Conservative government almost surely would have granted independence eventually.

Nevertheless, these differences in priority are not lacking in importance. Indeed, India might not have remained within the Commonwealth had not the grant been made when it was. France finally accorded independence to Viet Nam. But it might have been much better for France if Mendes-France had come to office a year earlier.

DISTINCTIONS BETWEEN THE INTERESTS OF DIFFERENT SYSTEM LEVELS

The distinction between the interests of different system levels rests upon the consideration that systems of action are analytic rather than concrete entities. This does not signify that they are unreal but only that classes of actions with relatively permanent characteristics are segregated and treated as independent systems. Indeed, a system may be dominant over the actors within it.

National systems of action, like other systems, are organized to satisfy system needs. Their essential rules represent their adjustment to their environments in terms of the relations of the actors within the system rather than in terms of specific instrumental goal objects.

For instance, curbs were placed on the movement of labor and capital in wartime England. When, however, the external environment became favorable, that is, when the war was won, it became possible to implement the values and thus to satisfy the needs of the national system better by removing some of the wartime curbs.

A national system cannot continue to regulate itself well unless it can satisfy at least some of the needs of at least some of its subsystems. Therefore, the national interest will include the satisfaction of at least some of these subsystem needs. However, even when the national system is not regulating pathologically, there may be conflicts between the interests of the national actor and interests of subsystems of the national actor system.

For instance, it may be in the interest of the political system to send an espionage agent on a dangerous mission or to nationalize an industry. Except for some peculiar conditions, these decisions will not be in the interests of the espionage agent or the industry or the owners of the industry. Although the industry may resist nationalization in the name of the national interest—and although in some cases it may be correct in this claim—the claim, theoretically at least, can be determined independently.

Analytically, the interests of individuals, subnational systems, national systems, supranational systems, and the international system stand on an equal footing. There is no natural order of priority such that one system level ought to defer to another.

There may be occasions when various system interests coincide. Although taxes in general are burdensome, taxpayers may, in keeping with their interests and those of the national actor, vote additional tax monies for defense purposes. Military appropriations may be directly valuable to the national actor and indirectly valuable to citizens whose interests are defended by the national actor.

On other occasions, the national actor may make a decision contrary to the interests of some individual, but it may nevertheless be in the interest of the individual to comply with the decision. Nationalization of industry may be a case in point. The decision may be contrary to the interests of the stockholders but—once taken—the penalty for attempted non-compliance may be sufficiently great to contraindictate that course of action.

On still other occasions, the decisions of the national actor may be so contrary to the interests of individuals that resistance is indicated regardless of the chances of success. Jews being herded into Hitler's gas chambers had no good reason to comply with the decisions of the national government.

There may be still other occasions on which the interests of the government are so opposed to those of the body of citizens that the government will collapse and be replaced by another form of government. The French and Russian revolutions illustrate this point. Reform was no longer possible within the old institutions. The attempt to defend these institutions was doomed to failure. Yet if some élites have interests allied to those of the governmental subsystem, they will be motivated to support them.

National systems may be so in conflict with the interests of individual citizens and groupings of citizens that they may be merged within supranational or international political entities. Efforts to forge a United States of Europe rest upon the claim that existing organizational entities are outmoded. Yet the interests of most élites in national actors may lie in resisting such efforts though the interests of other subsystems of the national system possibly may sanction attempts to destroy national institutions. Only if an integrative merger is the only way left to preserve some of the values of the national system, will the interests of the national actor and of its subsystems prove parallel. Even here, however, there may be conflicts with respect to speed and degree of integration.

There is in nature no inherent priority for the national actor system over any subsystem of that system or over supranational or international systems. As far as individual citizens are concerned, the interests of the national actor within which they hold citizenship have no natural priority over the interests of other national actor systems.

Should the anti-Nazi German have aided loyally in the defense of the Hitlerite regime, or should he have cooperated with the enemies of the regime? It was, in fact, to the interest of the anti-Nazi to cooperate with the Western powers and to the interest of the Nazi regime to discourage and to punish such treasonable and subversive activities.

Should decision makers within a small democracy sacrifice that democracy to give larger and more powerful democracies time to prepare against a totalitarian national actor? Individuals, after all, have no biological ties to the nation. They need not be destroyed with it nor need their values perish with the values of the national actor. Indeed, the destruction of the national actor may facilitate the preservation of individual values. In the first place, citizens may be able to flee and thus to escape the fate of the national actor. In the second place, if the national actor is sacrificed, other democratic or non-directive actors may be given time to destroy the directive national actor.

If the sacrifice is made, the nation may later be reorganized, or it may be absorbed within a supranational non-directive system. If, however, an accommodation is reached with the directive national actor, the national system may survive in a form contrary to the interests of the individual citizens.

Obviously, it is difficult to generalize in the absence of a concrete case. Nevertheless, the distinction between the interests of different system levels is compelling. Interests are objective, but what the national actor ought to do may differ from or conflict with what an individual or subsystem of the national system ought to do.

Some disagreements concerning the national interest may only represent errors in judgment. However, some disagreements may represent clashes between different subsystems concerning their interests but may be phrased as if those interests were the national interest.

Moreover, some disagreements may represent attempts to change the national interest, that is, to change the form and structure of the national system, to change its essential rules and its needs, and to change the relations of dominance within the system. In this sense, disagreement would concern not what the national interest *is* but what the national interest *ought to be* from the standpoint of or according to the interests of the subsystem making the claim.

DECISION MAKERS AND THE NATIONAL INTEREST

The sharp distinction between the interests of different system levels raises a specter. What if decision makers make decisions which implement their interests rather than those of the national actor system?

To some extent, fear that this may happen lies behind the democratic distrust of foreign policy officials. Within any system the agency dealing with a given sphere of activity will have some degree of subsystem dominance over that particular range of activity. Those who make the decisions scan for information which accords with their expectations. They are attentive to the problems which seem important within the communicative frameworks which structure their activities. They are responsive to their individual interests and to the interests of the subsystems to which they belong, whether by birth or by selection.

In general, no objection can be made to this state of affairs except in terms of different subsystem interests. Any substitution among the decision-making personnel would only change the values and subsystem interests to which attention was given. In terms of national essential rules, a different segment of the nation would become dominant over foreign policy.

There may, however, be cases in which foreign policy decision makers act contrary to the national interest because their subsystem interests conflict with the national interest. Decision makers, like other individuals, respond to their multiple roles. Their role in some other subsystem of the national system may conflict with and dominate their role in the foreign policy subsystem. There are a number of systems in which foreign-policy makers may hold roles which conflict with their foreign-policy-making role.

Political parties with international organizational ties may have interests opposed to the national interest, that is, opposed to the preservation of the nation as an entity with distinctive territorial bounds, or possibly, opposed to the preservation of the national political system except in so far as it adheres to essential rules consonant with the interests of the international party.

Religious, economic, and fraternal groups may have interests which are either consonant with those of some supranational system or independent of national interests insofar as their pursuit is not dependent upon the existence or non-existence of the national actor system.

To some extent, however, differences concerning the national interest may reflect differences concerning the external environment or concerning the consequences of given actions. Quisling activity represented to some extent interests at variance with the national interest. However, probably some who joined these movements believed that only in this way could they accommodate to Nazi victory and conserve any of the values of the national system.

The situation of decision makers at lower ranks who believe that the national interest is being violated by those in superior positions, either through ignorance or contrary interests, is poignant. Should such decision makers carry out policies they believe wrong or even disastrous? Or should they oppose such policies and brave the consequences?

The statement of this problem may stir the fear that anarchy will result if each decision maker, regardless of level in the administrative apparatus, implements the policies he thinks correct and fails to implement policies determined at higher national levels. If proper distinctions are made, such fears lack foundation. It would, of course, be anarchic if different policies were substituted at each hierarchic level in the administrative apparatus by decision makers who rejected the decisions of those above them in the hierarchy. However, common sense demonstrates that those lower in the hierarchy—regardless of their disagreements with those higher in the administrative hierarchy—are not likely to sabotage policy in this manner.

Many policies which *would* be better if adopted at higher administrative levels are worse if substituted at lower levels. Those lower in the administrative hierarchy—apart from lacking the information upon which the decision was based at the highest levels—are faced with different problems.

Lower ranking officials no longer have the problem of deciding high national policy; they have the problem of implementing that policy and of adjusting it to local conditions. Their very freedom not to apply that policy if it fails to satisfy local conditions maintains the flexibility of the administrative apparatus.

If the interest of lower ranking officials is consonant with the national interest, administrative flexibility in the implementation of decisions will raise no difficult problems. If officials are incompetent, they may overlook their paucity of information or the consequences for the national interest if they substitute their private judgment for that of their superiors.

But this becomes a matter of choosing competent officials. It would be equally bad to have officials who blindly applied policies regardless of local conditions or who were unable to make local adjustment without referring everything back to their superiors. During the war, for instance, one official without proper authority ordered a captain of a ship in port to unload a cargo of rotten potatoes which was causing the boat to sink. This was in violation of a directive to carry the potatoes to England. But common sense prevailed over red tape.

Suppose a higher ranking official is pathological. Suppose an American officer in charge of occupying a Japanese village had ordered his troops to burn it to the ground although the locals were cooperating with the occupying authorities. It is at least plausible that the national interest would be better served if the troops arrested their officer, ignored the order, and appealed to still higher authority to intercede. It is possible that the order might have been based upon secret information and that the troops therefore might have acted unwisely. But no rules for action are likely to apply to every possible contingency.

On the other hand, the interests of a decision maker may conflict with the interests of the nation. Although the previous examples illustrate cases in which national needs are best satisfied if orders from above are disobeyed, there may be cases when, rather than exercising discretion in implementing policy, a decision maker may be acting contrary to the national interest. Consider a German officer who refused to carry out Hitler's order to devastate a French village and to kill its inhabitants. Refusal to use terror might possibly injure the German war effort. Yet some officers might prefer to injure the war effort—or even to lose the war—rather than to engage in inhumane activity.

It is functional for national actors to have an interest in preventing decision makers from acting contrary to the national interest and to punish those who do. Exaggeration of the bad consequences of such actions or the convincing of decision makers that such actions are morally wrong is also functional. But there is no good reason—except *perhaps* fear of personal consequences—why an administrator who views national values with abhorrence should not sabotage the implementation of those values. Indeed, the myth that administrators have no responsibility except to carry out legally prescribed national policy has been responsible for some of the most sordid violations of individual values in the history of mankind.

From an abstract point of view, human beings are instrumental for maintaining the existence and interests of the political system. However, from the point of view of ultrastable individual human beings, the political system has value only as an instrument for implementing human values. There is no reason in logic or theory why individual needs should be subordinated by human agents to the good of the political system.

THE GOOD AND THE JUST

The national interest, since it satisfies system needs, is the good for a national actor, just as values or objectives which satisfy individual needs constitute the good for the individual. However, is there also a community of interest in the international system so that a concept of the just also may have relevance?

Analogies between human individuals and national actors are bound to founder with respect to some very important conditions. A nation rarely is dependent for its survival upon paternalistic national actors. There is no immediate and direct dependency between national actors likely to create bonds of solidarity nor is there any inherited biological characteristic which facilitates high affective valuation of the needs of other national actors.

The essential national actor is able to satisfy most of its sytem needs within its own national boundaries. It has no biological or psychological needs for intercourse with other national actors. There is no reason to believe that an isolated nation will become pathological as will an individual isolated from social and physical stimulation. The nation is able to develop a satisfactory image of the self through the interaction of individuals and groups within the nation. In fact, the national image is an image in the minds of men which expresses itself in national patterns of behavior.

National actors have no inherent constitutional need to communicate with other national actors. They may have a derived need to communicate with other national actors because their actions will affect these actors. If there is no communication, the consequences of actions for other national actors and the probable responses of these national actors to the actions will be misjudged. Thus lack of communication will lead to pathological international-actor behavior. However, it is possible, initially at least, to view these communicative needs from an instrumental standpoint.

Therefore, at least with respect to "balance of power" and bipolar international systems, relations between national actors are primarily instrumental. Yet to some extent this description is inadequate even with respect to the "balance of power" and bipolar international systems. American relations with Great Britain sometimes rise above the purely instrumental. At times aid is given or risks are run when other alternatives would be chosen if *only* instrumental considerations were involved.

Perhaps some of the hesitancy Asian nations have concerning the United States arises from the belief that aid has purely instrumental objectives, that they cannot count on American support unless that support is also instrumental to immediate American objectives.

The difficulty with instrumental aid is that it lacks dependability. It ceases as soon as the occasion which called it forth passes. Particularly within universal organizations, national policies cannot be expressed in purely instrumental terms and gain sufficient support to be adopted.

If such support becomes so important from an instrumental point of view that an instrumental attitude can no longer be taken toward it with safety, a solidary international community may arise. The channels of communication may block out information concerning the instrumental character of cooperative action. In other words, the necessity for cooperation may lead to a repression of information concerning the instrumental character of cooperation. But this fact itself may cause cooperative action to become intrinsically valuable at the level of individual actions.

Such considerations lie behind the formation of bloc actors. Blocs are so important to the member actors that maintaining them is more important than possible non-optimal consequences with respect to specific individual actions. For example, France may not like German rearmament, but that is a price France will pay to remain within NATO.

The level of instrumentality is the all-important consideration. It is important instrumentally to maintain the bloc or association. However, individual actions within the bloc or association are no longer considered on a purely instrumental level, although instrumental considerations may play a role with respect to some aspects of individual decisions.

The hypotheses concerning integration expounded elsewhere receive a more adequate explanation when these considerations are taken into account. To some extent, the cooperative structure, for instance, the supranational bloc actor, operates to channel information conforming with its purposes and to exclude information inconsistent with those purposes or objectives.

Moreover, discussion within the bloc stresses non-instrumental considerations, although instrumental considerations are not ignored at the level of implementation or adoption by the member actors.

Exclusive concern with instrumental considerations would undermine cooperative behavior. Therefore decision makers who participate in bloc activity will tend even to repress knowledge of the instrumental reasons for their cooperation. Bloc objectives will be considered as autonomous and as intrinsically important.

If national system needs increase the incidence of cooperative activity among national actors, cooperative objectives will gain an autonomous status. They will become intrinsic goals or values of national systems. In this event, the good will be supplemented by the just, that is, by the concept that other national states also have a right to satisfy certain system needs.

In this case, national action will represent some weighting of the good and of the just, that is, of the needs of a particular nation, given its specific environment, and of the needs of a supranational or international community.

If the essential rules characterizing any system of action are regarded as important by the actors in that system, these national actors will weigh possible gains from individual actions or decisions against the consequences of the action or decision for the set of essential rules. This is the insight behind the complaint that ends do not justify the means. In any precise sense, ends must always justify the means.[1] However, some actions, although gaining desirable immediate objectives, also undermine more important modes of inter-actor behavior, as expressed in the essential rules of the system.

For instance, one may lie to his wife in order to have some fun, but, if this lie is discovered, the marriage relationship may be injured. There is, therefore, a clear distinction between relationships between actors, that is, the essential rules of the system, and specific goal-orientated actions.

The essential rules of the "balance of power" and bipolar international systems are of less importance to national actors than the essential rules

[1] The utility of an action is a weighted product of the utilities of the alternate consequences.

of national systems and therefore will be subordinated to them in case of conflict. Nevertheless, there are limited areas, even in the "balance of power" and bipolar systems, in which the relations among some sets of actors acquire sufficient importance to subordinate gains in specific situations to maintaining the relationship among the actors. This is particularly the case in bloc arrangements in the loose and tight bipolar systems.

In the universal and hierarchical international systems, the essential rules of the international system will acquire even more importance than the essential rules of the bloc actors in the bipolar international systems.

Finally, cooperative or integrated action may be implemented by institutions or social structures in which large investments have been made. Failure to use these institutions may involve costs which are so large that they cannot be considered. In this case, the cost of maintaining the structure becomes a necessary cost for satisfying the needs of the actors within the system.

Yet, if the system is to be maintained, the cooperation of all actors within the system is necessary. Therefore, within the system the needs of the various actors must be recognized and appeals must be made to them as members of a common system in which the needs of all members are recognized as having intrinsic importance.

THE NATIONAL INTEREST

The national interest is the interest which a national actor has in implementing the needs of the national system of action. Some of these needs arise inside the national system, and others stem from factors in the environment.

Internal system needs include economic needs for raw materials and other material capabilities. But internal needs also include the need to maintain the essential rules of the system or to satisfy the wants which subsystems have or which the personality systems of human actors demand. To illustrate, a nation may be able to increase its material capabilities by mobilizing its economy and drafting its manhood, by eliminating political dissent and removing legal rights of citizens. Thus mobilized, it may be able to conquer other nations and to protect itself against any combination of external foes. Such action, however, may do violence to its most intense domestic needs. The nation may prefer strongly to endure some external risks rather than to repress its internal needs. Such preferences are in harmony with its national interest.

Environmental needs include defense needs. Such needs depend upon the structure of the international community and upon the presence or absence of dangerous foes. These needs do not vary directly with changes in internal structure. From this fact emerges the opinion that the national interest is unchanging and permanent. However, though these needs do not change directly with internal structure, the weights attributed to them in determining the national interest may change with changes in the needs of domestic institutions.

Internal national changes may make the nation either more or less susceptible to attack. For instance, the economic policy of a new government may work so well that allies or foreign sources of material supplies become less important to its defense. But also, the installation of a government dedicated to non-directive or democratic values may increase the cost of military ventures. Such ventures may weaken democratic institutions. Therefore, as the cost of external aggressive action is raised, it becomes less desirable even though it still satisfies some external needs.

Finally, external needs include cooperative needs, for few, if any, national actors are so well situated that they are safe without allies or bloc partners. Thus the national interest, in some circumstances, may place great importance upon maintaining the essential rules of the cooperative relationship. In this event, the national interest may subordinate gains from individual actions to the desirability of maintaining the alliance or bloc.

The national interest is objective but not independent of the circumstances and of the specific characteristics of the individual national actor. The self-centered interests of the national actor in the "balance of power", bipolar, and unit veto international systems are in part the product of the social structure of those international systems.

However, even in those international systems different national actors have different national interests which function with their values and internal system needs as well as with their international needs. Some national actors place greater value upon supranational and international interests in the "balance of power" and bipolar systems than other actors.

Moreoever, in the universal and especially in the hierarchical international system, the international interest becomes an autonomous and intrinsic value for the actors within the system. In the hierarchical system national actors, and consequently national interests, cease to function.

II

ON EXTREME

UTILITARIANISM

Utilitarianism is a familiar position among philosophers in the British Isles and has lately been presented in perhaps its most extreme form by J. J. C. Smart.[1] Smart argues vigorously against those he regards as holding an inferior and illogical view of utilitarianism, namely, the restricted utilitarians. The advocates of restricted utilitarianism, Smart says, hold that certain rules of thumb, which are good rules for a great majority of cases, ought to be followed generally, even in those cases in which they do not produce the best result. This, Smart contends, is an untenable position. I should like to show, to the contrary, that no rational man can in practice exclusively follow the extreme utilitarian doctrine, that is, choose the most advantageous action in a set of circumstances regardless of rules to the contrary, any more than any society could tolerate the doctrine as the exclusive basis for social action. The arguments I employ may raise some questions about utilitarianism in any form, but I do not wish at this time to push the argument that far.

[1] J. C. C. Smart, "Extreme and Restricted Utilitarianism", *Philosophical Quarterly*, XXIX (October 1956), pp. 344-54.

Smart argues that restricted utilitarianism—in which the consequences of the rule for action determine the action to be taken in any circumstance—either collapses into extreme utilitarianism or produces an irrational result. He cites an example designed to prove this contention. Consider, he says, the case of a weather almanac that is right in 99 per cent of the cases. Smart admits that its predictions might serve as a good rule of thumb for sailors if it is too difficult or too costly to make individual calculations, but he denies the rationality of blind adherence to the rule. "We could well imagine", he says, "a race of sailors who acquired a superstitious reverence for their almanac, even though it was right in only 99 per cent of the cases, and who indignantly threw overboard any man who mentioned the possibility of a direct calculation.[2] But would this behavior of the sailors be rational?"

In the example he chooses, it is difficult to disagree with Smart, for his logic is irrefutable. Why follow a rule of thumb that would produce a bad result in a particular case if an easy and cheap calculation can establish a better course of action? However, I believe that there are cases in which the calculation of the consequences of individual acts is undesirable and, therefore, in which it is desirable to follow the rule despite the fact that the calculation might lead to a "better" decision in the individual instance. In such cases, it may indeed be desirable to "throw overboard" someone who suggests a "direct calculation". I do not deny that there is always some sense in which only the decision with the best consequences ought to be made but hope to show that this sense coincides with the extreme utilitarian standard in only a trivial way.

Direct calculation may be permissible in individual cases, provided that the costs of calculation are not too high, if specific instrumental relationships are involved; but such calculations are highly undesirable

[2]By a direct calculation, Smart would seem to mean something of the following. Suppose the almanac asserts that storms follow coronas around the moon. If one sailor has access to a barometer and it indicates no storm, then this would be the direct calculation that Smart advocates in opposition to following the rule of thumb given by the almanac. We can get a better example from another area of activity. Suppose we know that left-hand batters hit right-hand pitchers better than right-hand batters in games of baseball and that a manager must decide whether to substitute a left-hand pinch-hitter for a right-handed regular against a right-hand pitcher at a crucial moment. He would do better, according to Smart, to find out whether this particular right-hand batter hits better against right-hand pitchers than the potential pinch-hitter. In fact, many managers overlook this and do act—unwisely—on the basis of the rule. In cases like this, Smart is correct.

in social situations which are dependent upon diffuse[3] and non-specific attitudes on the parts of the role holders. In the example of the sailors and the almanac the only issue is that of getting the ship safely to port. In such a case the rational criteria are those of efficiency, and the sailors are or ought to be oriented toward each other in terms of strict achievement criteria which are the most appropriate criteria for achieving the task at hand, the *common* purpose for all of them. In such cases more efficient methods for achieving the same end are to be applauded and, if this involves a "direct calculation" rather than the application of a rule of thumb, so much the worse for the rule.

Where, however, there is no common purpose or where achievement criteria are not involved, Smart's calculus may not be the best. There are social circumstances in which the worth of an arrangement depends precisely upon the fact that criteria of efficiency are not applied and in which the role holders look to each other for diffuse, affective support, in short, for love rather than for efficiency. Consider the stability of a marriage if husband and wife coldly calculated each day whether it were possible to find a prettier or richer mate, or if each had to fear that the other would leave if the first became ill. Suppose one did become ill and the other suggested a discussion to calculate the possible course of the illness and whether he ought to get a divorce on the basis of a probability estimate of the various outcomes.

I am not trying to prejudice the case by using examples which, I admit, will stir the moral sensibility of the reader. I use these examples because they seem to me at least to indicate that certain relationships which are very important to human beings require attitudes that are diffuse and non-instrumental if they are to achieve their purpose.[4]

[3]A diffuse attitude is one not confined to particular role relationships. Thus family relationships are diffuse; we expect to be supported by our families in all our activities. Most business relationships, on the contrary, are specific. Thus workers in an assembly line have a right to expect support from each other in carrying out the specific task of manufacture but cannot normally expect support in unrelated activities. Thus, in some contexts, diffuse support is required; in others, specific support. In fact, diffuse support within the firm would interfere with the profit or production orientation and with economic survival. On the other hand, specific attitudes within the family would interfere with the maintenance of the family.

[4]It may even be, although I do not propose to pursue this point, that the concept of the self and of its identity may be shattered by a completely instrumental attitude. One may experience the world as an "alien" and "cold" place. Dissociation and mental disturbance may result if all human relationships are subordinated to manipulation for advantage.

If my arguments are admitted, it may be pointed out in rebuttal that they establish only the disadvantage of acting contrary to the general rule in the particular case and that therefore they still collapse into the extreme utilitarian position. There is a sense in which this argument is correct, but, to the extent that extreme utilitarianism insists upon the calculation of consequences in the individual cases, I think the argument fails to hold. Thus, I do not contend that the bonds of matrimony may never be broken rationally but merely that the consideration of a decision to break them can rationally occur only after the consequences of the marriage are clearly undesirable rather than every time an opportunity to change for the possible better offers itself. And I think even the admissible calculation applies only to the timing and specific object of the change rather than to the decision to change.

Calculation of advantage with respect to individual actions therefore may be inconsistent with the maintenance of relationships that are much more important than the advantage that could be gained from individual decisions contrary to the rule. The rules of the society often perform the function of stabilizing these relationships and thus are validated by their consequences. If such rules did not exist, the specific instrumental attitude toward individual actions might then become optimal, but this would be a generally less desirable situation.

I do not think desirable behavior could be achieved even in principle, let alone in fact, by Smart's rational calculators. Smart uses an example to claim the contrary. Let us imagine, he says, a community where each man has a garden but where there is a water shortage. If water is used by most men to water the lawn, there will not be enough water for drinking and cooking. Suppose further that each man can water his garden secretly from the others, but does not do so because of his desire for the good of the community. Now suppose that there is a sick old lady in the hospital who loves flowers. Will one of the householders—out of his beneficent desire for her happiness—water his garden to grow flowers for her? Smart says that he will not because by a *reductio ad absurdum* he sees that if everyone behaves this way (presumably each will have a little old lady he wants to aid), no one will have water. I shall use the simpler but traditional game theoretic example of the prisoners' dilemma to establish that Smart is logically mistaken and that his extreme utilitarian calculus will lead to the result he wishes to avoid.

Two prisoners are held in separate cells by the sheriff. They have committed a major crime but the sheriff lacks proof. He therefore tells each prisoner in turn: "If neither confesses, you both will be convicted of a misdemeanor and receive very light sentences; if both confess, both will receive very heavy sentences; if one confesses and the other does not, the one who confesses will be freed and the other will receive the heaviest possible sentence". Assume that each prisoner values the penalties he must pay inversely to their length, that he is indifferent to the fate of the other prisoner, and that he makes his decision in isolation. On Smart's reasoning, both prisoners should remain silent. Each will see that in this way each will receive a very light sentence whereas if each talks each will receive a heavy sentence. Since the prisoners are both rational men and will act the same way, both will necessarily decide that they must keep silent.

Unfortunately, the reasoning is defective. Let us consider the matter from the standpoint of prisoner A, who mentally constructs a matrix for the problem and considers his alternatives. If prisoner B confesses, A avoids the heaviest penalty by confessing also. If B does not confess, A gets off free by confessing and therefore must do so. Therefore A rationally must confess regardless of B's decision. Since the same reasoning holds for B, both rationally must confess and receive very heavy sentences, although obviously there is a preferable cooperative solution if there were only some way to reach it. I may point out as an aside that the strategic criterion here is that of dominance[5] which, in game theoretic analysis, is much stronger than the minimax principle of von Neumann.

The same dilemma occurs in the case of the lawns and water shortage. Watering is dominant over non-watering. That is, if someone else waters his lawn, it is better to water one's own lawn; and if no one else waters his lawn, it is still preferable to water one's own lawn. Since, however, the water may be used up, the sooner one waters his lawn the better. Even where each wishes the good of the community, if he also desires some private good or some good for some other private person (the sick lady), each will water the lawn if there are many individuals with lawns, for in this case no individual use will diminish appreciably the supply of water. But the use of water by all—as specified by the extreme utilitarian

[5]One strategy is said to be dominant over another when, for any strategy chosen by the opponent, it produces a better result. This is clearly a stronger criterion than minimax which merely guarantees a minimal expected outcome but does not preclude the possibility that, for certain strategies of an opponent, one might do better than the outcome given by the minimax criterion.

calculus—will do grave harm. Individual rationality, in Smart's sense, produces bad results for all. Only moral inhibitions or a desire to live by the rules will protect the community from this result.

This is not true where each desire the good of the community, the number of individuals and lawns is small, and each individual use of water, therefore, appreciably diminishes the supply. In this case so much harm may be done to the community by any individual use that this harm will outweigh considerations of private good, whether egoistic or beneficent. One is hard put, however, to explain beneficent motivation on extreme utilitarian grounds, and it is a commonplace observation that humans are not motivated entirely on beneficent grounds. In any event, even assuming community-oriented beneficence, if there is any element of egoism or private beneficent motivation, there will always be examples in which the cost to the community of any particular individual's acting contrary to the rule is outweighed by the private gain although the result to the community of all acting contrary to the rule— as they must according to the extreme utilitarian standard—will be undesirable and possibly disastrous.

On the basis of reasonable assumptions concerning the nature of social problems and human motivation in present-day society, the acceptance of extreme utilitarian principles would be likely to turn society into a Hobbesian war of all against all. Unless all can agree to observe some rules of behavior and to punish those who do not, this war probably cannot be moderated. Even where all agree to observe these rules, the situation would remain precarious until the rules were internalized and thereby modified the desires of individuals, that is, until individuals refused to break the rules even to secure their advantage in individual cases.

One may regard such a development as an implicit maximization over time and thereby hold that it is merely another example of the extreme utilitarian principle. But, if so, one is maximizing whatever he regards as good by accepting the consequences of the rule, which, according to Smart's explanation, is the restricted utilitarian position. I think there is a difference. One might well want to throw overboard someone who suggested calculating advantage in individual cases. One can follow the rule to advantage only if assured that others will not calculate the possible advantages of breaking the rule. For the most desirable standards to be observed, men must have confidence in each other's behavior.

If a norm is accepted conditionally (that is, only for those cases in which it is not advantageous to break it), it will not motivate any one at any time except in those cases where the rule coincides with the action that would be taken in the individual case in the absence of the rule. This coincidence does not occur in the prisoners' dilemma or the lawn watering.

Where it is known or suspected that the rule does not correspond to the action that would be best in the case of "direct calculation", or where it is thought that other individuals might believe they did not correspond even when they did, it will become more difficult for others to observe the rule. In a lawless community, lawless behavior may be the most appropriate response. Therefore, in order to avoid this kind of situation, it is desirable for some rules to be followed automatically by all without calculation and therefore without the attempt to do better than the rule allows in some particular cases. This permits all to do well in a way not possible in the absence of such rules. Rules of this kind may be reinforced by secondary gains, that is, by the approval gained as a reward for being good and offered either by the community or by that internalized watchman, the conscience. Conscience permits the individual to live in a better society than would be possible otherwise.

The extreme utilitarian calculus would undercut the establishment of such desirable norms and therefore is to be condemned. It is hardly legitimate to save the principle by turning the rule or norm itself into something desirable, for, on extreme utilitarian standards, the rule is only a rule of thumb and not to be followed unless it produces the best results. But clearly, in many individual cases, provided only secrecy can be maintained, better results will be achieved by breaking the rule.

I recognize that Smart wants to talk about the beneficent calculators rather than egoistic ones. But it seems to me that this is merely another form of following a rule or moral standard of decency and thus begs the question. If we build into the desires of men the desire for the good of society, we automatically exclude many problems. I would not deny that if each marriage partner valued the happiness of the other more than his own, the calculation of advantage for the other would not upset the marriage, although in real marriages it might produce a cloying stickiness that would undermine the marriage. If, in the prisoner's dilemma, each prisoner values the other's freedom more than his own, clearly neither will talk. In the lawn watering if each prefers to have his neighbor use the water, none will use it. This may still not be maximal, for it would be less satisfactory than if someone used it but undoubtedly would be better than if everyone used it.

However, the moment even a small egoistic element, or even some element of private beneficence, is built into the problem in addition to the desire for society's gain—except in that case in which the individual use of water would exhaust or have a marked effect upon the supply—it generally becomes rational for each to use the small amount for the reasons of strategy dominance cited in the prisoners' dilemma. In any real society the egoistic element will be strong enough to establish, in my opinion, the undesirability of living in a community where all behave according to the extreme utilitarian position. It is a rare situation in which the individual's breaking of the rule has sufficient influence upon the total action of the society to outweigh the value of his dereliction. But, since this is true for all, the individual can live in a desirable society only if some rules are regarded by all as moral imperatives.

The extreme utilitarian may agree that he favors rules for society but not for himself; he may attempt to rise above the ordinary life of the community. In this case he must hope that others do not copy his behavior for, if they did, he would get the same undesirable result as the prisoners in the prisoners' dilemma. Therefore even the extreme utilitarian would have to favor social rules which penalize violators, and training, at least for others, which in the form of conscience provides an internal check upon action. But one can hardly isolate himself from his society's form of training. Smart may then rejoin that, if both sanctions are operative, extreme utilitarianism prescribes following the rule. I do not doubt this, but he then would save the doctrine by giving up the game. One may call this society's revenge on the extreme utilitarian who now so values the rule that he does not desire to break it or who has established so many social constraints that it now costs too much to break it. It is, therefore, practically impossible to be an extreme utilitarian.

Unlike, in Aristotle's terms, beasts or gods, men are socially oriented with respect to many relationships, and participants in these relationships will find it a disadvantage to have a calculating turn of mind. It is better for the husband to refuse to cheat on his wife because of consideration of long-run satisfaction than because of the fear of discovery. But I suggest that it is even better to be spontaneous and not to have such thoughts in the first place. In short, even restricted utilitarianism may be a better standard for the philosopher evaluating different societies and their rules than for the active man in his life.

If so, perhaps it is better to discuss utilitarianism (except in those cases where criteria of efficiency are the relevant criteria) as an evaluative yardstick for the observer trying to determine which moral rules are best for society rather than as a doctrine for real men. And then perhaps we can regard restricted utilitarianism as stating that in cases in which diffuse affective relationships are involved and in cases in which long-run maximization is desirable, rules of action are preferable to decisions based upon the specific conditions of individual cases. In other circumstances the appropriate criteria may be those of efficiency. Perhaps therefore it is better to refuse to regard either utilitarian standard as a dogma but to examine the conditions of life in which each is appropriate either as a guide for action or as a standard for evaluating actions.

I 2

RESTRICTED UTILITARIANISM

I wish to reply to Mr. J. C. C. Smart's cogent reply to my earlier discussion in *Ethics* concerning extreme and restricted utilitarianism. I wish to confine my remarks to a discussion of the prisoners' dilemma and the garden-watering examples, for these, I feel, are at the crux of the apparent remaining disagreement between Mr. Smart and myself, and a discussion may reveal whether this disagreement is fundamental or whether it can be resolved.

I have no disagreement with Smart's remark that, if the prisoners value each other's freedom, the matrix is changed and the strategy dominance that produced the dilemma is no longer present. This same point was made in my earlier discussion when I pointed out that the dilemma would not occur in the garden-watering example—where egoism did not function—except when there was an extremely large number of gardens and when individual watering had little effect upon the overall supply. The prisoners' dilemma was used merely to show what happens when dominance is present.

Even assuming Smart's universalism, however, the garden-watering example produces exactly the same result in large communities as egoism does in the prisoners' dilemma. The reasoning is clear. As the effect of the individual watering on the total supply of water approaches zero, the consequences for the community of each decision to water the lawn wash out in the matrix, and the individual need consider only the consequences to those affected by his individual decision whether to water the lawn or not, that is, to himself and the little old lady. As a result, the decision to water becomes dominant even though we have assumed Smart's universalism. At some point, however, as we increase the visible or clear effects of the individual decision upon the total supply, there is a growing divergence between the matrix where we assume egoism and where we assume Smart's universalism. As this occurs, dominance disappears and at some point—not necessarily exactly the point at which dominance disappears—the socially desirable decision is made.

Smart, however, does not wish to permit the same choice as in the dilemma, even in the extreme case where the effect of the individual watering upon the group supply approaches zero, for the consequence will be (where many individuals are involved) that everyone reasons this way, and so the total supply is dissipated. He therefore assumes symmetry of behavior, which gives rise to his mixed strategies and the avoidance of the dilemma. He admits that this involves a retreat from extreme utilitarianism. With this retreat I have no quarrel, although I would interpret the retreat as a broader one than Smart seems willing to admit.

The symmetry cannot be merely a consequence of the individual decision, even if all are universalists. If this were the case—that is, if the odds mixture I set regulated the odds mixture others set—Smart would be correct in reasoning that all would choose that odds mixture best for the community. But no individual has any warrant to believe that his decision will influence in any way the decision of any other individual. And we are back at the dilemma; for even a universalist, that is, a person who believes that what is good for others is as important as what is good for him, will still choose a dominant strategy. There will be symmetry, but it will be a symmetry in which each chooses the dominant strategy and produces the worst result. As long as the effect of the individual decision upon the total supply approaches zero, symmetry will not avoid the result identified with the prisoners' dilemma.

We can avoid the dilemma in one of only two ways. We can inculcate not watering the lawn in times of scarcity as a moral rule, in which case the penalty involved in breaking the rule will outweigh the gain from watering. Or we can assume a community in which all inculcate as a moral rule the injunction to choose that strategy which, if adopted by all members of the community, would optimize the total utility of the outcome under Smart's assumption of unversalism. This need not be interpreted in a Kantian sense, for the rule can be adapted to circumstances. And it is different from a system in which specific rules are inculcated. It will also avoid the dilemma. But it is a variation—at least so it would seem to me—of restricted utilitarianism.

If we adopt the latter type of rule as a moral rule, we can avoid the prisoners' dilemma—at least in any example I have explored. As noted earlier, the rule is not absolutely necessary in all cases: Smart's universalism would suffice in a two-person dilemma. Even so, there may not be a simple cut-off point where one applies the rule or simply uses universalism to produce the result. I expect that, as we increase the consequence for the community of the individual decision, the mixed strategies might be different for a large range of cases depending upon whether we merely assume universalism—that is, upon whether we merely assume that what happens to others is equally important with what happens to us—or whether we also value the rule which instructs us to do that which, if done by all (or by most), would produce the best result.

I will not pursue the point of whether there still ought to be inculcated, by training, specific rules, for it seems to me that here Smart and I agree on principle although we may differ on application. But I should like to stress that in my opinion he can sustain his general position only by some variation of the explanation I have just employed and that this involves more of a divergence from extreme utilitarianism than he seems to have stated. It may be, however, that this rejoinder will clarify the situation and that we are not so far apart after all.

13

A NIGHTMARE

In the scenario that follows the term "nightmare" carries several implications. The scenario is a nightmare in that it does sound like the product of a bad dream. However, if we extrapolate certain tendencies in society, as they could be reinforced by technological developments, the world that emerges would be a nightmare judged by the values that humane and sensitive individuals presently hold.

We do not argue that the scenario that follows is likely or even plausible. On the other hand, it requires a kind of blindness not to recognize that the seeds for this nightmare, bizarre though it is, lie in the present and that the arguments for many of the individual steps that might bring it to pass are not in themselves reprehensible. These steps could in some cases even be considered to represent praiseworthy motives. To recognize the less desirable potentialities of the present is a necessary, although not a sufficient, condition for avoiding them.

Much of what we have to say in this scenario is not original. Aldous Huxley in *Brave New World* and George Orwell in *1984*, as well as many other novelists, created anti-utopias in which omnipresent social controls changed radically the nature of man and of society. The anti-utopias usually have been regarded as merely imaginative extrapolations that were technologically infeasible. Unfortunately, a few short years later, as we now write, it is less difficult to extrapolate from existing progress in the sciences to the technological developments necessary to produce these anti-utopias. Huxley's Alphas and Betas would still seem scientific marvels; yet recent advances in genetics, with specific reference to the unravelling of the DNA code, show them to be within the range of possibility. Many of the scientific developments of the future could be even more consequential than nuclear fission, less controllable by current techniques, and more inconsistent with existing social institutions and cultural values.

Many of the demands for increased social controls will stem from the vulnerabilities of modern complex societies. Although modern complex society has both greater instantaneous and long-range flexibility than simpler societies, it also has less redundancy and more bottlenecks that could affect the whole society. Thus major interruptions that overwhelm its instantaneous or short-run adjustment capability, or occur too suddenly for its long-range flexibility to get a chance to work, might cause great damage to the society. Because simple societies are less interdependent than modern complex societies, their breakdowns are often much less total in their effects. The modern industrial society is highly differentiated and therefore requires greater integration in order to function effectively. The disrupted complex society, under at least some important conditions, might not be able to sustain even the low level of productivity that is normal to a simple society.

The greater wealth and improved technology of modern society provide us with many important advantages and freedoms. Diversity of life style, despite mass production and mass man, is possible today in a way that in the past was available only for a few of the élite or of the wealthy, if for any at all. The great diversity of modern society, however, requires a geometric increase in the organization of modern life. We become increasingly sensitive to the disturbances produced by others. And this sensitivity in turn requires greater and greater social control in order to maintain the peace and stability of the system. One need not assume the triumph of the police mentality, or the intrusion of motivations denigrative of human dignity, to foresee that many restrictions on human liberty will have valid and attractive rationales, even rationales related to the liberty of one's fellows. Federal safety regulations for automobile manufacturers and tests for drivers increase the "freedom" of the license-holding driver to drive in safety. Coercive treatment for the mentally ill raises the probability that they will be able to lead freely constructive lives. Plastic hearts might replace real ones and damaged brains might be linked to computers. Therapeutic abortions, through the death of the foetus, increase the freedom of the mother. And the biological adaptation of man to his ecological niche in an extremely complicated and over-populated society will increase his freedom to live a satisfying and useful life.

We have, of course, omitted the crucial qualification: under the new developing conditions. It is still possible that the terminus of the process will be inconsistent with anything we would regard as freedom or dignity or even human. The evolution of society might produce the devolution of man. The adaptability (and superiority) of man have heretofore consisted in his lack of specialized adaptation (unlike the lesser animals). In the not-too-distant future, man might be adapted in a specialized sense, while society through the control of genetic science maintains its general adaptability by fitting men to the various tasks that time and environment provide. The survival of the fittest may be replaced by the fitting of the survivals.

The nightmare is bizarre, but consider a few of the factors that could facilitate and seem to justify a controlled society, or a few that could make it feasible, although the two categories are neither necessarily nor entirely distinct. Overpopulation and organizational complexity have already been mentioned. The greater susceptibility of society in general to disruption could create opportunities for deliberate intra-societal attacks accompanied by blackmail, to say nothing of organized crime on a novel scale. When nuclear weapons become subject to criminal access (miniaturization will help to bring this about), and when criminal or political conspiracies become capable of bringing civil government to a halt through the disruption of the computerized networks upon which it will depend, the only alternative to a new feudalism (without the mitigating social features of the old) might be forms of surveillance and control far surpassing any now in existence.

Access to places of amusement and museums might have to be rationed, food substitutes developed, access to new forms of socialized housing (mile-high community units) regulated, scarce medical facilities (replacement organs, esoteric remedies, very skilled surgeons, and so forth) allocated. Some humans might have to be adjusted to environments different from the earth's surface.

Clearly it would be erroneous to compare man to the lemming, but every known animal species on which the experiment has been carried out is dysfunctionally disorganized by overcrowding. Rules governing mutual adjustment (whether social or legal) will necessarily be very stringent. There will be a strong emphasis on adjustment (other-directed orientations) in place of individualism. Resort to drugs, other worldly religions, delinquency, crime, and mental disease (as a way of "acting out") could increase significantly, requiring medical, social, and criminal sanctions to prevent or to contain those forms of disturbance that are excessively dysfunctional for the social and political systems.

The consequences of dislocations and of mistakes in the production, distribution, and control functions of business and government are likely to be so huge that the facilities for coping with them must take precedence over civil liberties or private pursuits and property. The blackout of the eastern United States in 1965 only suggests what can go wrong in the future. (That particular disturbance need not have occurred with proper systems design, including cutoffs and redundancy, with their concomitant costs—but that is the problem. On the one hand, there could be extremely sophisticated and prudent systems designs or, on the other hand, there could be extensive control and supervision to avoid the possibility or consequences of relatively farfetched disasters.) Needs for control and surveillance will likely develop to utilize the technological capabilities that are present in the system. Technological developments, in addition to meeting environmental requirements, will likely produce needs to satisfy the technological capabilities.

It is already possible to monitor conversations by the disturbances they produce on window panes and to photograph documents through windows at great distances. Television monitors both indoors and out might become common as the techniques become cheaper. Voices and faces might be checked immediately by advanced computers working through nationwide banks of identifiers. Quite apart from credit needs, the means to maintain continuous checks on the entire population and automatically to scan them for disturbing words or phrases will likely be available by the year 2000. It might occur that only those with enormous resources will be able—and in even these cases only partly and perhaps only by bribery or by political manipulation—to avoid some monitoring or to interfere with transmission of the data. At the minimum, if the monitoring exists, new code languages will develop in efforts to evade some of the consequences.

There are cases today of individuals who are kept biologically alive, in an attempt to avoid testamentary consequences, by bizarre and uncomfortable medical techniques long past the point at which the physician, the individual, or the family would otherwise prefer a natural death. As facilities for replacing human parts increase, including artificial stimulation or substitution for certain brain functions, court cases will almost inevitably arise over the issue of when a man ceases to be himself. (Consider the case of a man who has had most of his intellectual capabilities replaced by a computer or even by a transplanted brain.) Ultimate resort to these techniques would come under government regulation. If overpopulation and means for increasing longevity increase to some as yet unspecified limit, the right to bear children and to resort to longevity techniques could be controlled by the government. How these issues, which are so politically potent, could be handled presents a challenge to the imagination. If such issues arise, and they well might, then the consequences for what we now regard as civilized human standards are obviously enormous.

It is not unlikely that there will become available by the year 2000 drugs and other behavior controls capable of producing personality changes at will, of rewarding activities by hormonal flows (perhaps by remote control) that overcome rational ego or superego objections to continuation of the activities, and of punishing other activities. Alternative techniques include radio waves, ultrasonic impulses that cause uneasiness, induced hallucinations, and various forms of educative devices operating from infancy. These might be so effective that continuous control techniques would be superfluous, although available for obdurate cases. Much of this might be available or imposed under the rubric of mental hygiene, simply because such intrusions on individual freedom are not likely to occur except for highly persuasive reasons.

It is not difficult for an American to understand that a dictatorship—even a benevolent one—would use such techniques. The Soviet Union already has sent some of its important literary figures to mental institutions; it is well to remember that the United States sent Ezra Pound to such an institution, although it did so as an act of kindness. It is difficult to accept that such techniques would be used widely in the United States until we recall the extent to which they are already legitimized. Hundreds

of psychiatrists were apparently willing in 1964 to lend their names to
the conclusion that Barry Goldwater was mentally unsound although
they had not examined him. Our culture is attuned to the concept of
mental illness and its cure: the modern concept is to rehabilitate rather
than to punish criminals because of the belief that crime results from
mental illness. Delinquents are guided by social workers. Disturbed
schoolchildren are treated by guidance counselors. Parents read psychologists to learn how to raise their children. The rhetoric of our time—
and most of it is quite genuine and functional—is the rhetoric of mental
adjustment and treatment. Our national pastime is self-medication with
tranquilizers and with other drugs that affect the psychological condition
of the individual. Rather than doubting that Americans would use the
most advanced techniques that become available and as systematically as
possible, there is reason to doubt that there would be much effective
resistance. We do not need the rationale of a political ideology to justify
control of the masses. We have our own myth of adjustment and of
mental balance; anti-social behavior, as interpreted by the received truth
of the day, is sufficient to indicate the desirability of treatment. Even
some of the New Left—self-proclaimed rebels against societal conformity—have advocated (perhaps seriously, perhaps not) placing LSD into
dormitory food to free the mass of students from their "false"—hence
also "sick"—beliefs. Even those of us who criticize this abuse of terminology often think of some of the New Left or of other social rebels as
"merely sick".

As anti-social behavior becomes less tolerable as a result of the increasing complexity and crowding of society, are we not likely to treat
what we cannot tolerate? No doubt if we were ever presented with this
kind of future as a direct and systematic alternative to the present, we
would not opt for it. But we are not presented with choices in this
fashion. Each adaptation that helps partly to produce the future is considered on the basis of incremental costs and benefits, of marginal
changes; it is possible that each incremental change or marginal benefit
might seem to outweigh the costs, that the benefits will be clear and the
transition to the nightmarish future hypothetical.

So far the nightmare is one that could conceivably be produced by the
year 2000 or shortly thereafter. The ethical problems that could be
caused when we learn to produce man or variations of man in the laboratory are unlikely to occur until well after the year 2000. Laboratory men

who are indistinguishable from ordinary men, we hope, would be granted the rights of natural men. Specialized laboratory-created beings that differ from natural men, but that do possess the ability to reason, are more likely not to be granted full rights (a decision we would regard today as ethically monstrous). If they are not granted human rights, questions might then be raised about the rights of adapted and specialized men who are indistinguishable from manufactured adapted and specialized men. In any event, the scope and variety of restrictions upon full natural men will be enormously increased.

Further problems would arise if bionic computers are made that perform many of the tasks of men and develop creative capabilities. As the distinction between man and lesser creatures and machines begins to shade off, the uniqueness of man and the rights attributed to this uniqueness may begin to attenuate. The vulnerability of the political system to shocks and to disruptions could reinforce arguments for the restriction of man based upon the substitutability of manufactured men and bionic machines. A creature that is superfluous as well as dangerous might appear difficult to defend. If the esthetic function of man also degenerates, then the argument that man is an unique cultural being will also have attenuated. Bionic computers, for example, might be able to produce real art. Even now, some popular music (and even some classical records) are produced as much by equipment and by mechanical interventions in the performance as by "natural" performances with "normal" instruments. More than this, creative bionic computers might produce music that is genuinely more creative than some of the current musical fashions, for instance, aleatory music.

If athletes begin to make use of prosthetic devices as well as of drugs to improve their performances, we might gradually produce almost entirely mechanical athletes, for whom bionic robots might eventually substitute. As this process continues, man's confidence in himself and in his role might be seriously undercut. His vision of himself as an unique being, so essential apparently to his sense of identity, might be destroyed.

A variety of strange religions would spring up in efforts to explain this peculiar universe. Such religions might attempt to glorify man in ways that repudiate the rational and scientific interpretations that have flourished since the Renaissance; or they might be masochistic and denigrative of man. More likely both types would flourish under the suggested conditions.

Perhaps many (most?) men would be kept in a permanently drugged state (pacified?) and adapted to the ecology to which they are assigned according to some computerized calculation. The central government would so likely be swamped by the problem of keeping the system functioning properly that it would be concerned only with marginal and immediate problems rather than with the increasing repulsiveness of the entire system. In any event there might be no rational or moral (whatever these terms may mean in such a bizarre twenty-first century) feasible solution that does not reject modern technology or condemn billions of surplus humans to death or to deprivation. The twenty-first century would no more be able to return to the world of the twentieth century than we could return to the golden age of Greece.

Efforts to control the situation would doubtless occur—perhaps as desperate measures. For instance, the political and intellectual élite might distribute contraceptive drugs through the food supply that could be counteracted only by other drugs restricted to the élite. The rationalization could be persuasive: with bionic automation, production would not be disrupted and population might drop to tenable limits that permit humane standards.

Yet the cure might be more brutalizing than the problem. In any event, this "cure" assumes that a technocracy, or oligarchy, or "aristocracy" controls the political system. As technological innovations are made and biological manufacture and reproduction intensify, the legitimacy that invests political democracy might deteriorate; the political bases from which these encroachments can be resisted might be undermined. If at the same time the system becomes so complex that it can be worked only from the vantage point of the memory banks of a centralized national or worldwide computer system, political and military capabilities would in fact be concentrated in one (if not monolithic, at least centralized) control center. Particularly if creative bionic computers and man-computer feedback circuits are involved in the central apparatus, control may pass from man to machines, in which case, although population might be limited since it serves no useful function, humanity might be kept in a perpetually drugged and/or subservient state, to the extent to which it is permitted to persist. This would prevent rebellion and disturbance or other "undesirable" interferences with the maintenance of the system. By determining what information to feed back to the computer-linked controllers and by manipulating the logic of the problem, the computers might gradually gain control of the entire system. This might result not from some analogous organic urge to control or even to destroy, although the possibility that this complex might enter a condition equivalent to madness can hardly be dismissed, but from an effort to reinforce stasis; the bionic central computers are likely to view humans as defective both emotionally and logically.

Because of the enormous importance of the national computer networks for planning and control, they might become the focus of politics, conspiracy, and intra-élite coups in the event they do not secure the kind of control adumbrated above. Quite possibly efforts by political groups to seize control of the central computers might themselves disrupt the computer functions at least temporarily and produce crises or disturbances that affect the operations of and prognosis for the system. Advance weapons systems that operate on a computerized basis would make consensus among the population and support within the armed forces almost irrelevant. Some types of weapons could be individualized and could, in effect, "home in" on voice and sight patterns of particular individuals identified from the national population register as enemies. Others would be used against large groupings but would themselves not require any human agency other than the programming of the computer. These weapons would use advanced surveillance techniques to find and to destroy their targets or alternatively to incapacitate them. Again, the patterns they would home in on, whether group or individual, would be transmitted from a central registry. Pickup of prisoners would be automated.

The nightmare we have sketched is bizarre, implausible, inhumane, and evil. But it is not impossible. Incremental decisions could lead us from the present to such a nightmarish future. Even if this future were regarded as unlikely and improbable, it is worth considerable thought to reduce that likelihood and plausbility still more. Many unlikely and implausible things have occurred in the past. The nightmare we have sketched would undoubtedly place us beyond redemption.

PART V

On Empirical Systems Research

This section on empirical applications of systems theory, contains most of my article on international systems theory from *The New Approaches to International Relations*. Included within it, as the section between the ellipsis dots on pages 222 and 233, is an excerpt from an article first printed under the title "Some Problems in International Systems Research" in *International Political Communities*.

14

THE SYSTEMS APPROACH

TO INTERNATIONAL

POLITICS

International systems models are macromodels of international politics. They are not models of the foreign policy process or, although the Italian city state and Chinese warlord studies show that the macromodels of international systems theory can be applied to some regional and intranational systems, models of regional or intranational systems or of relationships between regional and international systems. The type of model that will prove useful depends on one's research aim, that is, on one's subject matter and on the question that one is asking. To expect that the loose bipolar model would explain behavior within the African subsystem when it is designed to explain the overarching system of international politics would be equivalent to expecting a model of monopolistic competition to explain the economics of the garment trade on the East coast of the United States. Yet the monopolistic model might (or might not, depending upon the facts of the case) be a relevant model for exploring the economy of the United States. If we confuse different aims, different structural levels of analysis, different levels of complexity, different levels of abstraction, different degrees of concreteness or descriptivity, and the differences between the theoretical and the descriptive, we will hopelessly muddle our efforts to advance the state of the discipline.

Systems models are merely tools for investigating reality. In the words of *System and Process*, "these systems are hypothetical only".[1] Indeed one might emphasize that the models developed in *System and Process* were quite crude; they were based at best on plausible reasoning. For instance, the injunction to increase capabilities in the essential rules of some systems did not specify by how much or under what risk conditions. Similar ambiguities necessarily occur elsewhere in the general statements of the models. For instance, using words it is virtually impossible to discriminate between the behavior of a system of nine nations and a system of seven.

Only when we were able to play out realizations of the "balance of power" model on a computer were we able specifically to link outcomes to the parameters that produce them. The theory itself is not mathematicized and it is not clear that this is possible. A realization of a model or theory involves building some features of the theory into the computer program as parameters of that program. These parameters can then be varied to explore the sensitivity of the computer program to changes in the parameters. Thus it is possible to explore changes in the number of players, the battle exchange ratios, the motivations of the players, and so forth. If the outcome is unstable, we can ask how to reintroduce stability, and by what changes in the parameters. We also must ask ourselves what relation each change has to the initial verbal model and why it helps shed light on that model; for the objective of this work is not merely to produce a stable computer realization. Computer analysis is used not to prove any specific propositions but to explore the interrelationships of propositions concerning the strategic structure of the model of the international system. For instance, consider the proposition: Would a "balance of power" system operate differently were the

[1] *System and Process in International Politics*, New York: John Wiley, 1957, p. 2.

actors security-oriented or hegemony-oriented? To explore this, we constructed a pilot computer model instructing national actors of the international system to optimize over each war cycle according to the appropriate utility schedule designed for them. We discovered that if there was a hegemony-inclined actor in the system, the system became unstable. Initially, a "balance-oriented" actor was the victim of this instability. Pursued to the end, however, it became clear that according to the logic of the model the hegemony-inclined actor would never succeed in becoming the greatest actor in the system and would eventually be eliminated by the remaining "balance-oriented" player. Thus there was an inconsistency between short-run optimization and long-run optimization for the hegemony-inclined actor. Consequently, for the pilot model, if hegemony-inclined actors could optimize over the long run, they would behave exactly the same way that more conservative security-oriented players do. This, however, is not a conclusion about the real world but about the logic of the model. Therefore the next step was to explore the conditions under which the hegemony-inclined actor could succeed in obtaining hegemony. Introducing imperfect information, uncertainty, and nonsimultaneous commitment to war is believed to permit success for the hegemony-inclined actor. On the other hand, there is no reason to assume that this result is a truth about the real international system; for we can explore those further counter-deviancy measures that would be sufficient to prevent the hegemony-inclined actor from exploiting his deviant tendencies.

The general literature asserts that in a system of five states wars will tend to be three against two and that wars of four against one will tend to destabilize the system. In our initial pilot runs the wars were almost invariably four against one; yet some of our runs remained stable for hundreds of war cycles with no indication that continuation of the runs would produce instability. We then had the problem of modifying our model to produce the three-to-two wars that are more characteristic of history. There are probably at least two ways to accomplish this: by reducing the cost of wars or by permitting side payments within coalitions. We intend to try still other modifications to see how they affect this factor of alignment size.

The two examples given should illustrate how systems theory utilizes computers. The computer is used to explore the relationships between assumptions. It is thus capable of assigning outcomes to causes, at least with respect to the structure of thought we have established to account for the real world of international politics. Thus, if we attempt to make inferences concerning the real world of international politics, we at least know how and why our hypotheses are related to our premises. We also have grounds for asserting that the real world outcome may be related to the assigned cause if in exploring the external world we find those conditions that produced the same outcome in the computer model and no other conditions (at least that we can think of) that would counteract this outcome were we to place these conditions in the computer model.

A second problem that we faced, which we are now systematically but slowly trying to overcome, was the paucity of historical information about international systems and their behavior. To overcome this deficiency, *Systems and Process* recommended, among other methods, a series of case studies based on the hypotheses flowing from the models.[2] Although historical scholarship may have successfully answered many questions of interest to historians, the questions a political scientist should pose to these data were largely unexplored in the literature. We did not know the characteristic behavior of the Greek city-state system, for instance, nor how it differed from behavior in the Italian city-state system. Nor did we have any good ideas as to why the differences occurred. We did not understand how the patterns of alignment differed or why they differed. We did not know how or under what conditions wars were waged or peace made. It was indeed difficult even to ask questions such as these, for they flow more naturally from the kinds of models employed in international systems theory than from the case-specific questions historians ask or even those political scientists ordinarily ask. A series of relevant cases is being studied in accordance with the original recommendations.

NATURE OF THE MODELS

The models employed in *System and Process* utilize five sets of variables: the essential rules, the transformation rules, the actor classificatory variables, the capability variables, and the information variables.

The essential rules of the systems state the behavior necessary to maintain equilibrium in the system—thus they are essential. The trans-

[2]*Ibid.*, p. xvi.

formation rules state the changes that occur in the system as inputs across the boundary of the system that differ from those required for equilibrium move the system either toward instability or toward the stability of a new system. This is necessarily one of the least developed aspects of the model; fully developed, however, it would provide models of dynamic change.

The actor classificatory variables specify the structural characteristics of actors. These characteristics modify behavior. For instance, "nation state", "alliance", and "international organization" name actors whose behaviors differ as a consequence of structural characteristics. The capability and information variables require no comment here.

There are three kinds of equilibrium in such systems. There is an equilibrium within the set of essential rules. If behavior occurs that is habitually inconsistent with one of the essential rules, one or more of the other essential rules also will be changed. If the set of essential rules is changed, then changes will occur in at least one of the other variables of the system. Or, conversely, if changes occur in one of the other variables of the system, then changes will occur in the essential rules also. If changes occur at the parameter of the system, changes will also occur within the system, and *vice versa*.

The models are not equilibrium models in the Parsonian sense, however. They are ultrastable, or even multistable, in Ashby's sense. Thus they are not static but respond to change, when it is within specified limits, by maintaining or restoring system equilibrium. Equilibrium does not have an explanatory function within such systems. Rather it is the equilibrium that is to be explained; and the model itself constitutes the explanation by indicating the mechanisms that restore or maintain equilibrium. The actors do not behave consonantly with the essential rules merely to maintain equilibrium but because they are motivated under the specified system conditions to do so.

Such models necessarily abstract from a far richer historical context. The theories therefore can be used for the derivation of consequences *only* under explicitly stated boundary or parameter conditions. For instance, the statements concerning alignment patterns of the "balance of power" model in *System and Process* apply only at the level of type of alignment, and do not specify the actual actors who participate in specific alignments. And they specify even this broad consequence only for stated values of the exogenous and endogenous variables. The first attempt to bring the models closer to the richness of history occurs in Chapter 3. In this chapter the models are varied for specified differences in the internal political and regulatory structure of nation states (these latter could theoretically be derived from comparative macromodels of national systems). The motivations of nation states, as dealt with in this chapter, may differ from the initial first-order approximations, as stated in Chapter 2. Thus, as we come closer to reality—and this is still at a high level of abstraction—we lose generality. We begin to employ procedures closer to the step-by-step engineering applications of physical theory than to the generalized theoretical statements of physical theory.

Even these gross characteristics of national actors are far removed from their historical complexity.

Any attempt to describe the actual actor systems would founder under the weight of the parameters which individualize these systems—even when their structural characteristics are similar. Such things as capability factors, logistic factors, and information, including history of the past, are specific to the system. . . .[3]

When we include the important factors that, from the standpoint of theory, are contingent, such as personality factors,[4] economic and political conditions, technological developments and inventions, and other intranational and transnational factors, the complexity becomes so great that serious efforts systematically to discuss them all and relate them all to models would become lost in the detail. If we want to apply the macromodels to concrete cases, i.e., to historical microevents, we must choose just those factors and just those values that we have some reason to believe operate in the particular instance we wish to understand and to explain. The chapters in *System and Process* on integration and disintegration, on values, and on strategy also attempt to bring to bear on the analysis in a highly generalized way some additional factors required to engineer the models closer to specific reality, i.e., closer to the microevent level.

Brief descriptions of the "balance of power" and loose bipolar models will be presented below both to illustrate more completely the nature of the models and to provide an introduction for the empirical systems

[3]*Ibid.*, p. 54.

[4]An effort is made in Chapter 6 of *System and Process* to relate such factors to the models in a generalized sense.

presented in this volume: the Italian city-state system by Franke and the Chinese warlord system by Chi.

"BALANCE OF POWER" MODEL

The "balance of power" model has the following characteristics:

1. The only actors in it are nation states and thus there is no role differentiation in the model. This is a somewhat counterfactual assumption, for during portions of the historical "balance of power" period there were other organizational forms, such as the Danube Authority and the League of Nations.

2. The goals of the major nations of the system are oriented toward the optimization of security. By this we mean that major nations will prefer a high probability for survival as major nations, even though this excludes the possibility of hegemony, to a moderate probability for hegemony combined with a moderate probability for elimination as a major actor. Most analysts would argue that Napoleon and Hitler did not operate according to this assumption. It is possible, although far from obvious, that the model would function differently were the assumption relaxed. There is sufficient factual validity to the assumption for large and interesting periods of history, however, that more than justifies its use as a first approximation.

3. The weaponry in the system is not nuclear.

4. There are stochastic and unpredictable increases in productivity that, unless compensated for, in time, might destabilize the system. Therefore each actor seeks a margin of security above its proportionate share of the capabilities of the system.

5. There must be at least five major nations in the system. A two-nation system would be unstable. If either of the two nations gained a clear margin of superiority, it would be tempted to eliminate the other in order to guarantee that the other would not eliminate it, if through some combination of circumstances the ratio of capabilities were reversed. In a three-nation system, were there a war of two nations against one, the victorious coalition would have some incentive to limit its demands upon the defeated nation. To eliminate the defeated nation would throw the victors into an unstable two-nation system. Under the assumptions, this result would be undesirable, un-

less one nation could gain such advantage from the elimination of the third that it could eliminate the second nation. But this result would also give the second nation an incentive to combine with the third against the first unless it misunderstood its own interests. On the other hand, if the first nation refrains from sacrificing the third nation, the latter may some day combine against it with the second nation in a subsequent war. And if one of the victorious nations in this subsequent war sees some advantage in eliminating the first nation, it is dependent upon the ability of the only remaining nation to recognize that its own interests require it to oppose this. The reasoning here is inconclusive; therefore three is not a highly plausible lower bound for stability. If there are at least five nations, however, it seems plausible that the argument for limitation in war would hold.

6. Each state, even though of great-nation status, is likely to require allies to obtain its objectives. Thus it desires to maintain the existence of potential future alliance partners.

The characteristics specified give rise to the following essential rules of conduct:

(1) Act to increase capabilities but negotiate rather than fight.

(2) Fight rather than pass up an opportunity to increase capabilities.

(3) Stop fighting rather than eliminate an essential national actor.

(4) Act to oppose any coalition or single actor that tends to assume a position of predominance with respect to the rest of the system.

(5) Act to constrain actors who subscribe to supranational organizing principles.

(6) Permit defeated or constrained essential national actors to re-enter the system as acceptable role partners or act to bring some previously inessential actor within the essential actor classification. Treat all essential actors as acceptable role partners.

The first two rules follow from the need for a margin of security in a world in which capabilities change stochastically. The third rule is essential to maintain the availability of future coalition partners. The fourth and fifth rules recognize that deviant actors may destabilize the system by their actions or by the actions of their followers or cohorts within other nations. The sixth rule is also related to the need for potential alliance partners and warns against restricting one's own choices unnecessarily.

These rules are not descriptive rules. They are prescriptive rules. That is, under the governing assumptions, states would follow these rules in order to optimize their own security. Thus there is motivation to observe the rules, abstracting from other considerations, but no requirement to do so. Under the appropriate boundary conditions, however, states would follow the rules and the model would be both predictive and descriptive.

If the major nations follow the specified rules under the specified system conditions, some of the consequences are obvious and others are not so obvious. Alliances will tend to be specific, of short duration, and to shift according to advantage rather than according to ideologies (even within war). In wars nations will tend to have limited objectives and to observe the rules of war and the doctrine of nonintervention.

Alliances will tend to be of short duration because permanent alliances would undermine the "balancing" characteristics necessary for the security of the member states. Thus alliances will have specific objectives as determined by short-term interests. And to use terms current in the eighteenth and nineteenth centuries, nations will be disposed to act in terms of interest rather than in terms of sentiment. In short, there is in this system a general, although not necessarily implacable, identity between short-term and long-term interests.

The limitation of war in the "balance of power" system requires no further discussion.

We shall mention only a few of the expected norms of international law. One would expect belligerents to behave in ways that maintain the essential rules of the system, since the rules are required for the security of all essential nations, including belligerents. Behavior during the war or territorial occupation that infuriated the enemy population might preclude the possibility of that state as a future ally. Although this might not be the only constraint operating to enforce the rules of war, nonetheless it is an important factor tending in that direction.

The rule against intervention in the domestic affairs of another state, a rule violated on many occasions, also tends to be sustained under conditions of the model. If the intervention—for instance, in favor of rebels —were to succeed, there might be a permanent alliance between them or a tutelage of one over the other. This arrangement would injure all the other states in the system and tend to draw their active opposition. For this reason the intervention would likely be unwise or unsuccessful. And if for any reason the intervention were unsuccessful, the state in which the intervention took place might have a serious revulsion for the intervening state that would make it a permanent enemy of that state. Although these reasons are not absolutely compelling, they are strong enough to make likely general observance of the rule of non-intervention in a "balance-of-power" type of system.

By and large, in real world revolutions, states did not tend to intervene on the side of the government either. Rather they maintained normal state relations and trade with the established government. If the rebels grew strong enough, then the rules of belligerency would apply; other states would behave neutrally toward the belligerents, at least with respect to shipping articles of war or trade goods. The reasons are similar to those given above; intervention would have had potentially destabilizing consequences for the system and would have elicited opposition from the other members.

For like reasons recognition of new governments or new states tended to follow universal norms in the "balance of power" system. Was there a definite territory? Did the government control the territory? Was there reasonable support from the population or at least the absence of large overt opposition? If the answers were yes, then the government or state would tend to be recognized, regardless of the form of government or its friendship for or antipathy toward particular states. Although the act of recognition itself was political, so that the fulfillment of the criteria above did not absolutely require the act of recognition, there was, with notable exceptions, fair concordance between rule and practice. Moreover, since nonrecognition was a political act, its consequences for international law were less than massive, the nonrecognized state merely being denied access to the privileges stemming from comity. Failure to recognize a state or government did not turn it into an outlaw, remove its obligations under international law, or free other states to behave toward it without regard for international law. Even before the facts establishing the legitimacy of a government were clear, other states were in effect bound by the rules of international law in their conduct toward the nonrecognized government or state. Intervention in its affairs would have been contrary to the rules of the system. Recognition may have been a political act and a negotiating tool in getting the new government or state to recognize its obligations under the rules of the international community, but it was not a weapon in a cold war designed to undercut its existence.

THE LOOSE BIPOLAR MODEL

A second model, which has some relevance to present-day international politics, is the loose bipolar system. This model contains two blocs, each led by a leading bloc actor. There is role differentiation in this model; in addition to blocs and bloc members there are nations not joined to blocs and universal organizations such as the United Nations. The weaponry in this model is nuclear—at least for the contemporary time period. In an age of efficient logistics and great organizational capacity, this latter feature is an essential element of the system. For unless factors of scale precluded it, we would expect one of the blocs to overwhelm the other unless deterred by a weapons system such as the nuclear type.

This system operates according to the following simplified set of essential rules:

1. Blocs strive to increase their relative capabilities.

2. Blocs tend to be willing to run at least some risks to eliminate rival blocs.

3. Blocs tend to engage in major war rather than to permit rival blocs to attain predominance.

4. Blocs tend to subordinate objectives of the universal actor to objectives of the bloc but to subordinate objectives of rival bloc to the universal actor.

5. Non-bloc actors tend to support the universal actor generally and specifically against contrary objectives of blocs.

6. Non-bloc actors tend to act to reduce the danger of war between blocs.

7. Non-bloc actors tend to be neutral between blocs except where important objectives of the universal actor are involved.

8. Blocs attempt to extend membership but tend to tolerate the status of non-bloc actors.

The first three rules reflect the uncertainties of a bipolar system and the need for at least a margin of security. Rule 4 is related to the need within the system for mediatory functions. Particularly in the nuclear age mediatory activities help coordinate conflicting blocs and achieve agreement short of nuclear war. This is similar to many other types of bargaining situations in which optimal solutions are facilitated by the mediatory process. On the other hand, although the blocs should sup-

port these processes, each bloc should also take advantage of opportunities for a somewhat favorable outcome. That is, maneuvering will take
place and it will be related to situational advantages. Moreover, it is
desirable, even apart from the concept of mediatory functions, to subordinate the goals of one's opponents to those of the universal organization and to subordinate the goals of the organization to those of the bloc,
provided it can be done with minimal inconsistency.

Universal organizations are major supports for the interests of actors
not belonging to blocs: the greatest protection for them insofar as they
can be protected by universally applicable rules of conduct. Therefore
non-bloc members have an interest in subordinating both blocs to the
universal actor. This would become difficult, perhaps impossible, in the
event of a major war. And minor wars might escalate into major wars.
Hence Rule 6, that non-bloc actors act to reduce the danger of war between the blocs. The non-bloc actors cannot properly fulfil this function
unless they remain neutral between the blocs. Lack of neutrality would
impede their mediatory functions and their support for the universal actor.
On the other hand, a neutrality that threatened to undercut the universal
actor would injure their interests. Thus Rule 7. Rule 8 emphasizes the
fact that although extending bloc membership is important to the bloc,
the mediatory role is sufficiently important for the bloc to tolerate non-
bloc membership—and under appropriate conditions even to support it.

The consequences of the rules are straightforward and for the most
part have already been stated. Consequences: Alliances are long-term,
based on permanent and not shifting interests, and have ideological components. Wars, except for the fear of nuclears, tend to be unlimited. The
fear of nuclear war, however, has a strong dampening effect on war. The
universal organization tends to support mediatory and war-dampening
activities. With respect to international law, there are few restrictions
on intervention and these arise mainly out of the fear of escalation.

Some of the reasons for these consequences may now be stated.
Alliances tend to be long-term and based on permanent interests. There
is a tendency in the system for a bloc to support its leading member even
on issues where there is a temporary divergence of short-term interests.
Moreover, there is a tendency for ideological congruity within the blocs,
for the kind of close association involved either requires organizational
uniformity, as in the Communist bloc, or the kind of public support and
cultural similarity that helped at one time to support NATO. If one

bloc were organized according to long-term interests, and other nations were not, the bloc might well gain its way on most important issues by splitting the opposition issue by issue.

There would be a tendency in this system for wars to be unlimited; neither bloc would regard the other as a potential coalition partner. The greatest inhibitor of a central confrontation lies in the nuclear component and also perhaps in certain factors of scale that would make administration of the world an extremely difficult, if not impossible, task.

As for the rule of intervention in international law, at least some of the constraints present in the "balance of power" system would not be operative in the loose bipolar system. The opposition to intervention would come from the other bloc and would not have the same massive quality as in the "balance of power" system, where most major actors could be expected to oppose it. Fear of confrontation and escalation would nevertheless inhibit intervention to some extent. In areas where one bloc had easy access and the other did not, intervention would not be unlikely. Where both blocs had relatively similar access, they might agree to insulate the area from bloc competition or alternatively they might decide to compete for it. The decision would depend on the specifics of the situation; the model could not be expected to give rise to a specific prediction on this point. One factor inhibiting intervention would be the fear that the erosion of this particular rule of law might tend to erode the general system of law. Although this fear might be a factor in decisions concerning intervention, the consequence feared is not so direct or massive in its weight that it would likely prove overriding. Moreover, most interventions would be indirect and covert.

One would expect the use of force to be permissible in a system resembling this model. The same factors that permit intervention also operate to permit the use of force, the Charter of the United Nations to the contrary notwithstanding. Historically Palestine, the Congo, Cyprus, Greece, Korea, Vietnam, Suez, Hungary, and various other episodes firmly illustrate the erosion of the so-called rule of law enunciated in the Charter. The bipolarity of the system tends to focus competition between the blocs and to produce a resort to force in those circumstances where one of the blocs has a clear preponderance of capabilities. The rule can to some extent be enforced against nonleading nations, as in the Suez case, or even as in the Pakistan-India case, but it runs into greater difficulties in the India-China case.

To some extent this difficulty stems from the fact that the bloc leaders have no desire for the continuance of a war that neither side supports, especially since any armed conflict might lead to a central confrontation, even if only with low probability. The bloc leaders see no reason to risk even the lowest probabilities of nuclear war if there is some convenient way of avoiding it and if the bloc leaders get no clear gain from the use of force. Where the universal organization tends to dampen the armed confrontations and to mediate quarrels among nonleading states, it therefore tends to reinforce the interests of the bloc leaders.

Recognition of states or of governments is based not on the criteria of control within a region with reasonable support from the people but, in large part at least, on the consequences of the act of recognition for bloc policy. Thus not recognizing East Germany, North Korea, or Communist China was, during the height of bipolarity, part of a program of political warfare designed to erode the positions of these governments. This did not mean that non-recognized states or governments were entirely without rights within the system or that unprovoked major acts of military warfare against them were permitted, even during the height of bipolarity. Yet whereas in the "balance of power" system the objective of non-recognition is to secure the compliance of the non-recognized state or government with the norms of the system, in the loose bipolar system the objective of non-recognition is to weaken the international position of the non-recognized state or government and, under favorable circumstances, to contribute to its demise.

.   .   .   .

Tight Bipolar System

The tight bipolar international system represents a modification of the loose bipolar system in which non-bloc member actors and universal actors either disappear entirely or cease to be significant. Unless both blocs are hierarchically organized, however, the system will tend toward instability.

There is no integrative or mediatory role in the tight bipolar system. Therefore there will tend to be a high degree of dysfunctional tension in the system. For this reason, the tight bipolar system will not be a highly stable or well-integrated system.

Universal System

The universal international system might develop as a consequence of the functioning of a universal actor organization in a loose bipolar system. The universal system, as distinguished from those international systems previously discussed, would have a political system as a subsystem of the international social system. However, it is possible that this political system would be of the confederated type, i.e., that it would operate on territorial governments rather than directly on human individuals.

The universal international system would be an integrated and solidary system. Although informal political groupings might take place within the system, conflicts of interest would be settled according to the political rules of the system. Moreoever, a body of political officials and administrators would exist whose primary loyalty would be to the international system itself rather than to any territorial subsystem of the international system.

Whether or not the universal international system is a stable system depends upon the extent to which it has direct access to resources and facilities and upon the ratio between its capabilities and the capabilities of the national actors who are members of the system.

Hierarchical System

The hierarchical international system may be democratic or authoritarian in form. If it evolves from a universal international system—perhaps because the satisfactions arising from the successful operation of such a universal international system lead to a desire for an even more integrated and solidary international system—it is likely to be a democratic system. If, on the other hand, the hierarchical system is imposed upon unwilling national actors by a victorious or powerful bloc, then the international system is likely to be authoritarian.

The hierarchical system contains a political system. Within it, functional lines of organization are stronger than geographical lines. This highly integrated characteristic of the hierarchical international system makes for greater stability. Functional cross-cutting makes it most difficult to organize successfully against the international system or to withdraw from it. Even if the constitution of the system were to permit such withdrawal, the integration of facilities over time would raise the costs of withdrawal too high.

Unit Veto System

Consider a world in which some twenty-odd nations have nuclear systems capable of a not incredible first stike. That is, each nation would have a nuclear system that would not completely reduce enemy forces in a first strike but that might nonetheless reduce the enemy forces so much, if everything went according to plan, that a war begun by a first strike might be contemplated. However, even a successful first strike would then leave a nation launching such an attack, because of its depleted arsenal, quite vulnerable to attack by a third nation—an attack that might not be unlikely either if its own attack had been without provocation or if the other nation were malevolent. In any event, the vulnerability of the attacker to subsequent attack by a third state would tend to inhibit such a first strike except in the most extremely provocative circumstances.

There would be little need for specific alliances in this world. To the extent that alliances did occur, one would expect them to be of a non-ideological nature. Nations might ally themselves in pacts establishing an obligation to retaliate against any "aggressor" who launched a nuclear attack, which exceeded certain specified proportions, against an alliance member.

In this system one does not expect large counter-value[5] or counter-force[6] wars. If nuclear weapons are used at all, they will tend to be used in limited retaliations for purposes of warning or in other strictly limited ways. The wars that do occur will tend to be non-nuclear and limited in geographic area and means of war-fighting. Sub-limited wars will occur more often than actual wars.

The system, however, might seem to have some potentiality for triggering wars or for catalytic wars. That is, if one nation engages in a

---

[5] A counter-value attack is directed against cities or other non-combatant installations that are of social importance.

[6] A counter-force attack is one directed against military installations. The term usually refers to strikes against nuclear installations.

counter-force attack, this in some views would likely trigger an attack on it by a third state. Or an anonymous attack or accident might catalyze a series of wars. These possibilities cannot be denied, particularly if tensions within the system become high. Nonetheless first strikes and accidental wars are unlikely because credible first-strike forces will not exist and because adequate command and control systems will be available. Thus the nuclear systems will be relatively stable against accidents. An anonymous attack will be a theoretical possibility but not a practicable one unless many nations develop Polaris-type forces—that is, forces such that an attack cannot be attributed to a particular nation. Even so, it would seem difficult to identify the rational motive for attack in such a world. An anonymous attack would not seem to have any reasonable political motive, since, by definition, the aggressor could not identify himself and thus secure the benefits arising from threats. Numerous nervous rivals would remain, and the attack might very well trigger a holocaust.

Because of the adequacy of nuclear systems and the relative unimportance of alliances, when contrasted with the "balance of power" international system, interventions would not be as ominous as in that system and therefore would not be as strongly interdicted. But since the gains resulting from such interventions would be smaller than in the loose bipolar system, they are unlikely to become characteristic of this system. The danger of escalation, moreover, would tend to limit them. If universal organizations exist in this system, they would act as mediators, as would non-involved states whether nuclear or non-nuclear. In general, though, the universal organization would have fewer and less important functions than in the loose bipolar system. Nations equipped with nuclear forces in the unit veto system will tend to be self-sufficient and to reject outside pressures, even if coming from universal organizations. In particular, the functions of the universal organization dealing with political change will tend to be minimized. This will be reinforced by the disappearance of the colonial question as an important issue in world politics.

The foreign policies of the great nuclear powers will tend to be isolationist. Alliances, as specified, will recede in importance. Hegemonial ambitions will be curbed—primarily by an obvious inability to achieve them. Protective functions will tend to be shifted to "other" shoulders, when aggression does occur, since no "natural" assignment of this function will be possible. (That is, almost any one of the nuclear powers could play the role; there is no particular pressure on any particular nation to assume it.)[7]

One would expect nations such as the Soviet Union and China to be less revolutionary, as the prospects for revolutionary solidarity recede even further, and as the frictions between nuclear powers, regardless of ideology, increase. As a consequence nations such as the United States would have less incentive to resist changes in the status quo.

The domestic corollary of the above would involve publics suspicious of foreign nations, relatively uninterested in the morals of quarrels or in social change external to the nation, and lacking the assurance necessary for an articulated goal-oriented foreign policy.

III

A number of models follow which may be considered either variations of the loose bipolar system or of the unit veto system. The variations will occur under conditions that are not consonant with maximum stability for either kind of system. Although perhaps not genuinely equilibrium systems, they correspond with conditions that conceivably might persist for critical periods of time. In this sense they might be considered to have some sort of local stability. They are worth exploration since they indicate some potential lines of development from the existing situation. Indeed the very loose bipolar system is descriptively reasonably close to the existing situation. Still, for purposes of model construction we simplify and reduce the number of variables involved. We look for those conditions which make for maximum stability within the limitations of the somewhat destabilizing constraints which we do place on the models. Other variants could easily be constructed.

[7] This is parallel to the situation between the two world wars, when the League of Nations sought to control aggression. The onus of stopping aggression could always be shifted to other shoulders and was not undertaken by any nation or combination of nations until very late in the game. At the time of Korea, on the other hand, in the loose bipolar system, if aggression were to be halted, only the United States was in a position to accomplish this. Thus the fact that the system singled out a particular nation for this role served to reinforce the performance of the role function.

Very Loose Bipolar System

This is a model that does not appear in *System and Process*. It has elements of great inherent instability and would not be presented at all, except that it has striking resemblances to contemporary international politics. In the loose bipolar system, the nations playing different roles are not differentiated in terms of history, culture, state of economic development, color, and so forth. In the real world, the uncommitted nations, by and large, are ex-colonies, in particular, ex-colonies of nations belonging to NATO, are in bad economic circumstances, are attempting to modernize and develop, belong, by and large, to the so-called colored races, and possess ideologies that make them hostile to much the NATO bloc stands for. Increased nuclear stability has reduced the fear of central war, except as a consequence of escalation. This has tended to dampen international crises of the classical military kind but has created a shelter for guerrilla and sublimited wars as well as for rare limited wars in areas where escalation is not likely. The blocs have weakened, although they still exist. Large areas of accord and common interest between the United States and the Soviet Union appear to have arisen. Meanwhile Communist China appears to many as a potential threat to the U.S. and the U.S.S.R. There has also been a limited degree of nuclear diffusion.

In this system, the universal organization is used in ways consonant, but not identical, with the revolutionary drives of many of the uncommitted nations. Within the universal organization both blocs will compete for the support of the uncommitted states with respect to the issues of decolonization and of racial equality. In this competition the bloc, which for the most part, supports the status quo will, by and large, be out-bid. The conservative bloc will be more effective in those areas in which it can intervene directly, or even indirectly, with military force and economic support.

Although the conservative bloc has sufficient support to prevent a rapid shift to the left within the universal organization, the competition for the support of the uncommitted nations will be shifted from the two blocs to a competition between the more and less radical wings of the revolutionary bloc. The process adumbrated above will likely coincide with the quasi-legitimization of intervention against existing "conservative" governments by revolutionary governments.[8]

This system will be characterized by the search for arms control, for accommodation between the blocs, and by the opposition to bloc policy by important members of both blocs. There will be a fragmentation, or at least weakening, of bloc structures. In the area of law, the rule of non-intervention will be breached even more than in the loose bipolar system. The universal organization will be used primarily to control the path of political change rather than primarily as a mediatory instrument. As a consequence, it is likely to have forced upon it more and more difficult problems that are not unlikely to be beyond the competence of the organization. They will likely involve strong conflicts of interest between the bloc leaders and may reach such a magnitude that the support of the bloc leaders for the universal organization may be called into question. Extreme self-restraint on the part of the bloc leaders will be required if the system is not to become unstable and if, in particular, the universal organization is to remain viable and to continue to perform its mediating functions.

The Détente System

The "détente system" world assumes that some of the favorable projections as to changes within both the Soviet and American systems occur. Soviet society becomes more open and less aggressive and the U.S. less defensive of the international status quo. Although no responsible, reasonable, and cautious social scientist would predict these changes, it still would be interesting to see if we can picture the kind of system which might occur if these changes did take place. In general, we assume the amelioration of the Soviet system, the domestication of the

---

[8]An example of this is given by the announced support for the Congolese rebels by the Egyptian and Algerian governments. According to the New York *Times* of January 2, 1965, after the Security Council's resolution calling for non-intervention in the Congo, the State Department, "believed, for example, that the United Arab Republic and Algeria will no longer be willing to admit that they are shipping arms to the Congolese rebels. The two countries may continue their shipments but at a restricted level that can be kept secret it is believed." This pathetic quotation indicates graphically the extent of the shift involved. (According to the New York *Times* of February 1, 1965, the Algerians announced their support for the rebels and the Egyptians, as a gesture of support to the rebels, asked the Congolese to close their embassy in Cairo.)

Chinese system, or at least the inability of the Chinese to create difficulty, and stability in much of the uncommitted world.

This is a world in which the U.S. and the U.S.S.R. are still strongly competitive but in which the competition is not conflictful. Tensions are relaxed and important arms control agreements reached. As a consequence Russia and the U.S. support nuclear forces capable only of mostly finite deterrence and there are portents that the forces are being reduced to those required for minimum deterrence only.

As a consequence of this "détente system", the internal organization of the two blocs loosens up. Some of the Soviet satellites begin to take occasional positions on foreign policy agreeing with those of the West rather than with the Soviet Union. Fissures within the Western bloc increase. Although most issues tend to find groupings revolving around the Soviet Union and the United States, the alignments have some tendency to differ from issue to issue. And on some issues the U.S. and the U.S.S.R. are in agreement and differ with China or one or more Western states.

The foreign policies of the U.S. and the U.S.S.R. tend to liberal interventionism. Anti-colonialism is carried to completion. The U.S. quits backing oligarchical but anti-Communist states. The Soviet Union learns how to live with non-Communist new nations and ceases its support of national liberation movements within genuinely independent nations. Some difficulties attend Chinese attempts to aid national liberation movements.

In the area of law, non-intervention in the internal affairs of other states is stressed. This is a necessary corollary of the "détente system". Although some of the rules of international law are changed to accord with new values—on the subject of expropriation, for instance—in general the rules of international law are strengthened and enforced. They are extended to outer space and celestial bodies.

The universal organization plays a strong role in the governance of space, celestial bodies, and the polar regions. It aids in the extinguishment of colonialism, in the regulation of arms control measures, and takes a leading role in the dampening of international breaches of the peace.

Breaches of the peace—or even wars—may occur in this system, but they will not involve the U.S. and the U.S.S.R., at least in direct confrontations with each other. Such wars will tend to be local, to be strictly limited in objectives, to involve minor nations, and to be strictly non-nuclear. Where this threatens not to be the case, the U.S. and the U.S.S.R. are likely to cooperate within limits to prevent occurrences that might escalate. And, if they do not co-operate in this endeavour, at least they will not seriously interfere with each other's actions towards this end. They will usually work through the universal organization in these cases.

The Unstable Bloc System

The world of "the unstable bloc system" is a world in which developments contrary to those assumed for the "détente system" world have taken place. This is a world in which tension has increased and in which the U.S. and the U.S.S.R. are highly suspicious of each other. Arms control agreements are minimal in this world. Third area conflicts are extensive. There are local outbreaks of violence. And national liberation movements continue to be a problem. Qualitative developments have made nuclear systems cheaper and easier to acquire.

The nuclear systems of the U.S. and U.S.S.R. vary in strength from mostly finite deterrence to not incredible massive retaliation. Four or five other states have nuclear systems but these are good for minimum deterrence only. All nuclear powers possess strategies calling for limited strategic reprisal under appropriate circumstances. But obviously it is easier and safer for the U.S. and U.S.S.R. to use this strategy, even against each other, and certainly against the small nuclear powers, than it is for the small nuclear powers to use it against each other. It is conceivable—but barely so—and not credible that the small nuclear powers would use limited strategic reprisal against one of the large nuclear powers. The chance is much greater that the small power attempting this would be left to its fate and that the retaliation then applied against it would not trigger off the other larger nuclear power than that it would. Thus the deterrent value of such a threat by a small nuclear power—unless led by an apparent madman—would not be great.

Alliance policy in this system is highly dependent upon military capability and policy. If the United States' posture, for instance, is clearly not adequate for deterrence against aggression directed at countries other than the United States, the strains on its alliances during periods of crises might prove overwhelming, except in those cases where its allies' capabilities, in addition to its own, might produce the requisite deterrence. One would assume that the Warsaw Pact powers would not be as susceptible to splitting tactics as NATO because of the "organic" political relationships among the members and because of the presence of the Russian army on satellite soil. Although this position is debatable, it is nonetheless plausible.

In general, bloc alignments would be subject to two conflicting pressures. The fact of crisis in a basically bipolar world would give the blocs greater reason for being and greater cohesion. The additional fact, however, that the U.S., or any other nation, might hesitate before inviting nuclear destruction on its own territory provides an opening for nuclear blackmail. That such blackmail might be dangerous and that it is unlikely to be practiced except under conditions of very great provocation does not negate this consideration. Moreover, the threat need not be overt. The fact that it is operative in the situation is enough to help shape expectations, attitudes, and national policies. How the two conflicting pressures factor out depends upon an interplay of considerations difficult to consider in the abstract.

The foreign policies of the U.S. and the U.S.S.R. in this model will tend to be interventionist. They will respond to the basic clash of interests and not to a general concordance of interests as in the "détente system". U.S. policy will tend toward conservatism, that is, toward the support of status quo conservative regimes. Change will tend to be viewed as a threat, despite some plausible arguments to the contrary.[9] There will be a consequent alienation of a considerable portion of the intellectual élite within the U.S. and in the other NATO states. Soviet policy will be oriented toward national liberation movements despite a desire not to "rock the boat" in the dangerous nuclear age. Additional "Hungarys" may occur, or other events may occur which disillusion Soviet intellectuals. Relations between Russia and China will influence Soviet policy. If, as at present, they are at odds, China will tend to preempt the revolutionary position and this might moderate Soviet policy to some extent. But, by assumption this would not go too far, or we would be back in the "détente system". It is also possible, but not likely, that with the retirement of Khrushchev and after the death of Mao, the

[9]For some of these arguments, see "United States Foreign Policy in a Revolutionary Age", in Morton A. Kaplan, ed., *The Revolution in World Politics*, John Wiley and Sons, New York, New York, 1962.

two nations become more closely allied. In this latter case, the conflict and tension between the blocs will likely increase.

Although most breaches of the peace in this system will not involve direct confrontations between the U.S. and the U.S.S.R., such confrontations are not entirely unlikely in this system. Moreover, there is a distinct possibility that nuclear weapons may be used in some limited fashion. If so, the use will probably be of the limited reprisal variety.

The role of the universal organization will be primarily mediatory and adapted to dampening the consequences of outbreaks of violence. Although each bloc will support political changes contrary to the interests of the opposing bloc, the efforts to secure a constitutional majority in the universal organization will generally prove ineffective. The universal organization will not acquire authority over outer space, celestial bodies, and serious arms control measures.

Intervention in the internal affairs of other nations will be rampant in this system and will be limited primarily by the fear of nuclear escalation. This system will not be noted for the growth of international law. If anything, there will be retrogression. Existing standards will erode and will not be replaced by generally agreed-upon norms.

Incomplete Nuclear Diffusion System

We will now consider another variation of the "unstable bloc system". The description of this system is roughly similar to the previously mentioned one, except that fifteen or twenty nations, additional to the U.S. and the U.S.S.R., will have nuclear forces. But these forces will be of the small vulnerable variety. Our analysis will stress only those features of this world that differ from the "unstable bloc system".

The United States and the U.S.S.R. will have nuclear forces that are not capable of first strike but that do give some significant advantage if used first. The smaller nuclear nations will possess what is ordinarily called minimum deterrence. This is similar to the French idea of "tearing an arm off". These forces would, in fact, deter most attacks against the homeland, but not all, particularly in extremely provocative situations. Their triggering capability would be quite small. And they would be quite vulnerable to surprise attack.

Alliances would be possible between major and minor nuclear powers or among minor nuclear powers. But the former type of alliance would be inhibited by the small state's possession of nuclear arms. Possession would by itself be a sign of independence and distrust. Moreover the large state would fear commitment by the small state's nuclear use. It would desire to insulate itself from a chain of actions that it could not control. And, although a general alliance among most of the small states possessing nuclear forces might create a reasonable deterrent, unless there were exceptional political or cultural circumstances the alliance would be very susceptible to nuclear blackmail and splitting tactics. Otherwise the discussion of the "unstable bloc system" is applicable with respect to alliance conditions.

Although wars in this system would tend to be limited, as in the "unstable bloc system", the degree of tension would be higher also; and the possibility of escalation would be greater. Limited and direct confrontations between the U.S. and the U.S.S.R. might occur in non-European areas. A central confrontation in Europe might also occur, but here the danger of escalation beyond the limited-war category would be very great. And for this reason the factors operating against a central confrontation would tend to be very great.

The mediatory functions of the universal organization would be more important than in the "unstable bloc system" world and would tend to be more stressed, although it would also prove more difficult to use them successfully. Outside of mediatory functions the universal organization would have even fewer functions than in the "unstable bloc system" world and would handle them less successfully on the whole.

The legal system would function even more poorly than in the "unstable bloc system" world, and intervention in the internal affairs of other states would be even more extensive. Foreign policy would be as in the "détente system" world, but the conservative interventionist nature of American policy would be even more pronounced. Soviet policy would tend to be more revolutionary. The alienation of some intellectuals would be increased, but the obvious dangers of the situation would also create a counter-current of chauvinism leading to a highly-dangerous bifurcation of intellectual opinion within both blocs and within the leading nation of each. Governments and their supporters would lack assurance and might become susceptible to ill-considered actions. There might be a swing between excessive caution and excessive adventurism.

.   .   .   .

Engineering the Model

As we already have pointed out the models constitute closed systems, while the real world in which they are to be applied is an open system. An example of the way in which application is made may be helpful. We would expect that in a "balance of power" system alliances would be short-lived, based on immediate interests, and neglectful of existing or previous alliance status. The rigid alliance systems of the European great nations between 1871 and 1914 and the relatively unlimited nature of World War I would seem, superficially at least, inconsistent with the prescriptions of the "balance of power" theory. We could, of course, resolve the problem by analyzing the period from 1871 to 1914 in terms of a rigid "balance of power" system. This solution, however, would require us to analyze every characteristically different state of the world in terms of a different systems model, thus depriving the concept of system of much of its theoretical meaning and turning it into a primarily descriptive device. The alternative procedure is to decide whether the underlying theory of the "balance of power" system can be used to explain the observed discrepancies.

We do not, of course, assert that if the theory of the "balance of power" system can account for the behavioral differences from 1871 to 1914, it therefore is *the* true explanation of the observed behavior. Undoubtedly other factors played important roles in producing both the specific sequence of events and the general form that the sequence took. We will merely have established that the asserted irregular behavior does not invalidate the theory, and that the theory may be useful for relating a wider range of phenomena than is possible without such a theory. This may increase the confidence we place in the theory and the satisfaction obtained from its explanatory power.

The reconciliation of theory and behavior follows. If we recognize, as there is reason to believe that Bismarck foresaw, that the seizure of Alsace-Lorraine by Prussia led to a public opinion in France that was ineluctably revanchist, this parameter change permits engineering the theory in a way consistent with the developments that followed. As long as Germany was unwilling to return Alsace-Lorraine to France, France would be Germany's enemy. Thus France and Germany became the poles of rigid opposed alliances, as neither would enter—or at least remain in—the same coalition regardless of specific common interests. The chief motivation for limitation of war in the theoretical system is the need to maintain the existence of other essential actors as potential future allies. For the foreseeable future, however, neither France nor Germany was the potential ally of the other. Consequently neither had an incentive—as would normally be the case in a "balance of power" system—to limit its war aims against the other. What had been an incentive for limitation became instead a disincentive. A somewhat analogous problem occurred with respect to the alignment pattern of the Italian city-state system. In this system, Florence, for a considerable period of time, functioned as the hub of opposed alignments. In the case of this system, the explanation involved a geographic factor.

This discussion of the problem of engineering the theory may also help to indicate the circumstances under which a theory will be extended or a different theory be called for. Where the theory can be adapted to the changed parameters economically within the explanatory framework the theory provides, it is not necessary to develop a new theory merely because the behavior looks different. Where such adaptation cannot be made, a different theory will be needed. Since many of the adaptations depend upon ingenuity and insight, it is possible that one theory will later be recognized to do the job that two theories were once required for. On the other hand, additional evidence may later cast doubt on a reconciliation between theory and behavior that once seemed intellectually satisfying. In some cases alternative theories may seem equally adaptable. And in still other cases, noninternational factors —for instance, domestic politics—may so dominate an international event that a theory of international politics may have only marginal explanatory power or perhaps none at all.

Designations of systems in terms of theoretical models are, then, not descriptive. The years between 1870 and 1914, for instance, are referred to as a "balance of power" period because the theory of the "balance of power" explains the observed behavior, which differs from that postulated by the model, by adjusting the theory for the change that French public opinion caused at the parameter. There are analogues to this elsewhere in political science. The British system during World War II is generally considered a democratic system (or whatever comparable terminology one prefers) under conditions of wartime stress; presumably democratic behavior would be restored with the return of peace.

This emphasis on theoretical equilibrium models does not mean that statements of variations of the models would not be useful for at least some analytic purposes, or that these variations must not be descriptive. But such models should be distinguished from the more important theoretical models that serve as the core of explanation.

The six theoretical models, or systems, of *System and Process* are equilibrium models. The more complex real world goes through phases for which these models are useful explanatory tools. *System and Process* (p. 21) leaves open whether the phases of the real world to which the different models are applied should be considered real system changes or merely different equilibrium states of one ultrastable international system. Thus in *System and Process* the transformation rules for the theoretical models suggest possible conditions for each of the models under which a world analyzable in its terms could be transformed into worlds analyzable by each of the other models.

Whether the real world system is presumed to have undergone system change or equilibrium change[10] depends on the reversibility of the process. The transitions between the types represented by the six models would seem to be not easily reversible—i.e., to involve more system ramifications than intramodel variations and consequently to require more than restoring the original value of the variable, the change of which precipitated the transformation, to restore the previous system behavior. Variations of the model, i.e., variations that can be explained by the same theory would seem to be more easily reversible. This question is not completely settled yet, however.

In any event, the two levels of analysis must be kept distinct. In a question of the relationship between a model or theory and observed events, we consider systems the same (of the same type) if the same theory or model explains behavior. In a "concrete" situation (when we ask if an external real world system has changed), the question of reversibility becomes dominant. The external world is said to have undergone a system change if the change from one model type to another is judged irreversible; otherwise there is merely equilibrium change.

The Greek city-states during their "balance of power" phase and nineteenth-century Europe are both examples of "balance of power" systems although there is no historical continuity; whereas 1945, or

[10]See *System and Process*, pp. 6-8, for a set of definitions distinguishing equilibrium change, system change, and system dissolution.

thereabouts, introduces the bipolar system, which is considered distinct from the "balance of power" system for purposes of theoretical explanation although there is historical continuity. In the latter case, both analytical and "concrete" system change have occurred, for we believe that nuclear weapons have introduced irreversible changes into the world.

The changes of systems types in real cases may be abrupt, in which case there is no doubt when they occur, or gradual, in which case there may be transitional periods when resemblances to one or another of the models is a matter of more or less rather than of yes or no. The analogy is to the transition between a "normal" personality system and a "psychotic" personality system, usually one of shadings in which the designation of the boundary line between the conditions, although important for a number of purposes, depends upon the application of criteria that may be subject to legitimate disagreement. Conceivably, although we have not yet discovered such cases, one theory might be applicable to certain selected aspects of the international system and a second to different aspects, just as certain aspects of the economic market are best explained by models of perfect competition and other aspects by models of imperfect competition. In any of these cases, however, the problem is empirical and the models are essential for both analysis and explanation.

Each historical system occurs in its specific environmental circumstances. In some cases the differences in circumstances do not produce behavioral irregularities or require explanations linked to variations at the parameters. In other cases the variations at the parameter may make for either less or more stability in the system than would otherwise have been expected. Take, for example, the mercenary system in the Italian city-state system; here we need to examine the ways in which the two systems are linked. The mercenaries have an incentive to behave consistently with the rules of the city-state system, for instability would undercut their own role. If there were a roll-up, mercenaries would not be needed in the system. And occasionally mercenaries did transform themselves into rulers in an Italian city-state—another incentive to maintain the system. Thus the operation of a mercenary system adds nothing to our model at the level of generalization that the model employs. On the other hand, it adds quite specifically and importantly to an understanding of the historical Italian city-state system. If, however, our investigations were to show that historical "balance of power" systems were stable only when some additional kind of actor were operating (not the mercenary system itself, for it is not universal to "balance of power" systems) then it would be useful to modify the systems model so that it would not be stable without such a factor.

We would also attempt to incorporate such changes into our machine realization of the "balance of power" system. If the new factor increased the stability of the realization, in the absence of still other changes, it would increase our confidence in our explanation of the historical system. If it decreased stability, it would then raise questions about the historical explanation. We would also ask ourselves which parameters of the realization to change in order to restore stability when this added factor impaired stability, and which to change so that the new factor is required for stability when it improves the stability of the system. This might, depending on the circumstances, lead us to change either the historical explanation or the model of the "balance of power" system. This is by no means as easy as it may sound; it is more a programmatic intention than an accomplished fact. Still it serves to illustrate the ways that feedback and learning may occur between the historical analysis, the verbal models, and the operations of the computer realizations.

Our perspective concerning the nature of international systems theory has been clarified in several ways since the earliest formulations. Although our present views are consistent with those expressed earlier, we have refined their expression somewhat. We are more cautious than we were originally about assuming the dominance of international factors in events of international importance, although interestingly the models seem to apply where we earlier expressed skepticism—for instance, the classical Greek period. Also, where behavior fits the models, we search more thoroughly for the parameters that help reinforce the result. We are now more aware than before that different combinations of parameters may be consistent with equilibrium.

III

We hope in our Chicago workshops to use our historical studies to provide comparative materials. Systematic comparisons may provide a refinement of inference and theoretical structure. The papers in this volume by Chi and Franke on the Chinese warlord system and the Italian city-state system respectively provide illustrations of the potentialities for this kind of comparative research. We here recapitulate briefly some of the comparisons that seem to be emerging from the workshops and their importance for an understanding of the theories of the systems.

The first factor is that in the process of forming regional groupings—before the regional actors could enter into strong interactions with each other—the Italian system produced at least five and the Chinese system only three strong actors at any one time. The Chinese case also contrasts in this respect with the system resulting from the breakdown of Alexander's Macedonian Empire. The Italian and the Macedonian systems were stable and the Chinese unstable. We hypothesize that the factor of number played a role in the contrasting stabilities.

A second factor to note is that the logistics of the Italian system were inadequate for striking at the heart of an opponent, while, after the initial phase of the system, the logistics of the Chinese system were good. The existence of rail lines permitted rapid penetration of enemy territory. Since the enemy force had no real support in the countryside, the attacker could disperse it relatively easily. The Macedonian case accords more with the Italian than the Chinese. Although armies could be and were transported long distances, these campaigns required long preparation and time for completion. The defenders had ample time to recoup.

The Italian cities had the support of their citizens, who did not view their governments as alien or external impositions. The Chinese warlords, however, conquered their territories and treated them accordingly. Although they exercised the functions of government, they exploited their domains. In this sense, the warlord system was not based on fixed territories and populations. Except for Ptolemaic Egypt, however, the Macedonian system was even less territorial than the Chinese, with more rapid interchanges of territory and fewer connections with the indigenous populations. Yet it was stable and the Chinese was not.

No capital city had legitimacy as the seat of government nor any public official as national ruler in the Italian system. The Chinese system devolved from a unified state, however, and all warlords paid lip service to the myth of unity and to Peking as the seat of Chinese government. Moreover, the belief in eventual unity was a source of weakness for the warlords. Control of Peking therefore conferred some values in internal politics and also in relations with foreign governments. Successive warlords captured Peking; with its effective organization and ideology, the KMT gained support as the potential unifier of China after the capture of Shanghai (until then the warlords had been unaware of KMT potential for reasons that cannot be recounted here). The Macedonian system also had a central symbol of legitimacy and unity; and there were putative successors to Alexander. When for other reasons none could succeed in unifying the Empire, legitimacy devolved to the generals who gained recognition as kings. All three systems contrast with the French. Paris had legitimacy as the seat of France and the ruler of Paris as king. Usually the king was stronger than any other noble. Even when he was not, however, the other strong nobles could not permit any one of their number to displace the king, for this would be too threatening to their own ambitions. Thus the French king, whose central logistical position was inherently superior and who potentially had access to superior assets, could afford to bide his time—whether or not he consciously did so—until conditions were ripe for unification.

In all the international systems studied so far, the success of hegemonial attempts depended as much on the individual abilities of a particular ruler as on the resources of the city or nation he headed. Attempts at hegemony might be cut off either by the aging of a city ruler or by his replacement by an ineffective successor. Thus the international system was given respite in many cases. In the Chinese case, on the other hand, with its good logistics, failures of leadership might, and did, permit an effective actor to take over. Time worked against stability. The Macedonian case was closer to the Italian and was, of the noted international systems, the most dependent on the qualities of leadership. In none of the Macedonian actor systems, with the exception of Ptolemaic Egypt, was there anything approaching an independent bureaucracy that could keep the wheels of government running effectively despite deficiencies of top leadership. The Roman system of choosing consuls provides strong contrast to these systems. Although not all consuls were great generals, all were experienced; and they were rotated under the guidance of a continuing Senate. In all systems studied so far, the actors who threatened the stability of the system were subsystem dominant and directive.

The Italian system was stable until members of the system invited the intrusion of France. The Macedonian (Greek) system was quasi-stable until members of the system got involved in the affairs of Rome. The Chinese system persisted only for a very short time and was rolled up by a peripheral actor with a superior form of organization and ideology. In three of our historical cases—the Kuomintang roll-up of China, the Macedonian roll-up of Greece, and the later Roman roll-up of Greece— a peripheral actor rolled up what might be regarded from some perspectives as a central system. Toynbee hypothesizes that such roll-ups are examples of classical civilizations conquered by ruder and more warlike systems. The Macedonians clearly were ruder and more warlike than the Greeks and also possessed a superior military organization. It is difficult to say whether the Romans, whose genius lay in law, were less civilized than the Greeks, whose genius lay in philosophy. Clearly the Kuomintang leaders were culturally more advanced than the more traditional Chinese warlords. Moreover, the Roman roll-up of Italy constituted a roll-up by a central rather than by a peripheral actor. We are more impressed by the fact that in each of the three cases where a "peripheral" actor conquered a "balance of power" system, it did not participate in the wars of that system until the system had run itself down. Although the actors within the "balance of power" system maintained reasonable relative positions, the series of wars ran down the absolute resources of the system while the "peripheral" actor either husbanded its resources, or actually gained resources as a consequence of military gains in outside systems. Then, when for one reason or another the "peripheral" actor became involved in the affairs of the "central" system, it was able to roll it up.

The Italian, Chinese, and Macedonian systems were all highly dependent on personal or group interrelationships that theoretically should have been inconsistent with stability. Both the Chinese and Macedonian systems rested on ties that stemmed from common military service or schooling. The Italian system was cross-cut by Guelph-Ghibelline rivalries. Yet only the Chinese system was unstable, and it is unlikely that personal relationships that interfered with external rationality played any significant role in the instability.

There was no nationalism in the Italian example. Loyalties extended to the city. There was a latent Chinese loyalty to the nation, however, that worked to the advantage of the KMT and later of the CCP. The Macedonian satraps thought of themselves as Macedonians, even after the devolution of loyalties. Rome's extension of her system of law and, under some circumstances, of citizenship was undoubtedly of some aid in the Roman conquest of the Italian boot—particularly so in view of the dangers stemming from barbarian inroads.

The Italian city-state system was stable enough so that none of the city-states had any incentive to acquire potentially destabilizing weapons at considerable cost. This was not true of the Chinese system where comparative advantages were magnified. Thus there was an acceleration of the scale and scope of war in the Chinese system. Demetrius did go to great expense in the Macedonian system to build his fleet in an effort to roll the system up. He failed, however. The mercenaries helped to stabilize the Italian system. A roll-up would have undercut their interests by reducing the need for mercenaries. Moreover, after long sieges of war, the defenders often found themselves in a position to buy the mercenaries off. Mercenary leaders also did not like to expend their soldiers, for they were their capital.

Note that the systems we are discussing were regional or local international systems imbedded in the general international system but apparently sufficiently insulated for long periods to permit independent treatment. A series of comparative studies of both regional and general international systems would help us fit the parameters of international systems much better than we presently can and better understand the interactions between parameters and system. Possibly such studies could provide clues to future possibilities by giving us a clearer understanding of the range of possibilities and of the factors that help to sustain one possibility rather than another. Such studies might also help us understand better the process of political unification. If we were to focus these studies on the normative aspects of the systems, we would probably learn more about them also. History is still a huge blank from the perspective of the information relevant to informed (international) political analysis. Much remains to be done before we are able even to attempt an intelligent evaluation of what we might learn.

INDEX OF
MAIN CONCEPTS